Studies in
Religion and Education

To My Children
**Imogen
Thomas
Elizabeth**

Studies in
Religion and Education

JOHN HULL

University of Birmingham

 **The Falmer Press**

A member of the Taylor & Francis Group
London and New York

First published 1984

ISBN 0 905273 51 6 (paper)
     0 905273 52 4 (cased)

Jacket design by Leonard Williams

Typeset in 11/13 Plantin
by Imago Publishing Ltd, Thame, Oxon

Printed by Taylor and Francis (Printers) Ltd
Basingstoke, England
for
The Falmer Press
Falmer House
Barcombe
Lewes, Sussex
BN8 5DL

Contents

Contents

Acknowledgments

'Worship and the Curriculum' first appeared in the *Journal of Curriculum Studies* Vol. 1 (1969) pp. 208–18. 'Worship and Education' was first published in *Educational Review* Vol. 24 (1971) pp. 26–33 and 'Recent Developments in the Philosophy of Religious Education' was published in the same journal Vol. 23 (1970) pp. 59–68. 'From Christian Nurture to Religious Education: the British Experience' is reprinted from the March/April 1978 (Vol. 73, pt. 2) issue of the journal *Religious Education*, by permission of the publisher The Religious Education Association, 409 Prospect Street, New Haven, Connecticut 06510, U.S.A. Membership or subscription is available for $25.00 per year. 'Religious Education in a Pluralist Society' first appeared in Monica Taylor (Ed) *Progress and Problems in Moral Education* NFER Publishing Company 1975 pp. 195–205. 'The Integration of Religious Education and Some Problems of Authority' first appeared in Ian H. Birnie (ed) *Religious Education in Integrated Studies* SCM Press 1972 pp. 77–92. 'Agreed Syllabuses, Past, Present and Future' first appeared in Horder, D. and Smart, N. (eds) *New Movements in Religious Education* Temple Smith 1975 pp. 97–119. 'Religious Indoctrination in the Birmingham Agreed Syllabus?' is reprinted from *Faith and Freedom* Vol. 30 (Autumn 1976) pp. 27–35. 'The Birmingham Agreed Syllabus' first appeared in *The Times Educational Supplement* 12/12/75 and 'Christian Nurture, Stances for Living, or Plain RE?' in the same journal 12/12/76. 'The Theology of Themes' appeared in the *Scottish Journal of Theology* Vol. 25 (1972) pp. 20–32, 'Christian Nurture and Critical Openness' appeared in the same journal Vol. 34 (1981) pp. 17–37 and 'What is Theology of Education?', also in the *Scottish Journal of Theology*, was in Vol. 38 (1977) pp. 3–29. 'Theme Teaching as a Method of Religious Education' was published first in *Lumen Vitae* Vol. 30 (March 1975) pp. 9–23. 'History, Experience and Theme in Religious Education' first appeared in the *Journal of Christian Education* papers 53 (September 1975) pp. 27–38. 'Perennial

Symbols: Preparing to Teach Religion Through Life Themes' was first published in the journal *Education 3–13* (October 1975) pp. 104–109. 'Open Minds and Empty Hearts: Commitment and the Religious Education Teacher' is reprinted from Jackson, R. (ed) *Approaching World Religions* John Murray 1982 pp. 101–110. 'The Divergent Teacher, the Plural Society and the Christian Faith' first appeared in *Papers from the Joint World Council of Churches and Centre for the Study of Religion and Education in the Inner City. Consultation, July 1–8, 1981,* Sacred Trinity Centre, Manchester pp. 14–21. 'Christian Faith and the Open Approach to Religious Education' is reprinted from *Religious Education for the 80's: Implications for the Student* Intedgrated Education Committee, St. John's, Newfoundland, 1980, pp. 91–105. 'Christian Theology and Educational Theory: can there be Connections?' is reprinted from the *British Journal of Educational Studies*, Vol. 24 (June 1976) pp. 127–143 and 'The Value of the Individual Child and the Christian Faith' from the same journal Vol. 28 (1980) pp. 199–211. In making these acknowledgments, I would like to express my thanks to the various editors and publishers mentioned for allowing these items to be republished in the present volume.

Introduction

For me, as for many religious education teachers in Britain, an awareness of the problems presented by religious education grew out of the daily responsibility for the planning and conduct of the assemblies in the London boys school where I was teaching in the mid-1960s. What should the place of religion be in schools today? What inner connection, if any, might there be between education in religion and divine worship? How could a reconciliation be affected between the critical, analytic and descriptive demands of education and the nature of the spiritual life? I had already faced this latter question as a theological student at Cambridge in my personal life, and my experience of teaching religion in school forced me to encounter the same question in a wider professional context. It is, therefore, appropriate that this collection should begin with the two articles on school worship which formed the seeds of what was to become my 1975 book *School Worship: An Obituary.*

If it was school worship which alerted me to the problems of religious education, it was working on the Birmingham Agreed Syllabus in the early 1970s which forced me to try to clarify and defend the new conception of the subject which was emerging. Lecturing in Ireland, Australia, New Zealand, Canada, and the United States during those years helped me to see that the British problems were not isolated, but appeared to be part of a cultural crisis being faced by many Western democracies, and led to the founding in 1977 of the International Seminar on Religious Education and Values.

My interest in classroom methods, however, had been sharpened much earlier by my involvement with teacher training. The many inspiring people I met at Westhill College during my two years on the staff there had deepened my interest in classroom methods, and the group of studies collected in Part III of this volume reflects the development of that interest.

Another crucial experience for me during the middle and late 1970s was my participation on the two working parties of the British Council of Churches which issued in the reports *The Child in the Church* (1976) and *Understanding Christian Nurture* (1981). The problems of the relationship between secular religious education in county schools and Christian nurture in the churches had already been encountered in the Christian Education Movement, from which professional fellowship I have always learned so much, and it was these influences which led me to a deeper concern about the possibility of a Christian rationale for the kind of open, secular, world religious kind of education which was coming to be regarded as the best way forward for religious education. Section IV of this book deals with this question.

I had gradually come to see that the problems of religious education and in particular the question of the relationship between religious education and the Christian faith were but a small part of a much larger scene, namely, the relation between theology as a whole and education as a whole. The creation of a Master of Education programme in Theology of Education in Birmingham University during the early 1970s had given me the opportunity to explore these subjects with mature students, and an invitation to deliver the Gunning Lectures in the Divinity Faculty of Edinburgh University in 1978 encouraged me to try to systematize such thinking as I had been able to do in this area. Further progress in this field, as well as in the theology of childhood, which I had been working on from about 1977, lies in the future.

The book thus represents a series of concentric circles, beginning with the central, immediate task of school assembly, flowing out to the wider problems of theory and method in religious education, and finally to education seen as a branch of practical theology. There is no doubt that religious education in Britain today constitutes one of the most lively encounters between religion and modernity, and it has been an education in itself to be associated with the many creative and courageous religious educators from whom I have learnt so much.

The book is dedicated to my daughters, Imogen and Elizabeth, and to my son, Thomas, because the enterprise which it seeks to promote is dedicated to all children everywhere.

John M. Hull
University of Birmingham
May 1983

PART I

Religious Education and School Worship

---

1. *Worship and the Curriculum*

The clauses in the 1944 Education Act dealing with school worship were warmly welcomed by those then concerned with religious education. This was not because the number of schools in which a daily act of worship was provided would increase, since the great majority of schools were already holding such services, but because of the official recognition which the act provided and the security which this offered. 'Now, and for the years to come, nothing less than the repeal of section twenty-five of the Education Act 1944 . . . can prevent the daily offering to Almighty God of the worship of the school children of England and Wales. Meanwhile, "the voice of prayer is never silent, nor dies the strain of praise away".'[1] The Oxford Diocesan Council of Education was one of many bodies to express approval in only slightly less lyrical tones. 'This new recognition by the state of the vital importance of worship in the life of every school within the statutory system is a landmark in English history, for it indicates that the lead which the Church has for centuries been giving in her own schools is now to be followed in those of the many local authorities.'[2]

The teacher of religious education of today looks back to this time of optimistic faith a sadder and perhaps a wiser man. It is generally agreed that the daily act of worship has not had the fine results which had been hoped for. 'Among the seriously concerned . . . there is a strong feeling that the Law has overstepped itself.'[3] 'I think we need to ask the question very seriously whether it is worth going on with school worship at all. Would it not be better – more realistic and more effective – to cut out the obligatory periods of worship, and leave the children free to go to church and learn to worship there?'[4]

It is easy enough to suggest reasons for the increased concern about school worship. Difficulties in practice are obvious. Pupils are less and less likely to be familiar with religious worship through attendance at church and sunday school.[5] Figures supplied by the National Council of

5

Christian Education show that the number of children in Sunday Schools dropped from 2,892,060 in 1946 to 2,345,905 in 1963 although in the same period the number of children of school age rose from 5,592,000 to approximately seven million. Expression of conscientious objection to worship is probably more common now than 20 years ago. Handbooks of school worship are often insufficiently varied and imaginative to arouse the interest of pupils. The increase in the number of children who belong to non-Christian religions is an additional complication. Worship in the Christian communities of Western Europe and North America, if not beyond, is passing through a serious crisis. The reasons for this are not fully understood, but it is not surprising that if worship is undergoing anxious scrutiny in the sphere of faith it is likely to become increasingly problematic within the increasingly secular environment of the maintained school.

More perplexing are the matters of principle which school worship raises. The discussion ought not to be so much about what the circumstances will permit us to do, but about what ought to be done even if the circumstances were favourable. What place ought worship to have in any educational system? What place ought it to have in the particular system of English and Welsh public education? Are the principles of worship compatible with the principles of education?

The literature of school worship reveals an almost total lack of consideration of such matters. The *Oxford Book of School Worship*, already referred to, is an outstanding example of this defect. Originally issued for use in church schools, it was revised in 1958 with the 1944 Act in mind and offered to both church and to state schools. But, as the Bishop of Oxford says, 'the substance (of the revised edition) remains the same.'[6] It is assumed that all pupils taking part in the assembly will be convinced Christians. When the Apostles Creed is said, 'the utmost care should be taken that, when it is used, it should be said by everyone as an act of faith, and in such distinct and reverential tone that every word can be heard.'[7] Pupils are to give thanks for their baptism and confirmation,[8] prayers are offered for the extension of the church,[9] for 'heathen lands,'[10] for 'our Bishops and clergy'[11] and so on. It is assumed that the religious life of the school has as one of its functions the service of the church. 'The aim in selecting prayers for this book has been to give the pupils such contact with the Book of Common Prayer that they may come to love it ...,'[12] '... the school prayers should lead naturally to a devout appreciation of the public services of the church';[13] 'there should be a steady stream of keen, well-trained congregational singers coming out from schools to take their part in the common worship of the

Church.'[14] No allowance is made for the differences both in atmosphere and in principle between the church school and the state school; indeed, it is not too much to say that the book, still widely used, proceeds on the tacit view that the Act turned the state schools into church schools. The substance, as the Bishop said, remains the same.

In the widely read writings of Revd J.G. Williams neglect of educational ethics is elevated to become an argument.[15] The peculiar problems of worship in the maintained schools arise from the fact that worship does not even begin 'to be possible outside the provision which God has made within the sacramental life of his Church.'[16] The answer is to make the school as much like the church as possible. Hence 'in school worship the claims of the Church must always be kept clearly in sight.'[17] No attempt is made to work out any independent justification for the state teaching of religion, and the discussion concludes that 'until our educational system is once again ... inspired by a theological outlook that gives unity and coherence to the whole field, we must continue to look to the Church school as the one place where education can be, in the Christian sense, complete.'[18] If this is so, Christian parents are conscience bound, as indeed official Roman Catholic policy still affirms, to withdraw their children from the state system and to place them in church schools.[19]

But the most disturbing feature of the treatment of school worship in this book is that it is frankly regarded as a powerful means of instilling religious doctrine: '... it is because in worship these attributes of God are simply taken for granted, and not argued or deliberately taught, that worship is the most powerful medium of all for communicating dogmatic truth. It is far more powerful than the direct instruction of the classroom, simply because it teaches incidentally and by implication; and it is the things that are taken for granted, the implicit assumptions, rather than any kind of explicit teaching, that sink most deeply into the subconscious mind and become the foundations of "faith" '[20] Indoctrination is regarded by J.G. Williams as being evil when it destroys the freedom and responsibility of the pupil[21] and this is just what he regards as being most valuable about the school assembly. It is effective because it deprives the pupil of his responsibility. He does not know what is going on. Mr Williams regards this as an inevitable part of any act of worship.[22] Perhaps this is acceptable if the committed are deepening their faith by immersing themselves in the believing group, but if as seems to be the case here, it is intended to be a way of influencing the uncommitted, it would be difficult to justify in any educational work, including such work which professed to be based upon Christian principles. Since large numbers of pupils are uncommitted it would seem to follow that to offer them worship is both bad education and bad Christianity.

Worship and the Modern Child is certainly more candid than most writings on this subject, but it is striking how seldom even in less forthright works one finds discussion of the objectives of the school assembly. It has often been taken for granted that just as within the Christian frame of reference worship being the affirmation of the divine glory can have no justification beyond its intrinsic worth, so acts of worship provided for pupils within an educational frame of reference require no extrinsic justification. 'Religious worship, in secondary schools, as everywhere else, must be nothing less than the rendering unto Almighty God of the honour, the veneration and – most perfect of all worship – the adoration which is due to Him as Creator and Redeemer, and the love which is due to Him as Himself eternal Love.'[23] Even a theme of worship, such as meditation on some special virtue, is not allowed by C.L. Berry, for the sole purpose of worship is praise. Confession and intercession are avoided on the grounds that worship is what we offer not what we ask or receive, and, he insists, that worship required by the Act must be 'on the part of' and not merely in the name of or on behalf of 'all pupils in attendance at the school'[24] This sort of argument is found but rarely now, but such clear statements of objectives in school assembly do serve a purpose if only in isolating the difficulty of assimilating worship strictly understood into the educational work of the school. Similarly, H.T. Salzer feels that too often in school assembly emphasis is placed upon man and his response to God rather than on God himself. 'The essence of true worship is that it should be, first and foremost, God-centred.'[25]

It is sad to see that even in the more recent Agreed Syllabuses little attempt is made to tackle the problems raised by this relationship between worship and education. The *West Riding Agreed Syllabus* gives approval to the assembly as a powerful means of unconsciously inculcating doctrine: '. . . all acts of worship are attempts to communicate a faith without giving direct instruction.'[26] The *Agreed Syllabus of the Inner London Education Authority* however marks a long overdue step in the right direction in a short article on the subject, concluding 'by adopting a broad definition of worship and linking it imaginatively with life as the pupils know it, it should be possible to achieve a sense of unity within the community, so that excusal for conscientious reasons is minimized, and the boys and girls enabled to appreciate and participate in religious experiences drawn from many sources and traditions.'[27] Full recognition is to be given to the fact that 'no membership of a Christian community can be assumed, and that a proportion of staff and older pupils may have intellectual doubts about the validity of worship.'[28] In this short article one can see that worship simply as worship is actually yielding to a variety of other religious, moral and social values.

Enough has been said to show that school worship is seldom if ever thought of as part of the school curriculum. No other part of the timetable has so successfully resisted change. Religious education thus presents a noteworthy paradox: worship, the content of which was not positively described in the Act, has been more conservative than the religious education classroom lesson, content of which is controlled in some detail through the Agreed Syllabuses. Perhaps if syllabuses had been imposed for school assembly, worship would have evolved as have other aspects of religious education. But assembly is not thought of as 'syllabus'; it is thought of as liturgy.

Some recent school assembly books make efforts to overcome the narrow (but precise) definition of worship we noticed in earlier writing.[29] Many schools are carrying out all sorts of new and valuable programmes for assembly. But what is needed is some consideration of the role of this daily school gathering in relation to the school's work as a whole.

Two preliminary steps seem to be necessary. First, we must ask whether the school assembly may have any potential for contributing to the general educational work of the school. Second, a theology of the school assembly must be developed which will be faithful both to educational and theological norms. As we have seen, it is doubtful whether this can be done as long as the assembly is thought of as worship. We begin therefore by asking what other potential it may have.

What educational potential has the assembly?

Of course, school assembly is already valued in many schools not because of its intrinsic worth as praise, nor for any specifically religious reasons, but for non-religious benefits which accrue more or less incidentally. These include the widely held belief that there is psychological value in an orderly start to the school day, the occasion for school rituals such as the creation of prefects, the opportunity for the head to build up some kind of relationship between himself and the school as a whole and so on.

Can the assembly be reasonably expected to fulfil any other non-liturgical functions? The following may serve as hypothetical functions with a *prima facie* plausibility; whether they can be more than that will be known after more prolonged observation after deliberate adoption.

The relation between the school and the community has been

growing rather more intimate in recent years but one still finds a few schools where apart from sporadic prayers for 'the nations of the world' and 'the leaders of industry' the potential of the school assembly for extroverting the school is not explored. The vast increase in the quantity and the emotional significance of the material offered to young people through participation in pop culture and through the mass media places a fresh demand upon the school to include within its total life discussion of such pressures. A number of the suggestions made below have a bearing on this theme, but here we may note the possibility of devoting assembly for a week to the affairs of a particular overseas country, with displays of work assembled by the geography department, recorded music of the country and visitors and perhaps films. Pupils with pen friends abroad may read their letters from their friends, and schools with a connection with a sister school abroad may centre the programme on the life of that school, with the playing of message tapes. If religion is an issue in the country deing dealt with, as it might be in almost any country, this would be treated as an attempt to understand the hopes and ideals of the people. The missionary societies, as they are still sometimes called, provide in their audio-visual aid catalogues a good range of materials which can be used to document assemblies of this sort.

But this kind of assembly will not be a geography lesson or a religious education class, although it will include some elements of both. The additional factor is the pupil in the presence of the whole school community which is expressing its concern for the lives and problems of another people. The pupil is engaged at another level of his self-identification, himself as a member of the school rather than as a member of a particular teacher's class. Whether the pupil would introject some of the qualities which he then perceived in the school community is a very complex problem, but emphases of this sort seem to be at least a step in the direction of moral education. The role of controversy is a vital one and will be discussed below.

Second, and this grows out of the previous illustration, assembly can be used to heighten awareness of current affairs not only with a view to creating concern for others but in order to strengthen the pupil's own sense of participation in the community and to help him to form attitudes about moral problems through hearing the relevant facts and arguments. Weeks of programmes should therefore be devoted to issues such as personal and national use of money, the use of leisure time, the problems created by advances in medicine, the question of human rights. Methods of presentation would include visiting speakers, panels of teachers and pupils, displays of posters, readings from newspapers, playing of taped radio and television items and the reading of essays and letters written by pupils. Weeks like this would often be linked with practical matters. The group of boys who went to put up the tents for the annual Darby and Joan Club fair would report on the event, appeals being held in the school would be backed with assemblies describing the cause, and the social service committee would have a day or two to give its terminal report.

If moral education is not a matter of the inculcation of the 'right' moral answers to problems but is based upon an understanding of the method of moral reasoning, the understanding of what moral arguments are and how choices may rationally be made between various moral alternatives, then the school need not offer the one true answer but will offer a variety of answers and corresponding choices.[30] The same is true of religious education.

Those in charge of assembly if it is to be used in this way, must grasp the nettle of controversy firmly. The fear of debate which emaciates many a school assembly must be overcome if progress is to be made in making it a truly educational period linked with the rest of the curriculum. Calm and clear controversy is the very life-blood of the moral, social and religious education of young people today. The view that it is harmful for pupils to realize that members of staff disagree about fundamental matters must be denied. The silent school, or the school inhibited by an imposed and superficial unanimity will be a poor place for the members of the pluralistic society to find their criteria.

This is particularly true when we consider a possible role of the assembly in the teaching of democracy. The practice of holding mock elections during national elections will perhaps become more widespread. Speeches from pupil candidates, and from representatives of the actual political parties should find a place in assembly.

The main concern of the life of the school should be exhibited in the daily assembly. The clubs and societies may hold an annual fair, taking lunch times and assemblies to present their activities to the rest of the school. The careers master will have a week during his career exhibition. The music department should from time to time present the fruits of its labours.

This leads us to think of some ways in which the assembly might help to relate the various topics covered in class by subject. This is being widely carried out in junior schools, where displays of work and assemblies devoted to work schemes such as 'Growing Things', 'People Who Help Us' and so on are common. The method could be taken much more seriously in the secondary school where subject divisions are more serious. Sixth forms working on integrated general studies courses will find plenty of ideas, but in other forms and in other schools the severity of the fragmentation of knowledge may be seen from the fact that it is often difficult to find any way in which the subjects share a common interest or contribute to the solving of the same problems. Weeks of assemblies deliberately exploring 'What the Subjects Say' may be of help here. Biology, history, religious studies, music, literature and all the rest may be able to join in a symposium on what the subjects say about war, about the future of man, about cities, about the imagination, and about death. The methods might consist of interviews of A-level candidates by those studying other subjects, comments by subject teachers, reports by groups of pupils who have been working on a project to discover what their subject said about the matter. Often the weeks devoted to social and international affairs will, by implication, be showing the way in which all the subjects are one.

Finally, in this list of *ad hoc* suggestions, it may be noted that assemblies of this sort may possess the added advantage of throwing members of staff together in the discussion which must precede many of these weeks. Subject barriers exist in the commonroom as well as in the classroom. Some teachers may be encouraged to explore the humane implications of their own subjects more deeply and this will in turn affect the quality of their own teaching.

Let us now turn to the theological implications of what has been said.

A threshold for worship?

A central feature of worship, and one which Paul Tillich has shown to be definitive for religion as a whole, is the idea of ultimate concern.[31] Worship is the response to that which is of ultimate concern. This can be seen by examining the words of the great hymns of worship, such as F.W. Faber's 'My God, how wonderful thou art' or W.C. Smith's 'Immortal, invisible'. These hymns evoke the spirit of worship by reminding the believer of the depth of his commitment to God, by repeating the aspects of God which are of ultimate concern to the worshipper.

Yet the religious impact of hymns of this sort upon school pupils is very limited. The words describe experiences which are foreign to too many of them. They cannot express the 'worth-ship' of that which is not valuable to them. We invite them to express the 'worth-ship' of that which is not valuable to them. We invite them to express concern over that for which they have no sense of concern.

What is the school to do? Shall we read the words to them before they sing? Shall the headmaster give a talk explaining the meaning of the hymn? Perhaps their understanding of the words will be increased. Will their understanding lead to concern? They may understand and respect the concern which they see some of their teachers to have, but will they make God an object of concern for themselves? If not, they cannot worship, and they ought not to be required to try.

School worship does not bite sufficiently deeply into the genuine concerns of pupils. We throw down a ladder, the lower rungs consisting of hymns and prayers and Bible readings. We hope that our pupils will be helped by these symbols to appreciate God. When they do not, we add further rungs, extending the ladder through use of more concrete symbols such as a cross, a vase of flowers or a white cloth. Still the symbols fail to express any level of pupil concern.

We must start from the other end. Pupils are possibly concerned about their families and friends, their health and hobbies, their success or failure at games and studies, and about their futures. Some, especially the older ones, will be developing concerns for the society around them and others will be beginning to share the international aspirations of humanity. It is here that a threshold of worship may be found.

But how shall we decide which of the many concerns of pupils are most appropriate for evoking and expressing ultimate concern, this prerequisite and essential ingredient of worship? A pupil may be very concerned because he has failed to do his homework, and may also be concerned when he learns that large numbers of people live in ignorance and sickness. We must look for the concerns which contain within themselves the potential for developing or implying a more profound concern, ones which lead on to concern which comes home to one in the most serious and unqualified manner. My concern that I might get wet if it is raining is a passing worry which does not grasp me with final seriousness. But if I were to be concerned as to whether I was wasting my life away, this might be a matter which in a moment of reflection could lead on to questions of great seriousness about my duty to myself and to society and, in the end, to God.

Our task in school assembly then is to take the most transparent, the most symbolic, of the concerns of our pupils, in the hope that they will be led from the trivial and the immediate and the local to the significant, the enduring, and the universal concern. When pupils do this, they are sharing in at least a part of what religious people experience in the act of worship.

It would be misleading however to describe assemblies of this kind as acts of worship. Much confusion is created by the attempt to maintain that, because the affairs of life, when considered in the light of absolute ethical and religious demands, may lead to religious experience and may be preparatory to prayer and worship, such ethical and religious considerations are themselves prayer and worship. Probably loving concern for others is an attitude without which intercessory prayer would be impossible, but to say that such loving concern is what prayer *is*, is merely to abuse the word 'prayer'.[32]

I am suggesting that we should abandon worship in LEA schools both because this worship tries to do what it cannot and ought not try to do, and because it is failing to fulfil an educational potential which it might otherwise realize. Those to whom it is important that pupils should have the option off coming to understand what worship may mean to the religiously committed will have the task of breaking worship into its components and taking any of these which may be compatible with the educational work of the LEA school, and then expressing these elements in frankly secular settings.

One such element will be that of ultimate concern. Another may be the element of affirmation. Worship is the joyful affirmation of faith, it is the response of gratitude towards God. This aspect of joyful affirmation may be included in assembly programmes, especially with younger children, for whom this is the most natural aspect of worship. Let the young child experience delight in colour and movement and in creativity. Joyful affirmation is in itself not worship, unless it is directed towards an object of ultimate concern, but unless the experience of the child includes such things, he may never come to worship at all. The object is not to worship in the school but to widen the options facing the child by providing the sorts of experiences without which the experience of worship will be unlikely to arise. Much more knowledge of the psychology of prayer and worship will be needed before this task can be carried out properly, and this must be connected with further knowledge of the religious growth of young people, in order to include in assembly the prerequisites of worship which will be relevant at various ages.

Of course, there is no reason why assembly should not from time to time be used directly to impart some understanding of other religions, and of the Christian religion, and this will take its place beside other aspects of community life which will be presented in assembly. The Imam of the local Mosque may be asked to come and read some well loved parts of the Koran and to say a few words about them. He may ask the school to listen while he reads a prayer that Muslims love to pray. The same sort of thing can be done with the Christian denominations during the week of prayer for Christian unity. But these assemblies will not purport to be services of worship, although individual believers may well enter prayerfully into the expression of their community faith. The aim of these assemblies is not to secure commitment nor to profess faith but to deepen understanding and facilitate choice. A similar end may be attempted by parties of pupils visiting religious buildings and watching the services there, and another method is the study of liturgical practices and texts in the classroom. Each of these approaches has its strengths and each has its limitations.

Finally, it may be worth observing that the sort of assembly outlined here will require even more careful planning and publicity. No one teacher should carry the burden of such a central educational session. The school will need to have a panel of teachers from various departments, and pupils from various forms. This panel will meet early in the term to plan the assemblies for the following term. The panel will have before it the syllabuses of all subjects for the following term so that points of contact can be noticed and the places where cross-fertilization in assembly might be attempted. Such a planning group might become a clearing house for syllabus ideas and might pioneer a closer degree of cooperation throughout the whole school.

If assembly is to catch the imagination of the school, publicity is essential. Posters setting out the themes for the following weeks must be displayed and followed up in the form of pages in the school newspaper or magazine devoted to reports of particularly memorable assemblies will help to deepen the impression of assembly as the focal point of school life. The panel will naturally receive criticism and will take reactions and further ideas into account when planning.

Religious education has little to fear from such a development. It would be incongruous to continue to modify the aims and methods of classroom work but to leave the assembly untouched. Religious educationalists will need courage to guide developments, for in many schools it will be the task of these teachers to initiate assembly reform. But the issue facing them is becoming clearer. Is religion, especially that of the assembly, to join the main stream of the school's educational work and play an important part in linking the subjects together, or is it to remain on the sidelines as the bit which doesn't fit?

Notes

1 Berry, C.L. *Teachers' Handbook to A book of Morning Worship*, J.M. Dent, 1946, p. 11.
2 *Oxford Book of School Worship*, Parts II and III, revised edition, SPCK, 1958, p. vi. See E.F. Braley, *The School without the Parson*, R.E.P., 1945, pp. 7ff for a common type of Christian welcome.
3 Loukes, Harold *New Ground in Christian Education*, SCM, 1965, p. 128.

4 Cant, Revd Canon R. 'The nature of worship' in *School Worship*, ed. C.M. Jones, University of Leeds Institute of Education Paper No. 3, 1965, p. 10. Cant's own answer is no. See also 'Opium of the children: The school assembly today' by H.A. Ree in *The Times Educational Supplement*, 13 November 1964, and the correspondence in following issues. For a recent defence of religious worship in schools see May P.R. and Johnson, O.R. *Religion in Our School*, Hodder, 1968, Chapter VI.

5 Alves, Colin, *Religion and the Secondary School*, SCM, 1968, pp. 57–9.

6 *Oxford Book of School Worship op. cit.* p. v.

7 *Ibid.*, p. 46.

8 *Ibid.*, pp. 70ff.

9 *Ibid.*, pp. 60–6.

10 *Ibid.*, p. 64.

11 *Ibid.*, p. 68.

12 *Ibid.*, p. xif.

13 *Ibid.*, p. 46.

14 *Ibid*, p. 175.

15 In, e.g., *Worship and the Modern Child*, SPCK, 1957.

16 *Ibid.*, p. 147.

17 *Ibid.*, p. 149.

18 *Ibid.*, p. 172.

19 A sign of a new conception of the relationship between the church and state religious education is to be found in the Report of the Special Committee of the British Council of Churches Education Committee which prefaces Alves, *op. cit.* p. 14: '. . . preparation for church membership is the duty of the churches, not the school.'

20 *Ibid.*, p. 151. The last word is placed in Williams' own quotation marks.

21 *Ibid.*, footnote p. 152.

22 *Ibid.*, p. 150.

23 Berry C.L., *op. cit.*, p. 20.

24 *Ibid.*, p. 27.

25 *School Worship*, Institute of Christian Education, 3rd ed., 1957, p. 5.

26 1966, p. 117. The philosophy of J.G. Williams, expressed in his *Leading School Worship* is specificially endorsed by the authority on this page.

27 *Learning for Life*, ILEA, 1968, p. 13.

28 *Ibid.*, p. 12.

29 For example, Doidge, R. and E. *Boys and Girls at Worship*, SCM, 1965; Bielby, A.R., *Sixth Form Worship*, SCM, 1968.

30 Wilson, John, *An Introduction to Moral Education*.

31 For example, Brown, D. Mackenzie (ed.), *Ultimate Concern: Tillich in Dialogue*, SCM, 1965.

32 See Rhymes, Douglas, *Prayer in the Secular City*, Lutterworth, 1967 and Robinson, J.A.T. *Honest to God*, SCM, 1963, pp. 99ff., both of whom seek to redefine prayer and worship without making it clear that this redefinition involves a substantial departure from the usual meanings of these words.

2. *Worship and Education: The Fourth R: The Report of the Commission on Religious Education in Schools*

Introduction

The *Durham Report on Religious Education*, which appeared in June 1970, offers an authoritative survey of the role of religion in education in England and Wales. Chapters on theology and education, on moral education and on religion in the educational systems of other Western societies offer much stimulus to thought, and the recommendations arising from the survey will be welcomed in most cases by moderate opinion. The suggestions that the statutory position of the Agreed Syllabuses should be abandoned and that the wording of any new Education Act should be much more flexible regarding the place of religious education are examples of the readiness for change which the *Report* exhibits at many points.

There is however one important area in which the *Report* is not entirely satisfying. School worship, far from being incompatible with educational principles, is thought to be required by them, and should therefore be retained in the county school.[1] A number of arguments are offered, but the one derived from consideration of educational ideals is 'the one most cogent reason why school worship must remain in English schools' (par. 297). It is this argument which will be discussed here.

The educational argument for worship

Two related arguments may be discerned in that part of the *Report* which deals with worship in county schools (pars. 284–320) and elsewhere in the volume. The first one which will be discussed here is derived from consideration of the content of religious education and the second from consideration of the aims of religious education.

The argument from the content of religious education

This may be summarized as follows: 1. Religion is educationally justifiable as part of the curriculum (pars. 112–16 and 201–18). 2. Worship is a 'significant feature' (par. 297) of religion. 3. 'Some experience of worship is essential ... if justice is to be done to the content of religious education' (par. 117).

The first proposition needs qualification and is indeed qualified both directly and by implication at various points in the *Report*. The truth of the matter seems to be that *some* aspects of *some* religions are justifiable as part of the curriculum. The doctrine of original sin, in some of its forms, is not a suitable basis for the upbringing of children but the concept of Christian love is highly significant for the whole of the educational process (par. 138). Certain parts of the Old Testament could inhibit moral development (par. 185). A religion with an exploratory approach towards its own theology is more consistent with modern Western educational requirements than a religion which might have a closed and static theology (par. 113). The teacher must select from the numerous sacred books (par. 213) and must go on selecting from the immense quantity of religious facts and beliefs those which he finds are most appropriate to his pupils and most consistent with the ethos of the educational environment within which he works. He asks if the proposed material is pupil-related, if it is relevant, and if it can be taught in an open-ended way (pars. 246–8). We conclude that there are aspects of a particular religion or of religion as a general human phenomenon which however significant they may be in their religious context might not necessarily be studied in the county school or in any school, perhaps because the material is inappropriate for the level of understanding of the pupils or because it is unhappy in its association with the ideals of the rest of the curriculum.

Worship is certainly a significant feature of the Christian religion and of most other religions but this in itself does not allow us to include the study or the practice of worship in the curriculum. If however there were no other overriding objections to its inclusion, the argument that an item was necessary to do justice to the full content of a subject would be a strong one. Private prayer is a significant feature of Christianity, and so is the mission of the church in evangelism, but teachers in county schools do not set so many minutes of private prayer as homework, nor a certain amount of missioning experience as a vacation task. On the other hand, service to others, which is also an essential aspect of Christianity, is encouraged by many religious education teachers (and others) and often officially supported by schools. Some important features of the Christian faith, such as participation in the Eucharist, are not insisted on in county schools partly for ecclesiastical reasons, and others such as private prayer and mission experience are not insisted on for mainly educational reasons. These examples illustrate the point that although certain important aspects of certain religions ought to be included we cannot claim that any particular aspect must be studied or performed at school merely in order to do justice to the subject. We may only claim this if there are no overriding considerations. Such considerations do exist, I think, in the case of performing worship, but not in the case of studying worship.

The argument from the aim of religious education

This argument, which appears at several points in the *Report*, may be summarized as follows. 1. The aims of religious education can be justified educationally (par. 215). 2. Experience of worship is a necessary stage in the fulfilment of these aims: (a) *The linguistic argument:* to understand a religious proposition it is necessary to see it in its real-life setting. This will include the ritualistic and worshipful contexts of religious statements (par. 117); (b) *The experiential argument:* worship is the practical application, the experienced reality, of religion corresponding to the practical aspects of other subjects (latter part of par. 117 on p. 61). Thus 'religious understanding' (one of the acceptable aims of religious education) 'cannot be developed without experience of worship' (par. 298 on p. 136). 3. Acceptance of the aims of religious education entails acceptance of regular school worship. (The argument is summarized in this form to highlight the aspects which concern us here. The *Report* does not omit discussion of why the worship may not satisfactorily be provided at home or church).

The linguistic argument, as it is here being called, is in itself a valuable comment on teaching religion. It is undoubtedly true that religious statements cannot be correctly understood if they are removed from the contexts in which religious communities use them. The devotional and liturgical setting is certainly important, and this should be studied. But there seems to be insufficient reason for thinking that this understanding can only come, or may best come, through the pupil's actual participation as a worshipper in regular services of worship.

Religious educators want their pupils to exercise empathy towards religious people and critical sympathy towards what they say. They rightly want them to understand, as far as the limits of the county school situation permit, what it feels like to be religious. Since it is not the object of teachers of religion to secure or 'even to press for acceptance of a particular faith or belief system' (par. 217) it is not possible to have pupils understand what it is like to be a Christian and to use Christian language by actually converting them. It must therefore be done by good teaching, by representation, by imagination, and by the growth of insight. It may be done by meeting, listening to and talking with religious believers, by collecting their prayers, and by visiting and observing (whether on or off the school premises) religious worship and seeking to comprehend the atmosphere and the intentions of such services. But the need to study the worshipful context of religious language does not seem to require actual worship, even if the number of services is reduced from five to two or three a week (par. 309). There are, in short, various ways in which one can 'look to the worshipping activities' (par. 117, quoted by the *Report* from Ninian Smart) of religions and actually worshipping is in some ways the least desirable.

The experiential argument, as it is here being called, is not satisfactory for the following reasons.

1   The practical, immediately experienced aspects of religious studies in schools are rather varied but include catching the inspiration of great lives, following a religious discussion between teacher and class, seeing how a teacher deals with a religious problem, painting or acting religious scenes or portraying religious emotions, and watching and as uncommitted guests courteously taking part in the ceremonies of various religious communities. There is a further sense in which all experience of service, of love, of alienation and of reconciliation may, as this *Report* shows so clearly, help the pupil to existentially understand certain religious expressions and symbols. It is misleading to narrow this wide range of ways in which pupils may be helped to experience the power of religion to their actual participation in worship. The error rests upon the supposition that in the classroom one is only talking about religion whereas in worship one is actually approaching God. We ought rather to say that experiencing worship is but one of the ways in which pupils may come to understand what it would be like if they believed in God. Then we should ask whether some of the ways are educationally preferable to other ways.

2   But although this variety exists in the means whereby teachers of religion may help their pupils to see the life-setting of religious language, and by imagination to enter into it themselves, there are also limits to the variety. We have already seen, and the

Durham Report rightly emphasizes, that teachers of religion may not seek to actually convert their pupils, although this would obviously be the most effective of all ways of helping them to grasp the existential meaning of religion, nor may they expose them exclusively to one religion in the hope that they will come to understand and value that one religion, nor may they take advantage of their superior knowledge, experience and perhaps intelligence to force religious views on their classes. The situation teachers of religion face is that some of the means of introducing pupils to religion are legitimate and others are not. Expecting, indeed requiring, pupils to worship seems to be in the latter category.

We have seen that the arguments which the *Report* advances to show that school worship is *required* by educational and religious educational considerations cannot be sustained. Not only do the arguments not compel the conclusion, but other difficulties arise which seem to count rather strongly *against* the conclusion. We will now consider only the main difficulties which the *Report* itself envisages.

Problems arising from the arguments about education and worship

A   The *Report* discusses the problems which arise from *the tension between worship understood theologically and worship understood educationally*.

(a)   *Worship understood theologically*. The central purpose of Christian worship is 'to respond appropriately to the love and grace of God as seen in Jesus Christ, and to make the divine power a reality in the lives of worshippers' (par. 295). In discussing the educational use to which worship may be put, the *Report* reminds us forcefully, 'It can only be worship if it is indeed the appropriate response of creature to creator and, as such, an activity to be undertaken for its own sake' (par. 298). The problem which immediately arises is faced in what follows, 'To regard it in this way is admittedly, as the secularist maintains, to assume the truth of certain Christian doctrines' (par. 298). (It should be said this is not only maintained by the secularist but by certain Christians such as the present writer.)

(b)   *The educational norms for religious teaching in county schools*. Religious education must be heuristic: '... the exploratory aspects of a discipline whose task of interpretation is never complete nor rounded off in a neat system' (par. 113): '. . . religious education is conducted in the form of an exploration, that no one view-point is considered automatically or regarded as invariably correct' (par. 248).

There is clearly some tension, of which the *Report* is well aware, between worship, which since it assumes the truth of certain doctrines appears to be a closed intellectual activity, and the rest of religious education, where no doctrine or truth is considered to be invariably correct.

The problem is dealt with in the *Report* is two ways. The first involves a consideration of the psychology of the worshipper. The theological point of view does not exhaust the description of worship. If held too exclusively a theological description may be 'too restrictive' (par. 296) and 'worship cannot solely be defined' in this way. Worship has 'diverse origins' and produces a 'diversity of human reactions' (par. 296). When we contemplate the psychological responses to any given act of worship or examine the composition of almost any worshipping group, it can be seen that 'attendance at an act of worship does not necessarily imply or pre-suppose total personal commitment to the object of worship' (par. 296) (This is probably the 'easement of conscience' which is referred to in par. 317.)

This point is supported by an analysis of worship into the expressive and the didactic. 'Needs and fears' may be expressed in worship as well as adoration (par. 299) and worship shares with classroom activity a certain teaching function (par. 300).

It is difficult to see that these replies are successful in meeting the force of the problem. Although not exhaustive, the theological description of worship is, as the *Report* rightly emphasizes (par. 298), essential for Christians and consideration of the variety of moods and reactions of those present at an act of worship in no way weakens the demand of the theological nature of the act. To what extent then does the observation that people vary in their reactions to worship offer relief to the conscience of the uncommitted person? For although it is valuable to respond with 'humility and awe' or with 'world-weariness and fear' (par. 296) is it also valuable to respond with scepticism, with unqualified disbelief, and with rejection of the assumptions of the act of worship? Attendance may not imply total commitment, but does it imply any commitment at all? It might be said that all it need imply is commitment to a search for religious truth. But worship assumes certain doctrines to be true. There is considerable difference between a search for truth and an assumption of truth. (It is interesting to see that in par. 357 the practice of confirmation in independent schools is described as having 'been all too often . . . a ceremony undergone by almost all pupils whatever degree of Christian commitment they have reached'. The same is true of county school worship.)

Moreover, members of staff and pupils are usually not only expected or required (as the case may be) to attend. They are expected or required to take part. They hold hymn books in their hands. They bow their heads. They stand and sit together at the same times. They sing and speak words addressed to God and to Jesus Christ. Is school worship ever conceived of as presented by the religious education department to mere spectators? The act of worship in schools normally assumes participation. And those who participate in the worship participate in fact or by strong implication in the assumptions upon which the worship is based and which it exists to express.

The division of worship into the expressive and the didactic is inadequate since the most significant constituent is omitted, namely, the affirmative. The nature of the didactic process in the worship is fundamentally different from that which takes place in the classroom.

The problem of the openness of worship is discussed in par. 298. Openness, the *Report* indicates, does not mean that the teaching of religion will proceed without any basic assumptions (pars. 136f) and adherence to these basic assumptions is held to be consistent with the required openness. But openness as defined in para. 248 is clearly not reconcilable with the position of worship as described in para. 298. In classroom teaching one certainly starts from basic assumptions. But no basic assumption is free from examination and criticism at some time or other in the teaching periods. In worship however one not only starts but finishes by assuming the truth of certain doctrines.

B   A second problem discussed in the *Report* is *the difficulty of finding an alternative to the present situation*. The *Report* is not however very consistent at this point. The secular type of assembly is allowed to take place occasionally (para. 312) although it is described in rather an unimaginative way. But in para. 306 the secular assembly is regarded with some caution, because, it is claimed, 'that would have very clear irreligious implications'. A secular ceremony is envisaged as 'studiously excluding all "religious" material'. But this fear is surely groundless. The *Report* itself asks that where secular assemblies are held they should 'at least sometimes recognize that religious values are a feature of ... humanity'. This is a moderate and reasonable request. There should be little difficulty in arranging school assemblies which recognize the religious in various ways not only sometimes but often.

The *Report* concludes that direction of school worship should continue to be a statutory provision. This is considered necessary in order to avoid changes of policy with changes of personnel and to avoid local controversy if responsibility for worship were to become local (para. 310). But in the complex situation of the multi-racial school, it is suggested (para. 315) that the pattern of school worship could be agreed by the local authorities, including the teachers of the school concerned. Why should not this become the usual pattern? Why should there not be occasional changes in local policy? The *Report* wisely recommends that the statutory position of the Agreed Syllabuses should be abolished (par. 219). 'We seek for religious education the same freedom which is enjoyed by every other subject' (par. 220). Why should not the admirable situation described in par. 220 where the content of classroom religious education is the product of local experiment and consultation also prevail in decisions about the nature and in the selection of the content of the school assembly?

Conclusion

There are, as has already been noted, other arguments in the *Durham Report* for the retention of school worship. But this, the 'one most cogent reason', the argument about the necessary association of school worship with religious education as it is currently being understood, fails to convince.

Note

1 See the discussion of these issues in the previous chapter.

PART II

The Nature of
Religious Education

3.   *From Christian Nurture to Religious Education: The British Experience*

Introduction

Religious education in Britain, as in many other Western countries, has been moving away from its traditional function, that of fostering the Christian faith, towards an open, descriptive, critical, enquiring study of religion (Knight, 1976). In Australia, this change has been marked by the publication of the Steinle Report (Waters, 1974) and the Russell Report (Russell, 1974), in Scotland by the Millar Report (Laidlaw, 1972) and in England by the Durham Report (*The Fourth R*, 1970), the Schools Council working paper of 1971 (Schools Council, 1971) and by the work of individuals such as Cox (1966), Smart (1968) and Smith (1969).

But whereas in Canada, the United States, Australia and New Zealand the movement, with various degrees of energy and success, has involved the *introduction* of a professionally-taught educational curriculum and the qualifying or suspension of a previous system which had been completely secular, or may have used clergy as instructors in 'released time' classes, in England and Wales it has involved a change of direction in a religious education enterprise which has been officially encouraged by legislation since 1944 and has been a regular part of public education since 1870. The British education systems have never been secular. The British experience has thus been an evolution within existing legislation using the same teachers. The situation is thus marked by continuity rather than by abrupt innovation. On the other hand, the result is a very patchy situation in which areas, and schools within areas, differ considerably in their approach to the subject. So in a large British city today, you may find one school justifying its descriptive study of world religions on the grounds of the large ethnic communities in the area, while a few blocks away, the same plurality of cultures will be used by another school to justify an almost evangelistic presentation of

Christianity alone. It may also be argued that it is more difficult to change the direction of a moving body than to start from scratch in the desired direction. You certainly have to distinguish in Britain between informed opinion as to what should be done in religious education and what is actually being done. The Lancashire Survey (Lancashire, 1975) found that only one secondary school in ten was using anything other than the traditional biblical syllabus, and a research report published in December 1977 (Bedwell, 1977) shows that of the secondary specialist teachers of religion in two mainly rural English counties about one-third are now expressing aims of an educational rather than a faith-nurturing kind. On the other hand, Britain is a relatively intimate society. The density of the culture, the ease of transport, the great number of conferences and consultations constantly taking place, the influence of centralized national bodies and agencies means that, in spite of the great range of local practice, it is possible to generalize about national trends and to speak of one or two fairly clear lines of overall growth, whereas in Australia, Canada and the United States, I have the impression that the state or provincial control of education means that official thinking may be at several stages and one almost has to describe the situation jurisdiction by jurisdiction.

It is interesting to notice that while in the other English-speaking countries mentioned discussion about the legal framework has centred on whether the existing secular legislation could accommodate any kind of religious education, in England and Wales (to which countries the 1944 Act applies) it has been a question of whether legislation which envisaged a faith-nurturing approach can accommodate a more critical educational approach. So the trend in other countries has been to include religion within a tolerant and mature secular system. But the British experience (because here Scotland and Northern Ireland may also be included) has been to secularize previously religious establishments. Generally speaking, it would be correct to say that in England and Wales only those in favour of a faith-nurturing approach are wholeheartedly in favour of all clauses of the 1944 Education Act. The majority of informed professional opinion favours retention of the Act in broad outline, believing that it is able to support the kind of educational approach which changed circumstances now require. There is a minority view which argues that substantial revision of the Act, or a completely new Act, is needed before the change from nurture to education can be really implemented (BHA, 1975; RE Council, 1976). Another result of the different roles played by the legislation in the different countries I have mentioned is that whereas in the United States and Canada the churches seem to feel that they are being asked to take something on, that is, to expand their mission in an educationally respectable way into the schools where they had not really been before, in Britain (where the faith-nurture carried out in the educational establishment was looked upon in earlier years as a triumph for the churches) and in Australia (where there has been a strong tradition of clergy entry to schools, pupils being divided for instruction along denominational lines) the churches are inclined to feel that they are being asked to give something up, to contract their sphere of direct influence, or to forego their traditional and sometimes hard-won rights.

The British situation to 1977

Although traces of the present British approach may be found in the non-directive 'discussion method' suggested by Harold Loukes (1961, 1965) and in the 'experiential Christian education' of Douglas Hubery (1965) it is correct to regard the then-called 'new RE' of the sixties as a Christian nurture movement along liberal and progressive lines (Horder, 1973). Some British commentators use the word 'confessional' or 'neo-confessional' to describe this approach, with particular reference to the sixties, and this is intended to indicate that the teaching of religion in schools was a confession of Christian faith, or sprang from a direct application of Christian faith in the classroom. But, although it is only a small semantic point, 'confessional' is less satisfactory than 'nurture', because both nurture and education can be and indeed must be interpreted as finding a rationale in applied theology and we ought to reject an implied distinction between a 'confessional' teaching which is an expression of Christian faith and an 'educational' practice which is not. The famous wave of Agreed Syllabuses which appeared in the later 1960s also expressed the ideals of this experiential faith-nurturing approach, the London Syllabus being the most progressive.

The major breakthrough in statutory religious education did not occur until 1975, when the Birmingham Agreed Syllabus and accompanying Handbook were published (Birmingham, 1975). The publicity which surrounded these events brought the new trends vividly before the general public for the first time, although the Syllabus and Handbook only summarized and resourced a kind of religious education which had been going on 'experimentally' for several years. A crucial factor was just that where the 1971 Working Paper of the Schools Council had been discussed by the teachers, the 1975 Syllabus was discussed by the parents and the politicians. This in turn led to a flurry of activity by various organizations including teachers' unions, churches, religious education associations and various working parties. Between the autumn of 1975 and the winter of 1976 no less than ten reports or statements on trends in religious education were published.

The approach of the Birmingham Syllabus may be summarized as follows:

1   The intention to nurture Christian discipleship, or indeed to foster faith in any particular religion or in religions as a group, was abandoned. The 1968 London Syllabus had gone some distance in this direction, and the Syllabus of the City of Bath (1970) had implicitly made the change, but it became explicit, almost to the point of bluntness, in the Birmingham documents (see especially the 'Introduction' to the Syllabus).

2   Various subsidiary purposes for religious education, barely mentioned in earlier Agreed Syllabuses, now became quite prominent. These concerned the contribution which could be made by religious education to community life in a plural society (the title of the Handbook is Living Together), the development of a critical understanding of religion, and enabling pupils to formulate their own personal philosophies and outlooks as a result of their encounter with the world religions. The units of work set out in the Teacher Handbook always try to include materials related to the three basic concerns – the communal, the phenomenological and the existential.

3   One of the ways in which religion is to be understood is by placing it in the context of the secular ideologies. Some familiarity with humanism is suggested on the part of primary boys and girls and in the secondary school study of at least one of the great secular stances for living is required. In order to assist the secondary teacher in meeting this part of the Syllabus, illustrative courses in humanism and communism were provided in the Handbook. Although the purpose of these studies is to further pupils' understanding of religion by contrast and comparison with their non-religious alternatives, the attitude of the Syllabus and Handbook is equally descriptive and objective when presenting the secular ways of life as it is when dealing with the religions. They are thus approached with fairness, objectivity and balance in themselves, although the overall intention of studying them is to contribute to pupils' religious education, just as the overall purpose of religious education is (for example) to contribute to community education, and yet the religions are

also presented in themselves as fully and fairly as possible. So the secular ideologies remain, in this syllabus, subsidiary and peripheral, and yet when they are studied, their integrity and possible validity are preserved and respected. They are not commended, except in the general sense that their inclusion itself indicates their dignity and value, nor are pupils warned against them, and that is true of the religions as well.

4 A principle of the treatment of all beliefs, whether religious or secular, is that no-one's faith or outlook is described in a manner with which believers would disagree. It would be going too far to claim that the religions are described in the way the believers would describe them, since believers do not always set out the life of their religious community in this sort of way, and in the context of their rivals and alternatives. But it can at least be claimed that the religious would not *disagree* with their presentation. Thus Christians helped with the Christianity courses, Muslims commented on the Islamic courses, and communist advice was taken when drawing up the communist optional course. The believer is the final authority on what he or she believes. Everything is to be taught as if in the presence of those whose life-faith it is. Criticisms as well as appreciations are offered of all ways of life, although it is also true that it was generally thought best to allow a religion to unfold without constant critical interruption, and pupils are expected to be respectful and thoughtful in their approach.

5 This means that the nature of agreement in such syllabus construction has undergone a profound change. Previous Agreed Syllabuses (with the exception of the fragmentary Bath Syllabus) had been ecumenical in that a common basis of agreed truth was sought. This had led, as long ago as the 1870s, to gibes about 'Agreed Syllabus religion', 'school religion' or 'religion of the lowest common denominator'. But the Birmingham approach seeks agreement not on truth but on procedure, and so asks, 'What do we all hold to be worth studying?' One result was that, since in Birmingham all participants agreed that without some knowledge of Christianity, nobody's religious education in Birmingham could be considered satisfactory, Christianity became the only religion which every pupil is required to study. Another consequence of the application of this principle was that Buddhism was not recommended for study before the sixth form (ages 17+) because Buddhism is not a large community in our city, and it was agreed that the ways of life most worth studying

by younger pupils were those significantly present in the school and reasonably visible in the surrounding community.

6   There follows a consequence for the teacher's own self-understanding. The immediate and obvious link between the teacher's own faith (if he or she has one) and the content of teaching is severed. There is now a gulf between preaching and teaching. The teacher's syllabus will not be controlled by one's own commitment. In some sense, this had always been the case but whereas previously, although forbidden by the Agreed Syllabuses to teach all he believed, he was at least teaching nothing but what he believed. Now he is teaching what he does not believe, except in the educational sense – he believes it worth teaching. The result of this is either to secularize the teaching force (no longer to see it as the lay apostolate of the church but as an independent body of professional educators) or to require a rather subtle theological grasp of how personal faith relates to educational practice. This calls for a new understanding of mission. Some forms of Christian faith find this presents greater difficulties than others.

7   In previous Agreed Syllabuses, world religions had not generally been studied before the sixth form, but in the Birmingham approach, pluralism in religion is presented to the child from his first year in school. He begins in the infant and junior school with the stories of the great religious leaders, with the myths and poetry of religions, with biographies, and with entrance into the rich world of religious festival and celebration. But not until the secondary stage is the world or religion divided sharply into the distinct world faiths. The young child learns about Diwali and the stories of Krishna, but Hinduism as such, as a separable and more or less coherent tradition, is unknown to him before age 12–16. Similarly, the child meets Jesus, Christmas, and the Saints, but Christianity is not perceived as a more or less self-contained sphere before the secondary school.

Thus it would be a mistake to regard the Birmingham approach as a study of 'belief systems'. These are but one aspect of the religious world. Beliefs are introduced, and in the later years of secondary school, belief *systems* become apparent. But it would be equally true to say that religion is presented as story and song, as ritual and custom. To attempt to organize the teaching of religion around 'belief systems' is to become unnecessarily narrow in an intellectual and perhaps sociological direction. So the syllabus deals with communism, as a political,

economic and cultural way of life exhibiting considerable variety, and not merely with Marxism, which, although perhaps a
less inflammatory word, suggests a study merely of the doctrines
of Marx.

Similarly, it is misleading to describe the Birmingham
Syllabus as consisting of 'comparative religion'. Religions are in
fact seldom *compared* until the later secondary years.

8   It would be a further misunderstanding to think of the Birmingham approach as being 'neutral', although this kind of syllabus
is often criticized on the grounds that an impossible or an
undesirable neutrality is required from the teacher. Or that a
'neutral' approach to religious education or to education as a
whole is demanded. The Syllabus is certainly impartial between
the religions and also (as far as eliciting belief goes) between the
religions and the secular ideologies. But this impartiality is itself
an expression of values, and springs from commitment. Religious education of this kind is not found in Islamic Pakistan,
Communist China or Christian South Africa. It seems to appear
only in the Western democracies, and its major advocate and ally
(although by no means its only one) is Christian faith. But to go
no deeper than professional ethics, what does the ideal of teacher
neutrality in world religions or in any kind of diverse classroom
mean but the right of all pupils to look upon the teacher as *their*
teacher? All pupils, whatever their family background, ethnic,
cultural, social class or religious origins or life, are entitled to
expect that their teacher will help them to understand, to grow
both in their own tradition and in the wider values of the
educated life. But this basic truth about teacher-pupil relations
immediately requires the teacher to teach each religion represented in his or her classroom, or school, (or world?)
with the same spirit of thoughtful, courteous appreciation and
enquiry.

9   Such teaching clearly calls for careful initial and in-service
teacher education, including the provision of a wider range of
resources. The City of Birmingham is meeting these needs
through a specialist Inspector for Religious Education in schools
and through its publication *Living Together, a Teachers' Handbook of Suggestions for Religious Education* which is a bulky
volume ('I found it hard to put down, but had found it even
harder to pick up', one teacher remarked) containing detailed
outlines of courses and lists of resources, as well as articles on
many aspects of teaching religion. This manual is under revi-

sion, and some dozen or so aspects are at present being considered by teachers' working parties.

Since the publication of the Birmingham documents in 1975, two more Agreed Syllabuses have appeared, from Avon (1976) and Cheshire (1976). Several other education authorities are in various stages of production. But it is not easy for an LEA Agreed Syllabus Conference to know where to go after Birmingham, and it is natural that there should be a period of caution while local councils gradually forget the controversies which almost engulfed the Birmingham proposals in 1973/74. We need time to debate the merits and the weaknesses of the Birmingham approach in conferences and journals, and time, too, for the accumulation of classroom experience and the assessment of pupil reactions.

No other LEA has yet adopted the Birmingham Syllabus, although it is not impossible that this will happen during the next few years. A useful step would be for the Syllabus to be adopted but for local bodies to produce their own versions of the Handbook. But if a Conference did not accept the Birmingham Syllabus, there might be a danger that the result would be to create an inferior form of the West Riding Syllabus of 1966 or the 1968 London Syllabus. It would not be easy to improve on *that* kind of syllabus, but if a different kind of syllabus is looked for, other than the Birmingham approach, then what? To go *beyond* Birmingham in an educational direction, rather than returning to nurture, will require a good deal of skill, because the problems raised by the Birmingham approach, other than those created by the fact that it is not a faith-nurturing approach, are quite complex.

It should be emphasized however that behind debates about the Birmingham Syllabus lies a deeper concern for the culture of Britain. Religious education has been thought of in some vague but emotive way as a significant conveyor of the culture, especially in terms of moral and spiritual values. What sort of a country is Britain today? Is this a Christian country? Is it a secular country? Is it a pluralist country? What is it becoming and what do we want it to become? These are the questions which in a time of economic uncertainty, recent entrance to the European Community, strife in Northern Ireland, and the growth of non-European cultures, have focussed on religious education in schools. Although the legal machinery of the Agreed Syllabus has the advantage of ensuring wide public and professional participation in curriculum decisions, this very accountability (which is a feature of school subjects unique to religious education) in England and Wales means that the specialists cannot just get on with subject development, as they can in the less controversial and less controlled subjects. Parents don't seem to write letters to the press about 'what is happening to our children' in geography classes.

British discussions of the Birmingham approach

Four areas of comment may be distinguished. First, there are those who are concerned less with the principles of the approach than its practicability. There is, they think, not enough time to teach so much; resources are inadequate; the teachers are not trained for it, or lack the right attitudes. These problems do exist, and would continue to exist whatever kind of syllabus were in use. One of the most effective ways to gain more than one period a week is to offer a valuable syllabus which obviously demands more periods, and to produce the teachers to do the job. Schools must be encouraged to pool resources, or to make use of the many resource centres which have been created in recent years (Restall, 1976), and Birmingham is particularly fortunate in possessing one of the best resource centres in the UK, at Westhill College under the direction of Michael Grimmitt.

The second and third areas of discussion may be grouped together because they represent opposite poles of interpretation. First, we find some humanists (BHA, 1975; Stopes Roe, 1976; White, 1976; and for replies, ACT, 1976; Atkins, 1977; Rankin, 1977) criticizing the approach of the Syllabus on the grounds that it is biased in favour of religion, so much so that it 'establishes religious indoctrination'. Then, on the other side, we have some Christians who see the Syllabus as symbolizing a de-Christianizing trend, who see it as a secularized and permissive approach, and call for a return to what they call 'Christian education', by which they mean Christian nurture (OCU, 1976). Both groups of critics are, I think, unconvincing, but I do not propose to devote time here to a detailed discussion of them. It is significant however that while what is emerging in Britain is religious education the humanist group (which by no means includes all humanists) dislikes it because it is religious, and the Christian group (a minority of Christians) dislikes it because it is education. The right response is to defend both words. Religious education should continue to offer a core of studies in the religions of humanity rather than become a study of all serious ways of life whatever; nor should it cease to be truly educational, in the open, enquiring sense.

The fourth area of discussion raises much deeper questions, and it is here that the outline of the next stage, which will go beyond Birmingham but not back to nurture, may be in formation. The fundamental point being discussed concerns the degree to which the Birmingham approach really is faithful to the nature of religion. Sometimes it is thought that in its very coolness, in its presentation of a variety of options, and in its careful setting of religion in a framework of viable and noble secular alternatives, the nature of religion as commitment is being lost. One leading British churchman has wondered if the approach might not turn out to be an initiation into agnosticism (Taylor, 1976). To this one may reply with the thought that it may not be possible to educate for life in a pluralist society without some initiation into agnosticism, if by this is meant some readiness to suspend an absolute adherence to one's own faith in favour of a readiness to listen to the other. Does not the very act of dialogue suppose some such attitude (Sharpe, 1975)? And the problem of whether such suspension can be a truly Christian response takes us into the question of the relation of Christianity to other religions. The Birmingham Syllabus is but a local (and painful just because it is local) case of a universal encounter between the religions.

A more probing analysis is offered by Revd Dr Daniel Hardy (Hardy, 1975, 1976). Hardy is still developing his critique and it may be premature to describe the questions he is asking, but one of his basic points is that religions do not in fact arise in this manner, and they are not apprehended by those who believe in them in this external way. The Birmingham ethos is not what it feels like when one is *in* a religion. Therefore the intention of modern religious education, which is to help pupils to understand what it would be like to take a religion seriously (Holm, 1976), is not fulfilled.

Hardy also points out that to separate religions, as is done in the secondary part of the Syllabus, to present them as contemporary cross-sections of religious experience and conduct, each divisible from the others, is to lose the historical and evolving nature of religious traditions, and to fail to realize the relations of syncretism or mutual consumption which have always existed between them. He also remarks that to imagine you can understand religion by looking upon religions as creations, assembled through the use of certain skills, is hostile to the self-understanding of the religions. The religious person is surely not one who has learned a skill at interpreting myths, in de-coding symbols, in drawing ethical conclusions from parables, skills of meditation and devotion, using these various learned responses in the construction of her or his own worldview. No, the religious person sees faith as coming from beyond; it is divine, it is a revelation. These are merely a few examples of the reflections offered on the Birmingham approach by Hardy.

It is still unclear however whether this critique is mainly methodological (that is, directed at *how* the Birmingham approach operates) or whether it is more fundamental and perhaps invalidates the whole enterprise of trying to teach religion educationally in a plural society. In as much as his comments amount to a theological criticism of this kind of phenomenological approach, the latter might well be the case; it might be that the only non-phenomenological way of teaching religion might be some kind of teaching 'from the inside' which might be difficult to distinguish from a nurturing approach, or at least one which carried nurturing assumptions, or positive truth-assumptions. But Hardy seems to be increasingly inclined to think that his comments are a theological-methodological criticism, and that a valid educational way of teaching religion consistent with the nature of religion can be found. *Learning for Living* expects to publish a third article by him on this subject during 1978.

But Hardy's articles do highlight the fact that the Birmingham approach is but one way of teaching religion educationally in a plural society. Another approach being developed in Britain sees religious education as a matter of developing understanding through concept-building. The basic concepts of a religion are distinguished theologically and philosophically, and then a psychological 'stage' approach is employed to build up the pupils' awareness from simple and preliminary concepts to more complex ones (Attfield, 1976). We also have the approach to religious education through local studies, which concentrates on field studies of the immediate environment of the school, and is increasingly being taught in integrated schemes with geography and social studies (Greer, 1977). A further approach arises from an analysis of what it means to understand religion, in terms of basic knowledge, then understanding beliefs, feelings and actions, and finally evaluating religious beliefs, feelings and actions by criteria both internal to the religion and drawn from other fields (Schools Council, 1977).

There is some discussion in Britain today about the place of evaluation in religious education, and I am thinking not so much of assessment by the teacher of the pupil's learning but assessment by the pupil of the religion he is studying. Some advocates of a strictly phenomenological approach (who perhaps misunderstand phenomenology?) suggest that the religious phenomena must be accepted for scrutiny without evaluation, since such subjective responses should be 'bracketed out'. I do not think this understanding of phenomenology is shared by its leading British exponents in the area of religious education but it is sometimes expressed by graduate students. Since religion is not to be appreciated because of its 'relevance' or its 'truthfulness', and since we should study it only 'for its own sake', because it is 'interesting', such student-teachers sometimes find it difficult to maintain motivation in their teaching careers. Most secondary pupils do not immediately and without explanation find religious studies interesting (although many do) and the teacher has to arouse the interest of his pupils by showing them its relevance to their lives and questions. But this involves evaluating the religion, and evaluating themselves in relation to the religion. Few young people care much about Parsee death and funeral customs until they have been interested in death as a problem for themselves. Then the response of the Parsees can have something to offer. Those who emphasize the importance of evaluation are usually religious educators (rather than professional research workers in religious studies) who are more inclined to ask about the educational contribution to be made by religion in the whole curriculum. They recognize that enabling pupils to evaluate religion, and themselves in the presence of religion (for the religion judges us even as we judge it), is a vital feature of the educational process, because it contributes to the pupils' growing autonomy.

Finally in this brief survey of the main questions being asked in the 'post-Birmingham' era, there is considerable interest in the problems of teaching Christianity. This is sometimes a defensive reaction to the charge that modern religious education is becoming de-Christianized, and sometimes it is proposed as a resolution of the problem referred to above, about teachers teaching religions not their own. Perhaps a revival of Christian studies, if carried out in a proper educational manner, might be a relief to many teachers. Others point out that Christianity presents special difficulties when treated 'as a world religion', and these are receiving some attention (Grimmitt, 1977). The problems spring not only from the cultural closeness of Christianity but also from the relative lack of formal behavioural features of Christianity (contrast Islam), the difficulty of determining its basic concepts, and the accompanying psychological problems when teaching so as to move pupils from elementary (that is, concrete) to more advanced (for example, abstract) thinking about Christianity.

Nurture and education

The British experience in recent years rests upon the distinction between Christian (or Hindu or humanist) nurture and education. Some British groups (OCU, 1976) appear unaware of the distinction, continuing to treat education as if it is or should be Christian nurture, if not Christian evangelism. Others adopt a rather equivocal position, such as *The Fourth*

R in which, although an educational position is adopted for classroom work, corporate school worship is defended in spite of its necessarily faith-nurturing or faith-assuming character. Of course, a lot of water has gone under the bridge since 1970, and it is likely that if this great Report were being written today, the distinction would emerge with greater consistency.

Still other groups (BHA, 1975) implicitly deny any middle ground between education and indoctrination, since they regard any religious teaching which intends to build up faith in religion, or is highly likely to have that result, as *ipso facto* indoctrinatory. It seems important however that religious communities should seek to show that between education (a term of approbation) and indoctrination (a pejorative term) there is indeed a middle ground. But this can only be done if the religious community nurturing processes within religious communities are clearly distinguished from both education and indoctrination.

It is probably true to say that in British religious education today informed specialist opinion accepts the education/nurture distinction (for example BCC, 1976), although the nomenclature varies. It has already been pointed out that the idea of nurture is sometimes expressed (less adequately, in my view) by the words 'confessionalist' or 'neo-confessionalist'. Some even continue to use 'Christian education' as opposed to 'religious education', and this usage usually conceals a confusion between (a) the processes and means whereby Christians bring up their children, (b) a Christian approach to, or philosophy of, general education, and (c) Christianity as curriculum content. But the vital distinction is not between a Christian approach to education and a non-Christian or (merely) religious approach, but rather between a Christian approach to critical, open religious *education* and a Christian approach to Christian upbringing or *nurture*. It is the processes which are to be distinguished, and *both* processes (nurture and education) may be equally although differently *Christian*. The assumption that it cannot be a Christian intention to do anything other than deepen Christian faith is disastrous for the Christian enterprise in schools, as it is disastrous for Christian vocation in any of the professions. To find a common ground in Christian faith for both nurture and education, without destroying the distinction between the processes or the unity of the faith, is the major theoretical problem confronting the churches in their dialogue with modern Western education. What we are dealing with here is thus not a semantic problem but a conceptual problem.

In what kinds of schools ought these different processes to take place? We might consider that the state or public schools in a pluralist democracy should not offer specific religious (or non-religious) nurture to anyone, but that such nurture is entirely a matter for the various religious communities acting through churches, synagogues and mosques. If we take this view, we must distinguish the *intentions* of state school education from its *results*. A good, open, critical, informative, freedom-enhancing education in religion certainly need not hinder Christian maturation, unless the latter is conceived in a narrow, protective manner which denies freedom and knowledge. Indeed, it has been suggested (Moran, 1972) that worthwhile Christian faith today is unlikely to emerge except as a result of such education. If this were the case, we are presented with a striking paradox. Only education can nurture faith. But not even education can intend to nurture faith. It is a matter of relative indifference to education whether Christian faith is nurtured or not. Nevertheless, such is the intimate relation of education and nurture to Christian faith that nurture may take place.

This situation, where the public schools ought not to intend to nurture faith at all, depends, for its continuing acceptance by Christians, upon maintaining this intimacy between Christian faith and education, which means enabling education to become itself. For while the school ought to give no more help to the pupil moving in the direction of religious faith than it should give to one moving in the opposite direction, it ought also to give no less. This means that we are opposed to schools being dominated by non-Christian or anti-Christian viewpoints just as sharply as we oppose the wish of some Christians to have schools dominated by Christian evangelistic interests. The churches' mission in education is to safeguard the open secularity of education and to preserve genuine pluralism.

Of course, there are Christians in all the Western democracies who judge that the public education systems have already reached an anti-Christian position, and accordingly we see some interest in the creation of 'Christian schools'. Well, these groups may be right, but I am reluctant to believe it. One must ask whether their protest is against non-Christian education in favour of Christian education, or whether it is against education in favour of Christian nurture. When such Christian groups claim that the educational approach to religious education is one of the factors which prompts them to form Christian schools, then I suspect that here we have Christians who want nurture *instead* of education. And this choice is not open to a church, only to a sect.

We can sum up the relation between nurturing intention and nurturing result like this: an intention to develop an appreciation of classical music may, in one way or another, lead to Christian faith. It certainly would not in any way hinder the emergence of Christian faith.

But such a result would be incidental to the intention to offer a musical education. But it may unintentionally become a threshold for Christian nurture, or for Jewish or Islamic nurture. The problem is to maintain a balance between swallowing education up and turning it into something else, and, on the other hand, losing rapport with education, until education is no longer amenable to a Christian rationale; and so becomes *hostile* to nurture. So the policy that the state school should not offer nurture *at all* depends upon maintaining a constructive Christian critique of trends in education.

The other possibility is that state schools should be *no more* responsible for *Christian* nurture than for humanist or Hindu nurture. In that case, nurture is no longer a possible but unintended result but an actual purpose of the state school, this being wider than education in the strict sense. According to this view, the evil lies in the injustice of a selective nurture rather than in the offering of nurture at all.

What then would be the position in schools containing none but pupils whose parents are willing for them to be nurtured in Christian faith? No invidious selectivity would then exist. Such conditions might well be found in some state schools, and could be presumed in all church-related schools, except those in areas where there were no non-church-related schools.

The first principle to be borne in mind is that whereas in the Christian family nurture can be offered *instead of* education, the school can only offer nurture *in addition to* education. But how can the nurture/education distinction be expressed in schools where it is decided to do both? Some of the English independent (private) schools have institutionalized the difference by having some staff who are secular educators teaching religious education, and others who are ordained ministers providing worship and confirmation classes. In the state schools, the religious education teachers sometimes distinguish between their classroom work and their voluntary lunchtime activities in supporting Christian groups, while a third pattern, which is common in the secular British universities, and could easily be extended to schools, is that, although the institution is secular and does nothing to advance or to hinder religion, this is compatible both with having a department of religious studies, and also with allowing any group of religious students to place before the university the name of a chaplain who will then be approved (but not paid or employed) and permitted to come and go on the campus in his ministry to the members of his religion.

There are three considerations which will enable us to choose between these two situations (education but not nurture, and nurture as well as education).

1   *The constitution of the school.* If a school is formally related to a church in some significant manner, then it surely has the right (but not necessarily the duty) of offering Christian nurture and of providing resources to carry this into effect. But only its educational activities should receive support from the state.

2   *The composition of the staff and pupils.* Can the school community be considered as much a part of the community of faith as the congregation which gathers for worship on Sunday? If so, it is right to offer nurture as well as education in the school. This could well be the case even in a state school which had such a membership, although it would, I think, still be the case that the nurturing activities ought not to be paid for by the state. There will naturally be every shade of opinion from school to school. Broadly it seems to me that the argument from natural justice should prevail against selective nurture in pluralist situations. If the minority of Catholic pupils cannot be nurtured, then the majority of Protestants must also look elsewhere than to school for nurture. No child should be placed in a position where he has to be withdrawn from the public, official curriculum of his school. I see no good reason for the provision of 'escape clauses' to justify continuance of a nurturing programme for the majority at the cost of the exclusion of the minority. Nurture is for some, but education is for all.

3   *Parents' rights.* In Catholic circles it has been customary to emphasize parents' rights, mainly in order to limit the right of the state to educate, and to ground the church's aid to parents in natural law. But the Lutheran Reformation laid stress on the civic duty to educate and placed parents firmly under the control of the public bodies as far as the schooling (and churching) of their children went. Perhaps the most promising approach for us today is to balance parents' rights not against the rights of state or church, but against the rights of children. The right of the parent to control the future by child upbringing must be limited by the right of a child to his own time. Time is the crux of the nurture/education distinction as it bears on human rights. Who has the right to withhold the past by denying nurture or to disminish the future by imposing nurture? Only a religion which is free concerning its own future can offer freedom to its young people. In that freedom lies the heart of the Christian support for both education and nurture, a freedom which insists on both, because it lives in hope.

References

[Abbreviation: LL *Learning for Living*]

ACT *Religious Education, a Considered View*, Association of Christian Teachers, 1976.

ATKINS, HENRY 'Stances for living', *Spectrum* 9, 1977, pp. 32–3.

ATTFIELD, D.G. 'A taxonomy of religious concepts', *LL*, 16, 1976, pp. 68–75.

AVON, *Religious Education Avon Agreed Syllabus*, 1976.

BCC *The Child in the Church*, British Council of Churches, 1976.

BEDWELL, A.E. 'Aims of religious education teachers in Hereford and Worcester, *LL*, 1977.

BHA, *Objective, Fair and Balanced, a New Law for Religion in Education*, British Humanist Association, 1975.

BIRMINGHAM, *Agreed Syllabus of Religious Instruction*, City of Birmingham Education Committee, 1975(a).

BIRMINGHAM, *Living Together, a Teachers Handbook of Suggestions for Religious Education*, City of Birmingham District Council Education Committee, 1975(b).

CHESHIRE, *Cheshire Agreed Syllabus*, 1976.

COX, EDWIN *Changing Aims in Religious Education*, Routledge and Kegan Paul, 1966.

GREER, JOHN *et al.* 'Religion in Ireland, a school-based curriculum development project', *LL*, 17, 1977.

GRIMMITT, MICHAEL AND READ, GARTH *Christians Today*, Kevin Mayhew, 1977.

HARDY, DANIEL 'Teaching religion, a theological critique', *LL*, 15, 1975, pp. 10–16.

HARDY, DANIEL 'The implications of pluralism for religious education', *LL*, 1976, pp. 55–62.

HOLM, JEAN *Teaching Religion in School*, OUP, 1975.

HORDER, DONALD 'Religious education in a pluralist society', *Religious Education*, special edition, 1973, pp. S.7-S.20.

HUBERY, DOUGLAS *Teaching the Christian Faith Today*, NSSU, 1965.

KNIGHT, C.G. 'The county school as an agent of Christian nurture 1944–1976', unpublished MEd. dissertation, University of Birmingham, 1976.

LAIDLAW, JACK 'The Millar Report', *LL*, 12, 1972, pp. 7–8.

LANCASHIRE, 'The Lancashire Religious' Education Survey', *LL*, 14, 1975, pp. 170–86.

LOUKES, HAROLD, *Teenage Religion*, SCM Press, 1961.

LOUKES, HAROLD, *New Ground in Christian Education*, SCM Press, 1965.

MORAN, GABRIEL, *Design for Religion*, Search Press, 1971.

OCU, *Ways Whereby Christian Education in State Schools Might Be Saved*, Order of Christian Unity, 1976.

RANKING, JOHN LETTER, *LL*, 16, 1977, p. 130.

RE COUNCIL, *What Future for the Agreed Syllabus? Report of a Working Party of the Religious Education Council of England and Wales*, 1976.

RESTALL, GERALD 'Resources for Religious Education', *LL*, 16, 1976, pp. 76–8.

RUSSELL, W.B. (Chairman). *Report of the Committee on Religious Education – Victoria*, 1974.

SCHOOLS COUNCIL, *Working Paper 36, Religious Education in Secondary Schools*, Evans/Methuen, 1971.

SCHOOLS COUNCIL, *A Ground Plan for the Study of Religion*, Schools Council Religious Education Committee, 1977.

SHARPE, ERIC J. 'The limits of inter-religious dialogue', *LL*, 16, 1976, pp. 9–12.

SMART, NINIAN *Secular Education and the Logic of Religion*, Faber, 1968.

SMITH, J.W.D. *Religious Education in a Secular Setting*, SCM Press, 1969. A revised edition of this book was published in 1975 under the title *Religion and Secular Education* by St Andrews Press, Edinburgh.

STOPES ROE, HARRY 'Education and the law in Birmingham', *LL*, 15, 1976, pp. 133–4.

TAYLOR JOHN V. 'Initiation into agnosticism', *LL*, 15, 1976, pp. 129–30.
The Fourth R: The Report of the Commission on Religious Education in Schools (The Durham Report), National Society/SPCK, 1970.
WATERS, KYLE 'Religious education in South Australia', *LL*, 13, 1974, pp. 200–22.
WHITE, JOHN 'Objective, fair and balanced, a reply', *LL*, 16, 1976, pp. 79–81.

4. *Religious Education in a Pluralist Society*

What difference does it make when the society in which religious education takes place contains more than one religion?

Religious education as the nurture of faith

Religious education has usually been nurture into the religious traditions and beliefs of the educating society. This idea presents few difficulties when the society is unanimous about its religion. In Norway the religious education offered in the state schools is Lutheran. More than 98 per cent of the population of Norway claims formal allegiance to the state Lutheran church. Whatever its merits, this is a perfectly straightforward situation.

But if the society is not unanimous about its religion, then there are problems. In the United States religion was denied access to the school. So diverse were the religious traditions that the school could not undertake the nurturing task on behalf of society and it was left to the individual religious communities to nurture their own young as they pleased. In Australia and New Zealand rivalry between Christian churches was intense, and since no single church was able to command a majority the schools systems became secular.[1] At a later date clergy were permitted to enter the schools and to nurture the young of their various persuasions in the classrooms. But the task to this day is not undertaken by the teachers.[2]

In England a compromise position was reached. The established church, unlike her Norwegian counterpart, did not command virtual unanimity. Even in Scotland, Presbyterianism, whether in its established or its dissenting forms, was sufficiently strong to make negotiated agreement with minorities unnecessary. So the Scottish pattern became 'according to use and wont' in each area, thus giving Presbyterianism a strong position, since 'by use and wont' it was the prevalent form of faith.[3] But Presbyterianism did not have the formal monopoly which the State Church of Norway possessed. England was peculiar in possessing both a strong established church and vigorous bodies of dissent. Had the range of plurality been wider, we might have seen something like the American or the Australian patterns emerge, accompanied by disestablishment. Had the range been narrower, we might have had something like the Scottish or even the Norwegian pattern.

The English compromise was reached in two stages. First, in 1870, there was agreement that if religion was taught in the maintained schools it would exclude 'formularies and catechisms distinctive of any denomination'. Second, from the mid-1920s by voluntary agreement and from 1944 by legislation, instruction would be given in the matters about which the participating denominations agreed. So a negative stage of exclusion was followed by a positive stage of inclusion, and so the Agreed Syllabus of religious instruction was created.

Plurality in English religious education

The English experience has thus been of plurality in religious education, and this experience is already more that a century old. But the device of the Agreed Syllabus made it possible to tolerate religious diversity without abandoning the traditional and expected role of religious education, that of nurturing the young into the religious traditions of the society. As rivalry between the religious communities declined, it was possible to move from the negative to the positive stage. But the agreement was only possible because the plurality was not very great. The English experience was confined to Christian churches.[4]

During the period of negative agreement, there was a high degree of rivalry but a low degree of plurality. During the period of positive agreement, there was a *low* degree of rivalry and a low degree of plurality. But what would happen if there were a *high* degree of plurality? If there were also a high degree of rivalry between the religious groups, religious education in the schools would not be possible. Even if there were a tolerant atmosphere, that is, low rivalry, it would not be possible to continue with religious education as normally and traditionally understood in a society with a high degree of plurality. The simple reason for this is that the more diverse a society, the more difficult it is to define the religious tradition of the society in such as a way to win enough agreement to make a syllabus. This is the situation in this country today and this is the main reason (although not the only one) for the profound changes which are taking place in religious education.

The plurality now existing is of two kinds. First, we have a larger number of people for whom life may be lived without reference to religion at all. Second, we have the appearance of a substantial number of believers in religions other than Christianity. Judaism, which never participated in the religious instruction provided in the maintained schools, has been joined by Islam, Hinduism, Sikhism, and on a smaller scale by Buddhism and the Parsis. The young person today not only encounters a wider variety of faiths, both religious and secular, but he may adopt any or none of them without losing his civic rights or his public standing.[5]

Even within the lesser plurality of the earlier period, there were limits to the agreement which could be reached in religious education. The Roman Catholics, although not prevented in law from participating along with the other non-established forms of Christian faith in the religious education offered by the state, chose not to do so. The Jewish community also took no part. The right of parents to withdraw their children from religious instruction in the schools indicates the limits of the agreement which were possible. But now *more* people are excluded. And when the number of pupils who are specifically not Christian reaches a certain point, questions of fairness begin to be asked. So today we ask whether, when the state offers religious education to children in its care, it should offer it only to some and not to others. When the state not only offers religious education, but insists (as it does) that it be received (subject to rights of withdrawal), then we must ask this question more urgently.

Of course, it is always possible for the non-Christians, whether they be secular persons or believers in other faiths, to be present at religious classes and to consider it as information. But it is not intended as information. It is intended as nurture into Christianity.[6] This is why it appears to be more and more necessary that what should change in religious education is not only its content but its intentions. And this is what is in fact taking place today.[7]

Consequences of pluralism for religious education

The interest in establishing valid educational objectives for religious education is a direct consequence of pluralism. For now that the religions are so diverse, it is no longer possible to nurture children into the faith of their society. There are now many faiths, and this would require many nurturing agencies. A natural reaction to this situation might be to remove religion from the school curriculum. Let it be the responsibility, we might suggest, of the various religious groups. In Britain however it seems unlikely that this reply will win much support. Religion is too important a part of the history, culture and current experience of mankind to be left to believers alone. There is a role for the school in preparing pupils for responsible participation in a political democracy; similarly, there is a role for the school in preparing pupils to take an informed and thoughtful part in a pluralistic society. When the society contains not one but several religions, the need for a thoughtful study of religions becomes greater not less. But preparing pupils to take an informed and thoughtful interest in what goes on around them is by no means the same as nurturing them into faith in one religion or even into acceptance (as far as this might be logically possible) of religion as a whole. It is the realization of this different role precipitated by the abandoning of its nurturing function which has led religious education to take such an interest recently in educational validity. There is a sharpening distinction between nurture and education.

Of course, religious groups have the right to provide schools and to apply for aided or controlled status. Aided status leaves the school free to nurture in the faith of the religion which sponsors it. So in England and Wales we have had the dual system, whereby agreed nurture was offered in the county schools and denominational nurture in the aided schools. The dual system was thus another feature of the compromise reached in the limited Christian plurality of earlier years. The problems created by the appearance of aided schools will grow greater as plurality widens. Since Christians, mainly Roman Catholics and Anglicans, are allowed their own state aided schools, and the Jewish community is similarly supported, it is inevitable that Muslims and perhaps others will seek the same advantages. These generous and tolerant provisions by the state offer security, acceptance and financial support to religious groups concerned about the threat which pluralism presents to religious community life. To that extent these provisions are likely to make an important contribution to the domestication and integration of recently established religious communities. On the other hand, it would surely be a hindrance to community relations in the long term if by the end of the century we were to have Muslim, Sikh and perhaps Hindu systems of schools alongside the Christian and Jewish ones. Northern Ireland has illustrated too dreadfully the consequences of an education conducted along sectarian lines. And if critical, descriptive, religious education should flourish in the county schools the aided schools might find it increasingly embarrassing that they are offering something which in the vast majority of schools would not be thought educationally valid.

The study of religions should therefore continue in the county schools, possibly coming to play a more creative role than the old Christian nurture out of which it is now growing. Let us look at some of the growing pains.

School worship

In schools with considerable numbers of young people from various religious traditions and from no religious tradition at all, it is not going to be possible to continue with official school worship 'on the part of all pupils in attendance at the school'.[8] Who are they supposed to be worshipping? Worship can and should be studied in the classroom and it is very much to be hoped that schools will continue to have assemblies at which a variety of religious and non-religious attitudes and beliefs will be shared and explored. But *sharing* different beliefs is not the same as being required to *worship* the one object of belief. Assemblies for sharing will take the place of assemblies at which official Christian worship is offered, ostensibly *on the part of all* the pupils. This change will come as a great relief to everyone involved in present experiences of school assemblies in pluralist situations.

But because it will be impossible to go on conducting official school worship (to go on assuming a unanimity of potential or actual faith), future Local Education Authorities drawing up Agreed Syllabuses under the terms of the 1944 Act will find their task difficult indeed. The Act can be adapted to pluralism in the sections which deal with classroom religious teaching. The expression 'other denominations', although normally taken to indicate the free churches, has been used to permit the inclusion of non-Christian faiths on Agreed Syllabus Conferences.[9] But such Conferences will have to choose between making recommendations contrary to the Act (and a Conference would not be competent to do this), making recommendations contrary to the spirit of their pluralistic syllabus, or saying nothing at all about school worship. The last is the most preferable and we can therefore expect that the traditional content of the Agreed Syllabus Handbook, which deals both with worship and classroom instruction, will be modified so that only classroom work is dealt with. Of course, it may be that pluralism will render the religious sections of the Act so archaic that no Local Education Authority which desires to recognize pluralism will be able to accept the restrictions of the Act, and that there will not be many more significant Agreed Syllabuses. It certainly is the case that pluralism is hastening the demise of the Agreed Syllabus as it has been previously understood. We may note, for example, that in nurture the parties agree to include in the Syllabus what they think is true. In pluralist education, they agree to include what they think worth teaching.

The content of religious education

One of the main problems for religious education in a pluralist society is to retain a specifically religious content. Even under the rather mild conditions which prevailed from 1870 to 1944 there was a tendency for teachers to omit religious doctrines lest they should give offence. Some Boards explicity forbade teachers when dealing with the Bible to comment on matters which were not philological, archeological, historical or moral.[10] And of course, the 1870 Act, like all its successors, forbade the teacher to include materials distinctive of any particular denomination. This meant that the religious features most characteristic of the participating denominations were excluded.

The biblical syllabuses which are still very widespread in religious education, especially in grammar schools, were the product of the impact of Christian pluralism. Alternatively, the schools treated religion as part of history, or as part of the cultural tradition. Religion itself in its living forms was rarely dealt with, because that would lead to controversy. The procedure of agreement was intended to remove the danger of controversy. Where there is low rivalry between the faiths, controversy fades away and this is why the Agreed Syllabuses of the period *c.* 1938 to the early 1960s are much more explicitly religious in their content, although still cast in the biblical pattern.

But if religious education is to be effective in preparing young people for life in a pluralist society, it must present the living religions present in the society. It may deal with their history, their cultural achievements and so on, but its main concern must be with them as living religions. Controversy cannot be avoided and indeed ought to be encouraged, but the way the school ought to deal with controversy is distinctive and lies at the centre of the contribution of the school, and of education as a whole, in pluralism. No teacher will teach a syllabus made up of his own enthusiasms and no teacher will teach his own faith in a manner which gives it any privileged position. Normally the partners in a controversy argue because they believe their respective positions are true. The school however makes no assumptions about the truth (or falsehood) of any of the religions. It simply presents them, describes them, holds them up in all their beauty and their ugliness, helping the pupil to understand without prescribing what the outcome for any pupil may be should he make choices or rejections.

This does not mean that the syllabus of religion in a pluralist society will be what is sometimes called comparative religion. Comparative religion is but one way of studying the religions. There are many others. Comparative religion is one of the most sophisticated stages of the study of religion, certainly too advanced for pupils below the middle and upper levels of the secondary school. The syllabus will however consist of the study of religion in one form or another. We will no longer teach the Old Testament and the New Testament as such. We will teach Christianity, and this will include some treatment of the Christian scriptures. And the same will be true of the other participating faiths.

A cluster of subjects

Religious education is in fact not one but a cluster of subjects. In many schools, social and community service is one of the responsibilities of the religious education department and a good deal of the classroom work is preparation for this. Some religious education, particularly in the secondary school, is social and political studies, often including current affairs and world problems, and is taught with an emphasis upon values and within a framework which is generally religious or at least humanitarian. Some religious education, particularly in the infant and junior school, is sensitivity training with an intention to expand awareness and widen the emotional repertoire of the child. Much of what is called religious education is moral education. Religious education also includes a good deal of ancient history and sometimes geography, usually relating to the Jewish and Christian origins and increasingly with older students it includes study of non-religious life styles such as humanism. Most importantly, it includes religious studies in the specific sense, that is, the study of the religions of mankind, their customs and rituals, their doctrines and myths, their sacred writings and their ethics.

The group of subjects has been held together within religious education because of a philosophy which saw all the various aspects as being part of the Christian enterprise in education. The teacher did not simply teach the ethical problems associated with the use of money; he presented the teaching of Jesus about money. He did not only discuss the various sexual moralities which may be found in our society today; he taught the Christian sexual ethic. He did not only introduce his pupils to world problems; he studied Christian Aid. The attitudes and emotions which he sought to develop in the young child were intended as a preparation for religion and this simply meant that the emotions (wonder, love, thankfulness, penitence and so on) were central to the Christian religion.

But the effect of removing religious education from its traditional context within Christian nurture is that there is now in principle no closer relation between Christianity and religious education than there is between Islam and religious education. There is thus some danger that the subject will disintegrate. Christian faith can no longer be related to religious education in the obvious and straightforward way that once it was.

When moral education is undertaken by the religious education teacher, it will be necessary to distinguish between the study of the ethical aspects of the various religions and moral education in its own right. When the latter takes place, teachers should beware of making the moral education lessons into a form of Christian nurture. Teaching material now exists which presents moral education work units in their own right and without reference to distinctive Christian teaching. If in these lessons the teachers also use materials supplied by Christian agencies and with specific Christian applications, they should make it clear to their pupils that the material does represent a Christian or a humanist or whatever point of view. The proper place for the study of Christian ethics will be within a course on Christianity.

There is really no longer any reason why religious education should continue to carry so much responsibility for moral education. Every subject has its moral implications and it is encouraging to see how many books now being produced for work in English and social studies are deeply aware of this.

With the arrival of pluralism and the resulting differentiation of the cluster of subjects, many of the older concerns of religious education must now be concentrated in Christian Studies, which, along with Islamic Studies and so on, will continue to be an integral part of it. The final word 'Studies' indicates the stance which the teacher ought to adopt. The Christian churches will become more significant as the providers of materials for Christian Studies, although there are as yet few indications that the churches have realized the different approach which materials of this sort will have to adopt. Most materials from the churches still assume a nurturing aim, even when intended for use in county schools.

There is a danger that teachers will become 'specialists' in one aspect of the concerns of religious education. One teacher will teach nothing but the Bible. Another will concentrate on social and international problems; a third will deal mainly with personal relations. But it is important that teachers of religion should see, and insist to their colleagues, that although they have a variety of humane insights to offer, their main contribution is the religions of man.

Secular philosophies

The non-religious lifestyles have an important place too. Their inclusion is another effect of pluralism, and it is right and proper that the religious lifestyles should be set against the non-religious ones in order to facilitate the understanding of both.

How should non-religions be chosen? Those which may be thought of as alternatives to religion, or which are in conscious rejection of religion, or which have some of the main aspects of religions, may be included in religious education syllabuses.

So, for example, humanism should have a place because it is in conscious dialogue with religion, rejects religion, and offers itself as a viable alternative to religion, in offering a purposeful life set within an overall understanding of man and the world. Communism and (although less relevant today) fascism may also claim their places. Study of the 'counter-culture', the drug culture and the various 'alternative society' groups might also be appropriate for older pupils. But study of the Conservative, Liberal and Labour parties would be less suitable. These do not consciously reject religion, and any links with Christianity which they might have should be studied as part of Christian Studies. Communism has a philosophy of history, a view of man, a kind of eschatology, a detailed ethic and so on. The main British political parties do not offer this kind of comprehensiveness and do not purport to be alternatives to religion. There is of course a proper place for political studies in secondary schools, but this should take place through an expansion of social studies, community education or some such thing.

The non-religious lifestyles which have enough similarity with the religions to make it right for them to be included within religious education syllabuses (humanism, communism, possibly fascism and the counter-culture) must be included in their own right and not simply as a foil for religion. They will be there in their own right just as sensitivity training and moral education will continue to share in this cluster of interests which we call religious education. But the central area will continue to be the religions of man. The secular areas are included both because they are important and no-one else will do them if religious education fails to, and (although of value in themselves) the criterion for their selection is their similarity with the religions. All areas of the curriculum interlock, and there is a limit to what a fairly small area of the curriculum such as religious education can be expected to do. Naturally, pluralism and the consequent differentiation of religious education vastly increases the claim of religious education to be significant, and if headteachers were able to offer three or four periods a week throughout the secondary school, everything could be dealt with. In the meantime, it is important that Religious Studies in the narrow sense should not be overwhelmed. Perhaps humanism and communism can best be studied during a joint offering to older students from religious studies, and the history, economics, literature and philosophy teachers.

Religious studies and religious education

Let us try to express the distinction in another way. Religious studies is the study of the religions. Religious education is a wider group of 'subjects' in which things like sensitivity training, moral education, personal relations, social service, study of the non-religions and so on are set around religious studies as the periphery around a core. Religious education may thus be thought of as helping the pupil in his own quest for meaning. Religious studies is the inquiry after other people's meanings. The study of non-religious lifestyles is also a study of other people's meanings. So the question concerns the relation between my search for meaning and my study of other people's searches for meaning. I could not, in searching for my own meaning, do it alone. I must be with others. Those others are not only the members of the great faiths; the members of my school also have a lot to offer me. But I would surely be impoverished if I were confined to my fellows in the school community, be it never so rich. My interest is also in what men and women in all lands and at many times have thought and believed. This is perhaps the way in which the whole cluster of subjects can be held together in pluralism through the idea of informed existential dialogue.[11]

Notes

1 Breward, I. *Godless Schools? a Study in Protestant Reactions to the Education Act of 1877*, Presbyterian Bookroom, Christchurch, 1967.
2 The situation is changing and some Australian states are considering the introduction of a critical descriptive religious education. See *Religious Education in State Schools* (The Steinle Report), South Australian Education Department, September 1973.
3 *Moral and Religious Education in Scottish Schools* (The Millar Report), presented to the Secretary of State for Scotland, March 1972.
4 The withdrawal clauses were sufficient recognition of Judaism and other minorities. Without these clauses, if a wider pluralism had been encouraged to participate in state religious education, it would not have been possible to instruct or nurture.
5 This is what I understand a pluralist society to be. In so far as some institutions are still tied to a particular religion or denomination (the monarchy) British pluralism is incomplete. Cities are naturally more pluralistic than towns.
6 '... the Syllabus is deliberately designed as an evangelistic instrument, and the

Christian teacher should have no reservations in using it as such. Before 1944 many teachers rightly felt that they had to be discreet in teaching religion because of denominational susceptibilities, but happily the situation has now been transformed. The subject to be taught is not Biblical knowledge nor morality but the Christian faith, and the aim is to lead the pupils to a personal knowledge of Jesus Christ and to active life within a worshipping community. To achieve that purpose the Christian teacher may zealously use all his influence.' County of Lincoln – Parts of Lindsey Education Committee, *Agreed Syllabus of Religious Institution*, 1964, pp. 10ff. Needless to say, this is a statement of nature and aim which almost nobody in Lincolnshire or anywhere else in England would espouse today.

7 The change antedates the impact of wide pluralism. Edwin Cox's *Changing Aims in Religious Education* was published in 1966.

8 Education Act 1944, Section 25, para. 1.

9 The fifth schedule of the Education Act (1944).

10 *Return: School Board Schools (Religious Teaching)*, House of Commons, 4 March 1879, *passim*.

11 Many of the questions raised in this chapter are discussed in greater detail in my *School Worship, an Obituary*, SCM Press, 1975. See also my chapter 'Agreed Syllabuses, past, present and future' in *New Movements in Religions Education* Horder, D., and Smart, N. (Eds) Maurice Temple Smith, 1975, pp. 97–119.

5. The Integration of Religious Education and Some Problems of Authority

Problems of authority arise at many points in the teaching of religious education. Pupils at both junior and secondary schools frequently ask their teachers about the sort of authority which passages from the Bible are thought to possess, and sometimes the teacher's own authority to say anything definite about religion is strongly challenged. Teachers of subjects such as the natural sciences or history are less frequently confronted with demands of this kind, probably because pupils have come to believe that such subjects are more obviously dealing with matters of fact and because they realize that religious questions are controversial in society at large.

When religion is taught in integration with other subjects questions of authority may take on new urgency and new problems of authority may arise. Let us first consider the various kinds of authority which a teacher of religion may have, then see how this authority is related to various other authorities in the school. We shall conclude by looking at one or two special areas where problems of authority become more acute with integration.

The authority of the teacher of religion

This has a number of aspects and teachers differ in the emphasis which they place upon them.

1   Like any other teacher he will have authority as a senior member of the school hierarchy. The teacher has this authority *ex officio*. It will take various forms in various schools and various situations. It may include his role as chairman of the class and as the director of its work. We may call this procedural authority.

He will also have authority as a disciplinarian, not only because of his personal qualities, but as the representative in the classroom of the authority of the headmaster, or of the staff or of the collective will of the school as a whole, as the case may be. This kind of authority we may call status authority or function authority, since it derives from the teacher's position simply as a member of the school staff.

2   He will also have authority as a subject expert. He is familiar with the facts about religion and skilled in the interpretation of them. Upon this and his status authority depend his authority as an assessor of pupils' work.

3   His authority as a member of a particular religious tradition. This is like his authority as a subject specialist except that now he speaks with first-hand inside knowledge. If he is a Methodist, he speaks with authority when Methodism is being discussed. He may see himself, if he is a Christian, as representing the Christian faith, or the church. This is likely to be the case particularly if he is an ordained minister or priest and in such cases there may be some tension in his own mind and confusion in the minds of his pupils about the ambiguity of his dual professional status.

4   We must include his authority as a representative of society as a whole; he may see himself as charged to convey the national heritage, or perhaps to pass on traditional values or, on the other hand, to represent to his classes the plurality of views and standards which actually exist in society now.

5   Finally, he may have authority as an experienced older person. This kind of authority is probably more important to the teacher of religion than to many other subject teachers because of the nature and form of much religious teaching today. Here we are reminded of the connection between the idea of authority and that of authenticity. What he says carries weight with his pupils if it has an authentic ring about it, speaking to their experience because it arises out of his own. We may distinguish between the authority of having had certain experiences (for example,, of travel, or of having been in various dilemmas or of having suffered illness or loss), and the authority of long experience (for example, as a married man, or as one who has lived in the light of certain beliefs for many years), and on the other hand his moral authority exercised through the fact that he possesses certain qualities admired by pupils (for example, his readiness to admit that he does not know for sure, or to accept correction, or

his fairness). We may even speak of the authority of vulnerability.[1]

The authority of the teacher and the structure of authority in the school

Which of these various patterns of authority becomes typical of a particular teacher's work will depend not only on his personality and on the attitudes and expectations which he brings to his teaching, and with which pupils and colleagues approach him but upon the type of authority dominant in the school as a whole. A school in which there is little participation in decision-making on the part of the assistant teachers or the pupils and in which there is a fairly rigid system of controls may encourage or even compel the teacher to rely on status authority. He may be misunderstood by pupils and colleagues if he adopts a different form of authority from that usual in the rest of the school.

In an independent school attached to a religious tradition, or in an aided or perhaps a controlled school, teachers may feel that they are expected to see themselves as representing the church. Indeed, this is still often the case with teachers of religion in wholly maintained LEA schools. The staff and pupils will expect the RE teacher to be an advocate and an apologist for the church. This attitude is probably now disappearing.

If the school is set in a deprived area, the teacher may feel less able to represent the authority of society as a whole for fear of alienating his pupils or through a realization of the middle-class nature of his conception of 'society as a whole'.

The authority of the compassionate and experienced person may not be possible for him because he is also a house master, or head of the middle school, and thus expected to exercise a probation officer kind of role. He may find that he cannot successfully operate both roles. Alternatively, he may find himself compelled to exercise the role of the wise counsellor and personal guide simply because many other teachers are using remote status authority and he becomes aware of a need for someone to act as a sympathetic figure.

These are just a few examples of the way in which the teacher may be limited in the freedom he has to adopt various kinds of authority roles. Other limits will be imposed by his acceptance of certain aims in his teaching of religion, or by the methods which he adopts. But can the teacher create freedom? The first step in the creation of freedom to move from one type of authority to another, or into situations where authority is given an unimportant place in his work, is the recognition of the limits. The legitimate area of freedom must first be circumscribed. It is necessary first to accept that there are types of authority which he may not exercise today.

This may sound a rather negative note, but such an approach is important now. Just as in 1944 teachers of religion explored what they were given power to do, so today a new way of looking at the nature of religious education compels us to explore what the teacher of religion may not do.

How will these various patterns of authority affect the content of religious education?

It is possible that too much emphasis upon the fifth type of authority (that of the experienced person) may lead the teacher to teach only things which he himself believes, and to stress only what is significant within his own experience. His syllabus will then be a collection of his personal enthusiasms.

The history teacher is not expected to have an equal affection for every period of history, nor is the English teacher expected to agree with the sentiments expressed by all the characters in the novels he presents. A teacher of religion cannot be expected to believe everything about which he teaches, for his choice of subject matter will be governed not only by what he thinks is true in his own experience but by what is educationally best for the pupil. This is obviously the case when several teachers are cooperating on the same subject or theme. The Cowper-Temple clause in the religious sections of past education acts, forbidding the teaching of truths distinctive of any particularly denomination, prevented the teacher from teaching *all* he believed; the rise of the study of other religions and the appearance of integrated studies make it necessary that he shall now present much which he does not believe or which is not central to his own view of life. But he will not teach that these beliefs are true; he will only teach that these are said to be so.

To some teachers, the thought that trends in the subject may require them to present materials about religion which they do not personally believe may be disturbing. It may seem to be an ethical problem. Is it not hypocritical to teach what you do not believe? It is certainly wrong for a teacher to pretend to a commitment which he does not have, and there are no doubt schools where for many years pupils have been so accustomed to religious education classes in which the teacher was evidently commending his own faith that they may be quite unable to realize that there can be a religious teaching which neither springs from commitment to a particular faith nor seeks to create such a commitment. In a school where confessional teaching with a desire to gain commitment is what is expected of the religious education department, the teacher who, being a Christian, teaches Islam, or being a Protestant, teaches Catholicism, or being a Free Churchman, teaches Anglicanism, may be misunderstood as a hypocrite.

But it is much to be hoped that as colleagues and pupils begin to understand what the new religious education is all about, expectations about the type of authority which the teacher of religion will exert will slowly change. There will be more and more schools where it is understood at last that the teacher of religion is not a preacher and that he is there in order to encourage informed debate about all sorts of religious, semi-religious and anti-religious topics. The task of the teacher will be seen as supplying accuracy and clarity rather than as offering a witness to his personal faith. As the present context of unhelpful expectations which inhibit a truly educational approach to religion is gradually dispelled, teachers of religion will find it easier to realize that presentation of a wide range of moral and religious ideas does not harm their own integrity. It will, indeed, be seen that the opposite is the case, that for the teacher to present highly controversial statements and beliefs as if they are commonly agreed is a hypocritical and misleading stance for a school to adopt.

If too much emphasis is placed upon the third type of authority (that of the representative of the church) the teacher may tend to teach only what the church teaches (in an aided school) or what all the churches teach (following an Agreed Syllabus of the older kind). This would not be appropriate in an LEA school, because then the content of the subject would be selected on ecclesiastical grounds. It is interesting to see the number of teachers in the Yorkshire survey of school worship[2] who were reluctant to include non-Christian religions in their syllabus, because they were afraid that pupils might be attracted to them.

The teacher whose main conception of authority is that of the subject expert speaks not as a member of the church but as a student of the church, not as a religious man but as one familiar with religion. This may tend to make his syllabus more objective and wide-ranging, but too much emphasis on this may turn the study of religion into an arid historical or biblical inquiry. Personal belief in the power of religion to illuminate human problems must not be rejected in favour of a false conception of academic study.

There are various ways of interpreting one's role as a subject specialist. One teacher will be the lecturer, another will be a resource man. The teacher of religion may be the man who knows, or he may be the man who knows how to help pupils to find out. Different classroom styles will follow from these different conceptions of subject authority, and to some extent the content of the subject will also be affected.

The authority of the religious education teacher related to the authority of his superiors, his colleagues and his pupils

We have already seen some of the factors which may limit the teacher's authority. We must also remember that the extent to which the religious education teacher can control his own syllabus may, under the present unfortunate legal arrangements, be limited by a strict imposition of the Agreed Syllabus supported by directives through the local education office or through the decisions of inspectors, although probably this does not happen very often. But there are from time to time cases where the authority of the headmaster is used to restrict the scope of the religious education syllabus (or to extend it). Sometimes a young teacher is unable to introduce syllabus change in religion because the head is devoted to the Bible-based work which has been used in the school for decades. Sometimes a headmaster aware of current developments is concerned because his religious education teacher is unimaginative. Sometimes comments or even protests from parents can bring about a change in the syllabus.

The introduction of integrated studies is certainly going to lead to some kind of change in the authority of the present Agreed Syllabuses. No teacher of any subject can take part in the planning of an integrated project if he knows from the beginning that what this document contains and nothing else may constitute his constribution to the topic. An Agreed Syllabus may seek to become more flexible and may offer itself merely as a collection of models of what kind of part religion might play in the curriculum. What is offered is then, however, no longer a syllabus but something much more preliminary. It is easy to see that as soon as teams of teachers have immediate control over syllabus creation, external control through a passively accepted syllabus devised by others is bound to be rejected.

In team-teaching, particularly with subject specialists from other areas, and even more so if the teaching is fully integrated, a compromise may have to be effected between what the teacher of religion believes to be important in his own subject and what his subject can actually contribute to the theme in hand. It is possible that the religious education teacher might take part in many schemes of work, and at the end still feel that the central concerns of religion itself have not been adequately studied.

Integrated teaching clearly implies a rejection of traditional subject authority as well as a willingness to allow the teacher's individual authority to be blended into the emerging authority of the team. This may create real difficulties for the teacher of religion because religion is likely to be the least understood and perhaps the least appreciated of the subjects. Colleagues, expert in their own fields, may be surprisingly ignorant of religion, and this ignorance may also be combined with strong views about religion. The teacher of religion may have difficulty in convincing colleagues of the importance and relevance of his subject or in reaching a reasonable level of acceptance for his aims, but on the other hand, a new authority may accrue to the subject if integration is successful. This depends on the confidence and capacity of the teachers of religion.

Religion is not alone as a subject of the existing curriculum in needing to rethink its nature and authority in the light of integration. Geography, for example, is, like religion, already a kind of integrated study composed of various aspects of various logical disciplines and it is not impossible that geography may disintegrate under the pressures of integration.

But there is a special reason why religion in particular needs to abandon its traditional subject authority. Teachers of religion have on the whole been less inclined to use educational arguments in justifying their subject. The arguments which are used to justify the place of certain items in the curriculum have in the case of religion not been congruous with the kinds of arguments used of other subjects. History teachers have on the whole long since given up the task of teaching patriotism. Teachers of religion, therefore, have to make a larger adaptation.

Other problems will be of organization. Even in a large school there may be only one fully trained teacher of religion, but he will be work⸱ with departments which may have half a dozen or more specialist⸱ will not be able to participate fully in more than one or two f⸱ teaching projects without curtailing his work in other parts of⸱ or entrusting it to non-specialists. Some integrated project⸱ carry on without any help from the religious education ⸱ this may, as team-teaching gathers prestige, create ⸱ the role of religion in the school as a whole. Th⸱ shared by the religious education department⸱ departments.

What authority does the pupil have i⸱ ways should he exercise authority over the⸱ content of teaching? Increased emphasis on t⸱

one of the striking features of contemporary religious education. 'The children are in effect themselves providing the syllabus.'[3] Many of the influences on the subject at this point are theological. The stress in thinking from the World Council of Churches on the idea of the world writing the agenda for the church has been significant. It has also been seen that since the pupil is the focus of revelation biblical material should not be selected because of its objective importance in the history of salvation but because of its capacity to illuminate the lives of the pupils.[4] Other influences have come from child psychology, and religious teaching cannot stand aside from the emphasis here on the primacy of the pupil's interests and needs in learning. It is obvious that the authority of the pupil's personality will affect the teaching methods used; this will be particularly true in the teaching of religion, where the psychological findings will be supported by theological views about the innate dignity and freedom of the human personality.

An authority appropriate to the teacher of religion today

The difference between the authority of the teacher of religion in the county school and the authority of the apostle is that the former does not derive his authority from God. The teacher of religion can no longer expect to find his pupils respectful towards the authority of the Bible or the church. The authority of the religious educationalist will be that of being a specialist, and his teaching will rest on the authority which is derived from being authentic. This will require a loyalty to truth and honesty in mutual seeking and learning. Integrity in the teacher's convictions will be combined with respect for the pupil's right to reach his own convictions. The teacher will have the capacity to think again and to decide again, and to help his pupils to think and to decide. Central to his classroom methods will be the authority which personality exercises over personality and he will know that this is the true basis of the authority of the Bible as well.

This style of teaching, found so often in the work of religious education teachers in the past, will become more essential still when with the growth of team-teaching and of integrated studies the whole tone of the school moves away, as it must, from traditional hierarchical disci-ne towards democratic agreement. This is so because the teaching by a of teachers of an integrated theme cannot be imposed or even firmly ed by one-way authority from above, or the project will fail h lack of teacher commitment to it.

can thus expect that the falling away from the Bible-based

syllabus, as a syllabus which was taught as having innate religious, theological and ecclesiastical authority by a teacher who derived his authority from it and from his role in the school structure, a falling away which was hastened by the discussion and life-situation methods of the 1960s, may be further accelerated by the arrival of integrated studies.

The right of withdrawal

From 1870, when religious teaching was provided in the newly established state schools, the problem of parental confidence in the content and objectives of this part of the school curriculum has been a matter of concern. The 1870 Act took two steps to retain parental confidence in state religious teaching. Religious teaching was not to include material of a distinctively denominational character. Parents were thus assured that the securing or reinforcing of denominational loyalty was not an objective of religious teaching. Second, where religion was taught, parents had the right to withdraw their children. The assumption here was that even with the safeguard offered by the Cowper-Temple clause forbidding denominational instruction, the religious teaching of the state schools would still not command universal confidence.

In 1944, with the arrival of compulsory religious instruction, the question of public confidence in what was now not only tolerated but required by law became a pressing problem. The withdrawal clauses of previous acts were repeated, and related to worship as well as to instruction, and a further step was taken in that the content of religious teaching was not prescribed positively as well as negatively. There were, of course, various motives behind the introduction of the Agreed Syllabuses as statutory documents, but one was certainly the hope that the general public, including both churchgoers and non-churchgoers, having access to the published syllabuses and being assured that the teacher of religion was obliged to teach nothing but what was in them, would have confidence in the teaching so given. But the continuance of withdrawal right indicated recognition by the state that parental lack of confidence might still be justified.

The reason was that the religious education given by the state schools from 1870 to 1944 and indeed until very recent years was undoubtedly evangelistic in general intention and doctrinaire in tone. Christianity was taught in the belief that it was true and in the hope that it would convince. Parents who did not share this belief and this hope were entitled to suspend confidence in this part of the school's teaching programme and to express this by withdrawing their children. This is what was meant by talk about 'rights of conscience'. The withdrawal right was thus an indication of the limits of the rights of the state over the rights of the parents. The withdrawal right is thus a classic example of a solution to a conflict about authority in education.

The problem we now face is that integrated studies as a method of teaching religion is not compatible with the concept of withdrawal. In the first place, withdrawal from a part of an integrated course is contrary to the ideals upon which this kind of teaching is based. The intention is that the wholeness of a subject should be seen by studying it from a variety of angles and a pupil's grasp of this will be seriously impaired if he misses the study of the theme through religion, or through English or through history, or through any other of the fundamental ways of human thinking. For such a pupil, the study would not in fact be an integrated study. I am here assuming that when religion is included in an integrated study, it will not be because of legal compulsion or because of a desire to show friendship and equality to the religious education department, but because it is thought that in this particular study the contribution of religion is a vital one without which the subject cannot be properly understood. To withdraw a pupil from any part of such a study would be to thwart the educational objectives of the whole thing.

Second, when religion is taught in this way, withdrawal is not practicable or, if it were practicable, this would show that the subject was still being presented in such unrelated compartments that exclusion from one was possible. In other words, only in a badly designed integrated study is withdrawal possible. It may, of course, be possible for the pupil to be withdrawn from the key lectures or lessons given by the religious specialists, but he can hardly be withdrawn from the panels, from the discussion groups, from the comments of other pupils and from the attempt to relate the various disciplines which is such a prominent feature of integrated work. The team of teachers would often, in a lively project, not be able to predict when the study would take a religious turn; and to stop discussion, often at a particularly controversial or interesting point, in order to remind certain pupils to leave, would be crass stupidity.

The situation is transformed, however, by the fact that the reasons which justified a parental lack of confidence in the religious education of earlier periods no longer exist, at least in theory. Religious education is no longer thought of as evangelistic or doctrinaire. The whole conception of the function of the subject has undergone a remarkable change in recent years. Since the aims of religious education, whether integrated or not, are objective, seeking to describe and evaluate and educate, to encourage critical thought and comparison and facilitate choice for or against religion, there would not seem to be any reason why in principle this subject should be singled out as the one in which parents may not trust. It seems sensible and logical, therefore, either to remove the withdrawal right altogether or to extend it so that a parent can withdraw his child from any part of the curriculum which fails to win his confidence. The objections would then probably be less related to a subject or an aspect of a subject than to a particular teacher and his method of handling the subject.

Two factors complicate the situation. It has to be admitted that many teachers of religion, perhaps a majority of older teachers, are not in fact yet teaching their subject in an objective and educationally justifiable manner, nor have they yet come to realize that it is a professional obligation for them to do so. It will be some years before the attitudes and methods advocated in the current literature and accepted in work being done in teacher education have thoroughly affected the whole profession.

Second, many parents are insufficiently informed of the changes, and even in areas where they have no cause to lack confidence in the religious education of the school, they continue to hold views based perhaps on their own experience at school or based on misconceptions about trends in the subject. It may be that even if withdrawal can no longer be defended in theory and becomes less necessary in practice, the time lag in public appreciation of this will make it politically impossible to change the withdrawal right, however educationally desirable it may be to do so.

It is clear at least that the teaching of religion in an integrated way does depend on establishing and maintaining the confidence of the parents, and in difficult areas and with sensitive topics teachers will have to explore ways of reassuring parents. Improved communications between the school and the home may accomplish a great deal. But if this cannot be done, integration will founder as far as religion is concerned, and that will seriously impoverish the experiment as a whole.

It is obvious that the situation highlights the need for the teacher of religion to teach in such a manner as not to raise legitimate doubts in the minds of parents, and to set the highest standards of professional behaviour. In the same way, parents have an obligation to inform themselves of the position in religious education, to appreciate and sympathize with the religious educational work of the school as far as they possibly can, and to exercise the withdrawal right only when they are deeply convinced that real damage will be done to their child.

Worship, integration and authority

The authority of worship over the worshipper is sacred. It is the authority of the creator over the creature who approaches him. An unknown God can be worshipped but only if it is believed that there really is an unknown God and that he might be worthy of worship. The worshipper does not discuss; he listens and obeys. He does not carry out an appraisal; he adores and gives thanks.

The authority of worship is ultimate upon the one who seeks to live before God. But we must ask if the LEA school, containing a wide variety of pupils of various religious and non-religious traditions, of various degrees of commitment and non-commitment, supported by a community similarly diverse, can any longer expect its pupils to accept this kind of authority until they are ready for it. They would be ready for it when they became old enough to respond to the demand of the God who is totally worthy of worship, and had in fact responded in this way. School worship must not be used to evangelize the uncommitted.

The situation gives rise to a number of problems.

1   To what extent is the situation different with younger children? This is certainly the case with some other aspects of authority. For example, it is often agreed that with young children moral education must first depend upon the authority of the parent and the teacher, and that a framework of morally desirable attitude and habit should be established even if, since the child accepts and obeys out of respect for authority and not from inward conviction, the child is not at this stage truly moral. Similarly, one might wonder whether worship should be introduced to young children even although they cannot yet be expected to respond in intelligent freedom at that stage. True morality and true worship must both be internalized, but it might be wondered whether children would ever have the option of experiencing true worship unless they grow into the habits and attitudes from which worship springs in their earlier years.

2   It seems that the authority of the religious education offered in the classroom differs from that offered in school assembly. In addition to the factors arising from the very nature of worship which we have considered, it is obvious that in schools the assembly is an official occasion. What takes place there has the tacit or the overt support of the head and of members of staff. There are still schools where assembly is used to exhibit and reinforce the school hierarchy. The headmaster reads the lesson

on the opening day of term, and is followed on the second day by the deputy headmaster. Then the members of staff read in order of seniority and when they have done, the prefects begin. There are members of staff who attach importance to the prestige of conducting or taking part in assembly before the whole school.

More important to the religious education department is the fact that whereas in the classroom what they say is offered for discussion and criticism, in assembly what they say, if it is really presented as material for worship, is offered as representing the total demand of God over man. This split in the authority of the religion in the school is perhaps less evident with young children who cannot, of course, bring the same critical spirit to what is said in the classroom.

It seems clear that the authority of the Bible cannot be the same when read in school as it is when read in church, and that this will become more apparent with older pupils. In church the Bible comes as, is received as, the word of God summoning to radical obedience. In school, although it is always possible that individual pupils will respond inwardly to the reading of the Bible as the word of God, the staff cannot expect or require them to respond in this way. The authority of the Bible when read in the secondary school assembly must therefore be the same as the authority of any other literature. It will be read for profit, for what morality, truth and beauty it may contain and for such critical discussion as it may evoke, but not as the word of God.

The problems of authority in worship will become more acute if the teaching of religion is integrated with other subjects. The fact that religion is operating on two levels of authority will become more obvious. The question will also be raised about the reason why one subject should have almost exclusive rights in the daily assembly when there is so much that could be contributed by other subjects. *If classroom religion is to integrate, assembly religion must also integrate.*

Already in many infant and junior schools, the daily assembly is being used to express a theme or a project which the school as a whole has been working on. There seems to be no reason why that sort of thing should not be extended into the assembly of the secondary school. A. R. Bielby has, in his books of assemblies,[5] used material from many subjects.

Appropriate for use in assembly would be any aspects of an integrated study which

(a)   were sufficiently simple to be comprehensible to pupils not taking part in that particular theme; it seems unlikely that the whole of a secondary school can work at the same time on the same theme as junior schools sometimes do; and

(b) give rise to questions of ethics, of values, of the consideration of relationships, of man and his place in society and nature, and of philosophy and religion, in personal and public life; and

(c) are convenient to treat in a public way in a large gathering. This means that the topic must be suitable for treatment through speakers, readings, debates, drama, music and meditation and the other things which it is possible to do in an assembly.

These criteria, if applied to almost any integrated theme, will yield plenty of suitable material for many assemblies. But it is important to see also that the principle of team-teaching is applied to such assemblies as well as to the teaching in the classroom. So many assemblies should be allotted to each team of teachers under the supervision of a coordinating committee of staff and pupils, representing a variety of subjects and religious views. There is no need for the religious education specialist to have any special prerogatives on this committee, although it will need to consist of persons awake to the humane, moral and religious possibilities of their subjects, since it is in this general area that public gatherings of this sort can be most useful educationally. Often the religious specialist will fall into this category and might be the natural chairman, but sometimes he will not.

In assemblies of this kind it would be fundamental that the treatment of the theme would take place without assumptions of religious commitment or of religious truth. Such assemblies would not therefore consist of worship as ordinarily understood, but they might fulfil a valuable educational role in binding the school and its studies into such unity as is feasible today and they might also provide much new material for further classroom work in various subjects. In this way the school assembly might become a model and an inspiration for the educational ideals of the whole school.

Notes

1 *Christian Commitment in Education*, the Report of the Methodist Conference Commission on Education, para. 77, Epworth Press, 1970.
2 Jones, C.M. *Worship in the Secondary School*, Religious Education Press, 1969, Ch. 2.
3 *Learning for Life*, the Agreed Syllabus of Religious Education of the Inner London Education Authority, 1969, p. 32.
4 Moran, Gabriel, *God still Speaks: The Basis of Christian Education*, Burns & Oates, 1969.
5 Bielby, A.R., *Sixth Form Worship*, SCM Press, 1968 and *Education through Worship*, SCM Press, 1969.

6. Agreed Syllabuses, Past, Present and Future

The present legal position

The 1944 Education Act requires that religious education in England and Wales 'shall be given in accordance with an agreed syllabus adopted for the school....' The Fifth Schedule of the Act prescribes the procedure for the adoption of an Agreed Syllabus. The Local Education Authority shall convene a 'conference' consisting of representatives of

(a) such religious denominations, as in the opinion of the authority, ought, having regard to the circumstances of the area, to be represented;

(b) except in the case of an area in Wales or Monmouthshire, the Church of England;

(c) such associations representing teachers as, in the opinion of the authority, ought, having regard to the circumstances of the area, to be represented; and

(d) the authority.

Each of the four 'committees' so constituted has one vote and all four must vote in favour of the proposed syllabus. They may decide to adopt an existing syllabus prepared by another authority, or parts of several such syllabuses, or they may prepare their own syllabus.

The resulting syllabus is also to be used in the controlled schools although denominational teaching may also be given in certain circumstances. In aided and special agreement schools, denominational teaching may be given in accordance with the trust deeds or the customs of the school, but in certain circumstances teaching according to the agreed syllabus of the area may also be made available.

These provisions are unique to religious education. Religion is the only subject which by law the schools are required to teach, and the Agreed Syllabus is part of a wider agreement by means of which the

73

church schools and the county schools have become more closely integrated.

Earlier history of the Agreed Syllabus

From 1870 to 1944 religious education was not required by law in England and Wales. Whether religion should be taught or not was a matter for local decision. But if such teaching was provided, then it should include 'no religious catechism or religious formulary which is distinctive of any particular denomination'. This, the famous Cowper-Temple clause of the 1870 Act, was repeated in the 1944 Act. If the schools were not to teach anything distinctive of the various denominations, what were they to teach?

In fact, almost all the school boards or the Local Education Authorities did require the schools in their areas to offer religious instruction, and from the earliest days of the public education system, local authorities would issue guidance to the schools on the content of the instruction they were to give their pupils. Many of these syllabuses were modelled on syllabuses already in use in the church schools but with denominational peculiarities removed. The Anglican catechism would thus disappear but the Apostles' Creed and the Ten Commandments would remain. Some ecclesiastical authorities issued revised editions of their own syllabuses for use in the 'council schools'. Sometimes a local authority would ask local clergy to help in the drawing up of a special School Board Syllabus and clergy were often entrusted with the task of inspecting the instruction given in the council schools.

These early syllabuses were very brief, being perhaps no more than a paragraph or two in the local school regulations or perhaps a page of biblical passages and other materials to be studied and memorized. But as the denominational rivalry of the nineteenth and early twentieth centuries declined, more substantial cooperation between the local authorities and the churches appeared, and by 1920 many quite detailed, thorough and relatively enlightened syllabuses were circulating among the various areas.

It is not possible to point to any one document as being the first of the modern Agreed Syllabuses, but developments in Cambridgeshire were certainly amongst the most important. In the years after the First World War the Cambridgeshire Education Committee had been trying to reorganize its schools into senior schools (eleven plus) and 'tributary junior schools'. This was possible in areas where all the schools were of one type, that is, all were council schools or all were church schools. But where (as was the case in most parts of the country, particularly the towns and cities) there was a mixture of types of school, the religious problems created some difficulty. Not only was there the problem of how the schools were to be administered, but what was to be done about religious education?

In March 1923 two Advisory Committees were set up, one to consider the practical problems of a single administration and the other to see if it might be possible to draw up 'an *agreed* [their italics] Syllabus of Religious Instruction and observance which would be acceptable to all religious bodies' (Cambridge, 1924). The result was *The Cambridgeshire Syllabus of Religious Teaching for Schools*. The committee, although not divided into representative groups as became the later practice, did include headteachers, churchmen and academics, both Anglican and Free Church.

The appearance of this Syllabus gave considerable prestige and inspiration to what was rapidly becoming a national movement. Within five or six years numerous authorities had appointed committees of teachers and clergy and had adopted the results as an 'agreed syllabus'. By 1934, 224 of the 316 local education areas had adopted syllabuses of this sort and about 40 different syllabuses were in circulation. The Cambridgeshire Syllabus was easily the most popular, being used in 87 areas, but there were still some 90 areas in which the older kind of syllabus was still in use (Yeaxlee, 1934). In 1939 Cambridgeshire added still further to its influence by issuing a new edition of its now famous Syllabus.

So it was that, when the Agreed Syllabuses became mandatory and the machinery for their production and revision was codified in 1944, a tradition had already been well established and the Syllabuses themselves had already reached a certain maturity and stability. Not until the later 1960s was there to be any substantial change in the directions laid down in the 1920s and 1930s (Hull, 1975).

A typical syllabus of the older type

The Agreed Syllabus, as it evolved between about 1924 and 1964, was almost entirely a syllabus dealing with the past. Interest in the present was directed towards the nurturing of the religious lives of the pupils. But the present was not *studied*; the present was nurtured through study of the past. The Bible was studied, including the history of Israel, the life and teachings of Jesus, the growth of the Church in New Testament times and the history of Christianity in particular areas. The latter was often the only distinctive feature which a particular syllabus could offer. There might be religious biography, usually missionary and social reforming heroes, and, usually in the sixth form only, some discussion of social and ethical problems studied from the Christian point of view. There might be some comparative religion (as it was called) in the sixth form. But usually the sixth form syllabus consisted of more advanced biblical study with some systematic or philosophical theology.

Let us take, as an example, the widely used 1945 Surrey Agreed Syllabus:

> The aim of the Syllabus is to secure that children attending the schools of the County ... may gain knowledge of the common Christian faith held by their fathers for nearly 2,000 years; may seek for themselves in Christianity principles which give a purpose to life and a guide to all its problems; and may find inspiration, power and courage to work for their own welfare, for that of their fellow-creatures, and for the growth of God's kingdom (Surrey, 1945).

The suggestions for infants (ages 3 to 7) include a good deal of material which 20 years later might have been called 'experiential'. Talks on light, food, shelter, flowers and trees are suggested under the heading 'God's gifts to His children', and 'God's wonderful world' and 'God's provision for Animals' are found under the general heading 'God our Heavenly Father – His Love and Care'. But although 'the child's interest is in his immediate surroundings' many of the lessons 'may appropriately consist of simple, fully-illustrated talks about the objects, animate and, inanimate, which form the background of the Bible stories' (Surrey, 1945). A good deal of the work may thus be thought of as emotional and conceptual enrichment with a view to the appreciation of the Bible. There are, of course, many stories from the Bible, both Old and New Testaments, suggested right from age 3. The reference to 'God's provision for the Animals' in fact occurs under the main heading 'The Bible and Its Teaching'.

Throughout the whole Syllabus, from infants to seniors, the work for each year falls under two main sections. Section one is 'The Bible and Its Teaching'; section two is 'The Christian Life'. Section two of the final course for seniors deals with 'Christendom' and consists of an outline of Church history concluding with the appearance of the British denominations followed by 'Christian Work in the Modern World'. 'Some of the Problems of Religion and Life' appears only as an Appendix. This then is a typical syllabus of what might be called the classical period of Agreed Syllabus creation.

The Agreed Syllabus of the later 1960s

From the late 1950s there was, in religious education, a much more thorough emphasis upon the centrality of the experience of the child, and in response to an upsurge of activity and renewal in the early 1960s, a new generation of Agreed Syllabuses began to appear. The first, and still one of the most influential, was the West Riding Agreed Syllabus, *Suggestions for Religious Education* (1966). The custom of arranging the work in yearly units was abandoned, and greater stress was laid on the development of the child by arranging the work into broad categories such as 'late childhood' and 'early adolescence'. The material for each stage was headed 'Themes and Activities' and it was emphasized that the pupil needed to discover Christianity for himself. Much more material was concerned with the present. For middle adolescents, two of the three themes suggested are 'Personal Relationships – Discovering Oneself' and 'Christianity in the Modern World'; and for 'late adolescence' there is but one theme, 'Religion and Life in Contemporary Society'.

The other influential Syllabus of this period was that of the Inner London Education Authority, *Learning for Life* (1968). Here the techniques of theme teaching are developed more thoroughly, with material on 'neighbours', 'holidays' and 'the family' for juniors, and a thematic presentation of the Gospels dealing with work, death and money is offered to adolescents as an alternative to a more traditional type of study of the life of Jesus. (See also Wiltshire, 1967; Lancashire, 1968; and Northamptonshire, 1968).

Cambridge, Hampshire, Essex and Cornwall

By 1970 it was becoming clear that the machinery of the Agreed Syllabus was not sufficiently flexible and rapid for the needs of religious education. Designed as a system of checks and balances among the denominations, the authority and the profession itself, it supposed tensions which in fact seldom existed. Cambridge had asked its Standing Advisory Council on Religious Education in 1966 to consider the possibility of a revision of the Cambridgeshire Syllabus and while discussions were in progress, the Advisory Council, thinking that teachers might be too scrupulous in teaching from the existing Syllabus, issued a statement to schools 'assuring them that trial and experiment in religious education were not only permissible but warmly supported by the council' (Cambridge, 1970). Following discussion with teachers, a Religious Education Development Centre was set up at Homerton College, Cambridge. In September 1968, three working groups of teachers began to meet at the Centre under the auspices of the Advisory Council to prepare material for trial in schools. This material was published in 1970 and by then it had been decided that there would be no more Cambridgeshire Agreed Syllabuses. The existing Syllabus, although not formally suspended, was by-passed in the decision to encourage wide ranging experimentation, and when the Chief Education Officer wrote the Foreword to the 1970 collection of papers he said, 'Some other Authorities have recently produced revisions of their Agreed Syllabuses but our Standing Advisory Council have decided to encourage in religious education the same sort of development which is taking place in other areas of the curriculum.' The Education Committee, in its own Introduction, remarks, 'These suggestions are not in any way a new syllabus; they are to be considered as part of continuing curriculum development . . .' (Cambridge, 1970).

In 1967 Hampshire had convened a statutory Conference to consider the question of its agreed syllabus. The Hampshire Syllabus then in force was the 1954 Syllabus and the 1967 Conference gave approval to the additional use of the 1966 West Riding Syllabus. But no revision of the existing Hampshire Syllabus was to be attempted. Instead, the two working parties of the statutory Conference produced a 'Handbook of Suggestions' which 'is not a new agreed syllabus; nor, indeed . . . is it a syllabus at all. It is quite deliberately compiled in a form different from that of any previous agreed syllabus of Religious Education produced by the Authority' (Hampshire). The Handbook is intended to offer teachers practical help and consists of many articles, collections of ideas, work units for classroom teaching, resources and so on.

The Essex Education Committee authorized the use of the West Riding Syllabus (1966) in September 1969, and, rather like Hampshire, decided to supplement it with a series of papers for teachers. As in Hampshire, the Primary and Secondary Working Parties, originally set up to consider revision of the syllabus, undertook the production of this material. It was felt that 'in a climate of much educational change there should be continued consultation and discussion, looking forward to a possible new syllabus' (Essex). The material was published under the title 'Interchange' two or three years later.

In Cornwall, the Agreed Syllabus of 1964 was in need of revision and a Standing Advisory Council met in 1968 and established working parties, and the new Syllabus was published in 1971. As the Chairman of the Education Committee pointed out, 'This is probably a unique Syllabus as it was, with the approval of the various Church authorities, written by teachers for use of teachers in all types of schools' (Cornwall, 1971).

In these four developments we can see the machinery of the agreed syllabus being used in a fairly flexible way. The distinction between a Conference for the recommending of an agreed syllabus (which an authority *must* set up) and a Standing Advisory Council for Religious Education (which it *may* set up for general purposes) is becoming blurred, teachers are taking a more prominent role, the problems of reaching agreement between the churches on what they hold in common are not in evidence, and the materials in use are open to continuous addition. Agreed Syllabuses are becoming instruments not of syllabus creation but of curriculum development. Bath took a slightly more radical view towards both the machinery and the content than any of the four authorities we have just considered; Birmingham used the machinery with scrupulous exactness and came to grief because the letter of the law was invoked against it – an ironic fate for a Syllabus which had made a greater effort than most in the early seventies to observe the customary legal procedures. (For a summary of Agreed Syllabus revision, see Birnie, 1971.)

The Bath Agreed Syllabus

Although it has received little national attention, the Bath Syllabus (1970) presents us with an interesting example of the changes which agreed syllabuses are undergoing at present.

The City of Bath Conference to revise the 1953 Bath Agreed Syllabus had its first meeting in May of 1969. The Fifth Schedule of the 1944 Act was strictly observed. Ten of the 32 members of the Conference were representing the churches and 16 members represented the teachers. The Conference began by considering the aims of religous education. A statement was drawn up which was presented for approval to the Education Committee in October 1970 and went forward to the full City Council the following month.

In this three-page statement, the Conference recommended that the 1953 Agreed Syllabus should be withdrawn. No revision was to be attempted. The Conference also recommended that no 'independent syllabus' for Bath be prepared but 'teachers will be encouraged to make use of suggestions in some of the new syllabuses (for example, West Riding, ILEA, Wiltshire, etc.) and also to devise schemes of work particularly suited to their own situation, which shall be incorporated into the handbook' (Bath, 1970). A loose-leaf handbook would be issued. This would contain the opening statement itself, a number of other papers prepared by the Conference on aspects of religious education, and 'occasional working papers' would be circulated from time to time for addition to the folder.

The Conference next recommended that a working party 'mainly representing the teachers' should be set up 'to act as a clearing house for ideas' and to stimulate new work in religious education. This would be channelled through the existing Teachers' Centre. The statutory Conference would then consider its obligations under the 1944 Act to be complete and would continue as a Standing Advisory Council 'to cooperate with teachers'.

The statement then discusses the aims of religious education.

> The primary aim of religious education is to help young people to understand the nature of religion. This does not simply mean teaching about religion if by that is implied an historical survey of the doctrines, practices and institutions of the major religions or even of only the Christian religion. It means helping young people to understand and appreciate religious phenomena, to discuss religious claims with sensitivity, to be aware of the nature of religious language and to recognize the criteria and standards by which truth and falsehood in religious beliefs are distinguished ... (Bath, 1970).

Several implications of this basic aim are then stated. The first is that 'religious education must remain open ... both in its selection of material and methods of enquiry and in its respect for the individual so that pupils can eventually make free and responsible decisions about the claims of religion.' The second implication is that while in this country 'it is appropriate to examine the Christian faith more closely than other faiths' nevertheless 'in a pluralistic society there must also be an attempt to understand views other than Christianity (eg Humanism, Communism, Buddhism etc)' (Bath 1970).

When the document was discussed in the Bath City Council, several councillors expressed concern about the single reference to humanism and communism. The debate was reported in the *Bath and West Evening Chronicle* on 4 November 1970 under the heading 'Religious education report starts row'. The report, the newspaper account said, 'could lead to the revolutionising of religious education in schools' but 'a move to get this reference [to humanism and communism] removed from the report before its adoption by the council was defeated.' One councillor, urging that the report be rejected, said, 'It is the duty of a Christian council to oppose this insidious breach and erosion of the [agreement about religious education] which has been arrived at over several life times.'

Another commented, 'If they want to teach atheism in schools, why don't they just call it atheism?'

A lively correspondence on the subject was published in the newspaper in the next few days. 'Lessons that make me see red', 'Christianity is best', 'The truth about that "teach Communism" report' and 'Hysteria sets in' were some of the headlines.

The Chairman of the Education Committee of the City Council made a statement in which it was made clear that there was no intention to 'support the teaching of Communism ... [but] that an attempt be made to "understand" what Communists believe'. The Conference on the Agreed Syllabus met again in December 1970. The section in question was reaffirmed and not altered. When this recommendation came back again to the Education Committee and in due course to the full City Council no objections were offered. The matter received but the barest mention in the local press and there was no further public controversy. In effect, this document became the adopted Agreed Syllabus of Bath and so replaced the 1953 Agreed Syllabus.

From this time the Standing Advisory Council for Religious Education (the heir to the Conference although a smaller body) fostered the idea of a 'developing syllabus' which would in principle be unfinished. The folder was issued and the document which the City Council had approved, now called 'Introduction: Suggestions for Religious Education' became the first paper in the folder. Between May 1971 and February 1974 five more papers were circulated for addition and just before the new administrative area of Avon was created on 1 April 1974 a paper from the Bristol Agreed Syllabus was added to the Bath collection in order to unite these two parts of the new unit.

The Bath events throw some interesting light on the problems of producing an Agreed Syllabus in the conditions of today. What the City Council adopted (Paper one, 'Suggestions for Religious Education') is not a syllabus at all and does not claim to be one. It is a statement about the aims, principles and difficulties of constructing a religious education syllabus but it is not actually a syllabus. Paper three, 'Using the New Syllabuses' (May 1971), fulfils the intention declared in the opening paper that teachers would be asked to consider materials from several of the new Agreed Syllabuses and it sets out a number of headings of work, themes and topics from these other syllabuses; but this paper never came to the attention of the Education Committee let alone the full City Council. What the City Council had done, in effect, was to offer religious education complete freedom of content, subject only to the guidance of the opening paper and the continued cooperation of the Standing Advisory Committee for Religious Education. Religious education was thus set free to pursue the normal paths of curriculum development followed more or less by other subjects through teachers' centres, work parties, conferences, publication of experimental work and so on. Although the main procedures of the 1944 Act were followed and although there was certainly a *bona fide* intention to meet the legal requirements to the full, the Bath Agreed Syllabus is a departure from the tradition and a radical reinterpretation of the workings of the Act. There was no legal challenge.

Many other matters which became burning issues only two or three years later in Birmingham were raised in Bath. The question of humanist participation was discussed at the very first meeting of the Bath Conference. It was decided to invite humanist comment at a later stage. The procedures adopted gave very much more responsibility to classroom teachers than had normally occurred before. The question of the inclusion of secular philosophies and movements was the most controversial one and the area which gave rise to maximum misunderstanding between religious educators and the public. On the other hand, because of the absence of significant immigrant communities in Bath, the question of participation by the non-Christian religions did not become prominent nor was the question of school worship resolved.

The Birmingham Agreed Syllabus

The first Agreed Syllabus of the City of Birmingham was adopted in 1950 and reissued in 1962 with an expanded section of suggestions for teachers. The Syllabus and the accompanying articles have no particular merit but simply restate or reprint material which was standard in such works.

> We speak of religious education, but we mean Christian education. To believe that Jesus Christ is the key to reality, that the full revelation of God's nature in a human life has been made in Him, that through Him alone we have peace with God, is not to deny that the Holy Spirit has been and is at work in other religions and philosophies. But the aim of Christian education in its full and proper sense is quite simply to confront our children with Jesus Christ ... (Birmingham, 1962).

By the late 1960s it had become obvious that a new Agreed Syllabus was needed. Considerable numbers of Sikh, Muslim, and Hindu children were attending Birmingham schools and religious education was seen as a key point in community relations. The Conference was convened in 1970. The committee representing the 'other denominations' included not only Catholics, Orthodox and free churches but also representatives of the Jewish, Sikh, Hindu and Islamic faiths. At a later stage, a humanist was co-opted on to several of the working parties and on to the Coordinating Committee with speaking but not voting rights.

The Religious and Cultural Panel of the Birmingham Community Relations Committee had been meeting since March 1969 and spent some time in discussing what kind of religious education would be suitable for the city in the 1970s. The panel, which included Sikhs, Jews, Muslims, Hindus, all the major Christian churches and representatives of the teachers' organizations, presented a paper to the Agreed Syllabus Conference called 'Religious Education in a Multi-Religious Society' (Birmingham, 1971). The panel recommended that:

> it should be part of an education for life in this country that children come to know something of the traditional religion of the land, namely Christianity ... children should not be ignorant ... of the main features of the major world religions; and that in Birmingham ... Christian children should know something about Hindu, Islamic, Judaic and Sikh faiths ... just as children of these various faiths should know something both of Christianity, as the majority faith of the country, and of the other minority faiths ...

The panel concluded that there should be

> a deeper and more particular study of one religion, normally the tradition to which the pupil adheres. In multi-religious schools this would be made possible by allowing in the new Agreed Syllabus for options in part of the curriculum, the particular options that would be appropriate in a particular school depending upon the composition of its pupil body (Hull, 1971).

Work on the Syllabus and the Handbook which was to accompany it was virtually complete late in 1973. It was decided that the Syllabus itself should be very brief, merely setting out the broadest principles of the syllabus and giving some slight indication of its content. This one-page document was recommended by the Conference as the statutory syllabus and it was that which required the statutory agreement of the four committees of the Conference. The 1970–3 Conference was at this point following the example of its 1962 predecessor. In the 1962 Birmingham Syllabus, the actual syllabus is printed in red on the two-and-a-bit central pages of the book and described as 'Basic Syllabus'. The rest of the 1962 book of 107 pages is accompanying articles and suggestions for teachers. The syllabus for the age range 12 to 16 in the 1973 document said

> Three areas of investigation should be studied. A (i) Religion as it manifests itself in our own and other societies, and the claims upon which it rests. (ii) Non-religious stances for living, their basic assumptions and their outworking in personal and social life. B Aspects of personal life and behaviour which call for moral judgements. C The problems currently facing mankind national-ly and internationally which involve ethical and religious consi-derations. [At the time of writing, the Birmingham Syllabus and Handbook had not been published. I quote from my own documents as a member of the Conference.]

The Handbook which accompanies this brief syllabus, part of which has just been quoted, is a bulky volume of some 600 pages, with extensive articles on aspects of religious education, and detailed courses for every level of the school with lists of resources and bibliographies.

> In the present Syllabus and Handbook religious education is seen as an intrinsically valid educational activity, justified by its particular contribution to preparation for life in contemporary society. It is not propaganda for a given religious standpoint. . . .

The Introduction continues by pointing out that previous Agreed Syllabuses when dealing with world religions tended 'towards a compari-son of other faiths with one considered as self-evidently superior to the rest; whereas the approach now is to study them objectively and for their own sake.' In the secondary school there should be

> a detailed study of at least one religious tradition in all its dimensions. Each pupil should have the right to choose for himself or herself the subject of this study from the following options: Christianity, Hinduism, Islam, Judaism and Sikhism. In addition to this detailed study some further study of one or more of these options should be undertaken, including Christian-ity if this is not the religion chosen for detailed study. All secondary school pupils should also study one, at least, of the non-religious stances for living.

At the secondary stage, the Handbook then sets out for both detailed and less detailed study courses in all five of the prescribed religions and courses for less detailed study in two non-religious stances for living, viz. humanism and communism. It is anticipated that a detailed study would occupy about a year and a less detailed study about a term.

At a final meeting of the full Conference in the autumn of 1973 all four committees voted in favour of the Syllabus and recommended the Handbook. These documents went on to the Finance and General Purposes Committee of the Education Committee of the City Council in February 1974 where they were accepted subject to the deletion of the references to communism. This decision was front page news in the local press and was also reported in several national newspapers. The Education Committee and the City Council itself refused to delete the offending portions, and a controversy developed along party political lines, with the minority Conservative party opposing the communist course and the majority Labour party seeking to retain the Syllabus and Handbook intact. The fact that this affair coincided with a national election did nothing to calm things down. A lengthy correspondence was published in both *The Birmingham Post* and the *Evening Mail* with headlines such as 'Subversion', 'Communist textbook', 'The teaching of communism' and 'Happy Marx'. Publication of the Syllabus and Handbook was delayed.

The legality of the Syllabus was questioned and counsel's opinion was sought. In June 1974 the barrister retained by the City's Solicitor expressed the view that the Syllabus did not fulfil the requirements of the 1944 Education Act. The Bishop of Birmingham had also expressed some reservations about the Syllabus and Handbook and his Director of Education sought the advice of the National Society (Church of England) on the legality of the documents. Legal opinion was again quoted against the Syllabus. 'Communism in syllabus is outside law, says Church' was the headline in *The Birmingham Post* on 10 June.

Section 10 of the Fifth Schedule of the 1944 Act provides for appeal from the local authority to the Minister should the conference be unable to agree or should the authority fail to adopt a syllabus unanimously agreed upon by the conference. The legal opinion engaged by the City thought that the City, although believing it had adopted a syllabus, had not in fact done so because what the conference had submitted to it was not in fact a syllabus of religious instruction. It was not a syllabus because the brief document in question did not provide sufficient indication of the main heads of the proposed content, and it was not entirely a syllabus of religious instruction because it included non-religions, to be studied in their own right. These could only be included, counsel thought, if their study contributed to the advancement of religious knowledge. The matter was therefore referred to the Secretary of State for Education in Mr Harold Wilson's government, Mr Reginald Prentice. In the late summer the City was advised that the Conference to draw up the Agreed Syllabus had not yet completed its work. Until it had done so, no opinions on the legality of its recommendations could be given.

Many of the problems glimpsed in Bath came to a head in Birmingham. Since affairs in Birmingham present us with the clearest case to date of the difficulties and the profound changes taking place in the Agreed Syllabuses, we must examine some of them in greater detail.

What does 'agreement' mean in an Agreed Syllabus?

The Agreed Syllabus had always been an ecumenical document in the sense that the churches, agreeing not to permit the teaching of anything denominationally distinctive, agreed to teach what they held in common to be the truth. The Bath Syllabus revealed how irrelevant this kind of ecumenical cooperation has become today. In any maintained school in the future, when religious education deals with Christianity, it will do so 'without implying the need to commend or to be exclusive'. Not only is religious education not 'teaching Communism' in that it is not fostering belief in communism; it is not teaching Christianity either, in that it is not concerned to foster faith in Christianity. When the aim of religious education is 'to secure an understanding and appreciation of religion' then the subject will be controlled by whatever methods might be suitable to the study of religion. Statements from Christians about what they believe in common will of course be valuable in helping the teacher to present Christian beliefs accurately; but the assumption that the churches needed to agree about a syllabus because their common faith would be taught as being true can no longer be viable.

The Bath Syllabus revealed the irrelevancy of the older assumption but the Birmingham documents replaced it with a new assumption. All the Conference today is required to agree about is that the various subjects it recommends are all worth including. That is all. Christians after all do not believe that humanism is true and Muslims do not believe that Hinduism is true. Although from time to time during the meetings of the various working parties the view was expressed that belief in God was the common affirmation which linked the Syllabus together (Buddhism is not presented in detail until the sixth form) this can hardly include the non-religious stances for living, and since these are treated in exactly the same spirit (descriptively and sympathetically) as the religions, the theistic basis collapses. Agreement is thus not about the truth of the content at all. The various groups represented all agreed that their respective beliefs were worthwhile, noble, and that a child's education would be the poorer if he were denied some opportunity to encounter them. This new assumption about agreement cuts the ground from under the whole philosophy and rationale of the older Agreed Syllabuses including those which appeared in the 1960s.

A descriptive approach to the world religions

Non-Christian religions were included, if at all, in the older syllabuses only in the sixth form and only in an apologetic or missionary context. The London 1968 Agreed Syllabus created an important precedent when it included representatives of the Jewish and Muslim communities. But although the contribution of the Asian pupil to religious studies is emphasized, London does not recommend any specific study of a religion other than Christianity earlier than the sixth form. The problems of teaching other religions are discussed in a helpful way, and it is rightly pointed out that religions not actually represented in the school will be more difficult and less valuable to teach, but in a city like London there must have been many schools even in 1968 where something more than this would have been appropriate well before the sixth form. The biographies suggested for study in the primary school may, it is suggested, include people of all beliefs and none, but leaders of the non-Christian faiths are not mentioned by name as are the Christian heroes. Similarly, the joint work of Christians and humanists is commended but no humanist seems to have been co-opted on to the conference at any stage, and although the contribution of the uncommitted teacher in religious education is recognized, the usual description of the religious education teacher is 'the Christian teacher'. Nevertheless, London had blazed the trail which Yorkshire and Birmingham were to follow.

Early in 1974 the West Riding of Yorkshire Education Committee published a Supplement to their well known 1966 *Suggestions for Religious Education* (Agreed Syllabus). Called *Religious Education in the Multi-faith Community*, it appears to be the first recognition through an agreed syllabus that in a religiously mixed society religious education in the county schools cannot commend one faith and simply refer in passing to others. Such a policy would force the non-Christian communities to withdraw from religious education and would encourage the development of whole new systems of aided schools.

We have seen how from its inception the Birmingham Conference was committed to a religious education syllabus which would make a positive contribution to community relations in the city. It was gradually realized that this meant the creation of a syllabus which could be taught by any well informed teacher of good-will, regardless of his faith, to any interested pupils, regardless of their faith. So, in the Birmingham documents, a new relation between the teacher's teaching and his personal faith is envisaged. Previously a teacher taught what he believed (Christianity) although the Cowper-Temple clause might prevent him from teaching *all* he believed. Now he is asked to teach (that is, encourage pupils to study) many things which he does not believe and to refrain from commending in any special way the things he does believe. The abandonment of the Christian hegemony in the agreed syllabuses in these various ways represents a small but significant shift in the relations between church and state in Britain.

The non-religious stances for living

Previous Agreed Syllabuses made tentative steps in this direction. The Lancashire Agreed Syllabus of 1968 mentions 'Humanism' and 'Dialectial Materialism' as possible discussion topics in the sixth form, and in a somewhat similar context the London 1968 Syllabus refers to 'rationalism, materialism, Marxism, existentialism'. But these secular life styles were approached from a Christian point of view; they were thought of as 'challenges to faith'. The 1966 West Riding Syllabus describes communism and humanism as 'alternative to the Christian faith' and the short book list contains only works by Christians.

The tendency to include the non-religions in religious education received significant support in *The Fourth R* (Durham Report) in 1970.

> By religion we mean some pattern of belief and behaviour related to the questions of man's ultimate concern. For some, it is an Eastern religion; for some it is Christianity; for others it is one of the secular creeds of the West, for example Marxism; for others it is agnostic humanism ... (p. 100).

Religious Education in Secondary Schools (Schools Council, 1971) remarks, 'It may be argued that some of the alternatives to religious faith, such as secular Humanism, Marxism and Maoism deserve the same sympathetic study and attention. We would agree' (p. 66). There is a well established group of new textbooks for religious education which deal with the non-religions alongside the religions. (See, for example, Herod, 1969 and Sherratt and Hawkin, 1972.)

The Birmingham Handbook goes much further than previous agreed syllabuses in that, instead of a few words directed at the sixth form, it provides thorough courses for the fourth or fifth forms in both humanism and communism, and accepts the advice of Working Paper 36 that such beliefs should receive 'the same sympathetic study' as the religions themselves.

The fact that the Birmingham documents are not concerned with the teaching of politics is apparent from the fact that humanism has been chosen, along with communism, as an example of a non-religious stance for living. Humanism has less organized political expression than either Christianity or communism. But what then are the criteria for the inclusion in a religious education syllabus of non-religious stances for living? A candidate for admission must satisfy all three of the following criteria. First, the ideology or way of life must explicitly reject religion. Second, it must claim to be a substitute for religion. Third, it must nevertheless exhibit certain characteristics of the religions, such as a theory of history, a total view of man and his destiny and a system of ethics. Although a necessary ground for inclusion, these criteria are not a sufficient ground. Fascism for example, although it meets the three criteria, may not be thought sufficiently significant in Britain today to justify inclusion in a hard-pressed curriculum, or it may be deemed morally unworthy of inclusion. The main British political parties are clearly excluded by the criteria. The Liberal Party does not offer itself as a substitute for religion, the Conservatives do not claim to present a comprehensive interpretation of every aspect of life, the Labour Party does not reject any doctrine of Christianity. Such influences from Christianity as there may be in any of these political philosophies would be dealt with in Christian Studies. Capitalism is an ambiguous case. Perhaps it would be helpful to make the same sort of distinction between the implicit and the explicit in the study of the non-religions as it is customary to make in the study of the religions. Capitalism would then be seen as an *implicit* non-religious stance for living. No doubt it is full of all sorts of implications for ethics and religion. Capitalism implies a view of man but it does not preach a doctrine of man. It adopts an attitude towards the world but it has no teaching about the world. In these respects it differs from communism and should probably be excluded.

Doubts about this widening of the content of the Agreed Syllabuses have been expressed in two quarters, and they are concerned mainly with communism. There is a significant body of Christian opinion which is doubtful (and other religions are similarly sometimes doubtful). The debate turns upon problems to do with the Christian response to secularity and the nature of Christian mission. The relationship between Christianity and education is also an important problem. There is also a significant opposition from politicians, both at the local and the national level. This opposition springs from a misunderstanding of the task of the religious education teacher. The politicians assume that if a teacher teaches about Christianity, it is because he is a Christian and wants others to share his views. Similarly, they assume that if the teacher wants to teach about communism, it is because he is a communist and wants others to share his views. Just as the clergy used to interpret trends in religious education in terms of the pulpit so now politicians are interpreting them in terms of the hustings. It seems difficult for them to understand that the teacher is neither an evangelist nor a propagandist but an educator. The teachers' unions have taken a lively interest in the controversies about the Birmingham documents because they have seen that the professional integrity of the teacher is at stake.

An assessment of the continued significance of the Agreed Syllabuses

It seems unlikely that Agreed Syllabuses will ever regain the influence which they had from about 1924 to about 1970. This is partly because there have appeared other sources of authority and guidance. These include the Schools Council curriculum development projects, the materials published by the Shap Working Party on world religions, the Primary Mailing of the Christian Education Movement and the broadsheets prepared in many counties by the many advisers in religious education employed by the local authorities. It is also clear that, because of the cumbersome machinery required to bring them into operation and the limitations presented by such elaborate committee work, Agreed Syllabuses will normally be rather conservative documents. Teachers are asking for a more active role in shaping their own syllabuses, and the patterns of teacher training and the work of the many in-service centres encourages this. It is symptomatic of this trend that many local authorities have published recommendations for religious education which have by-passed the Agreed Syllabus machinery entirely. Use has been made of the Standing Advisory Councils which the Act permits the authorities to establish, or the authority has published work submitted by teachers. These documents have no statutory authority but they have tended to present the more active growing edge of the subject. We may also notice the tendency in the Agreed Syllabuses to present articles rather than a detailed syllabus, and it is interesting to notice that, even immediately after 1944, the Syllabuses, in spite of the fact that they really did have mandatory power, continued to insist in their forewords and introductions that they were only suggestions and that teachers were to be encouraged to be selective and creative.

In spite of all this, the Agreed Syllabuses retain a certain moral and professional weight which no other document has. They give official approval and recognition to trends already well established. They offer a platform for public discussion and for cooperation between many interested parties. Their most significant feature is usually not merely what they say but how they came to say it. Change in the classroom is not effected by presenting to a fully trained teacher a syllabus in the making of which he has had no direct part. But the Agreed Syllabuses do a great deal to register the climate of the subject and to set out its norms.

In the future some means must be found which will retain the interest and commitment of local authorities and churches in religious education and which will provide a forum for the sharing of concerns between the teachers and the public. There must however be no more statutory controls. Officially sponsored advisory bodies seem the most promising solution.

References

BATH, *Agreed Syllabus of Religious Education*, City of Bath Education Authority, 1970.

BIRMINGHAM *Agreed Syllabus of Religious Instruction*, 1950, revised edition, City of Birmingham Education Committee, 1962.

BIRMINGHAM, 'Religious education in a multi-religious society', *Learning for Living*, 11, 1, Community Relations Committee, 1971, pp. 26–28.

BIRNIE, I.H., 'Carry on agreeing', *Learning for Living*, 2, 1, SCM Press.

CAMBRIDGE, *The Cambridgeshire Syllabus of Religious Teaching for Schools*, Cambridgeshire and Isle of Ely Education Committee, 1924; *Religious Education: Suggestions for Teachers*, Cambridgeshire and Isle of Ely Education Committee, 1970.

CORNWALL, *Handbook for Religious Education*, Cornwall Education Committee, 1971.

DURHAM REPORT, *The Fourth R*, National Society and SPCK, 1970.

ESSEX, *'Interchange' Working Papers in Religious Education*, Essex Education Committee, n.d.

HAMPSHIRE, *Approaches to Religious Education: A Handbook of Suggestions*, Hampshire Education Committee, n.d.

HEROD, F.G. *What Men Believe*, Methuen, 1969.

HULL J.M. *School Worship – An Obituary*, SCM Press, 1975.

ILEA *Learning for Life*, Inner London Education Authority, 1968.

LANCASHIRE, *Religion and Life*, Lancashire Education Committee, 1968.

NORTHAMPTONSHIRE, *Fullness of Life* (Primary) and *Life and Worship* (Senior section), Northamptonshire Education Committee, 1968.

SCHOOLS COUNCIL, Working Paper 36, *Religious Education in Secondary Schools*, Evans/Methuen, 1971.

SHERRATT, B.W., and HAWKIN, D.J. *Gods and Men*, Blackie, 1972.

SURREY, *Syllabus of Religious Instruction*, Surrey County Council Education Committee, 1945.

WEST RIDING, *Suggestion for Religious Education*, County Council of the West Riding of Yorkshire Education Department, 1966; *Religious Education in the Multi-Faith Community*, County Council of the West Riding of Yorkshire Education Department, 1974.

WILTSHIRE, *Religious Education in Wiltshire*, Wiltshire County Council Education Committee, 1967.

YEAXLEE, B., (Ed.) *Religious Education*, Vol. 1, 1934.

7. *Recent Developments in the Philosophy of Religious Education*

In the middle decades of this century there was a generally accepted philosophy of religious education. The whole of education was to be consistent with, and where possible directly derived from, Christian beliefs. The school was to be considered a Christian community. No clear distinction was made between the roles of the church and the state school. The function of religious education as part of the curriculum was to create Christian discipleship. All teachers were preferably to be Christians; teachers of religion could not be effective unless they were Christians. Worship was the natural climax of the whole thing: here the Christian community, led by believing teachers, explicitly affirmed faith in God.[1] At the same time there was steady emphasis on the freedom of the child, this being a consequence of the Christian idea of personality, so that while intending and hoping to create Christian discipleship, Christian education would foster independence and seek for a free response.

This philosophy was never articulated in detail. As late as 1956 Rupert Davies remarked on the variety of half-formed ideas and commented on the need to explore the matter more thoroughly.[2] He himself however accepted the general outline I have described. This will never now be worked out in detail, since the very foundations of the approach have been shaken.

The changes which are taking place have sprung from a realization that the old philosophy is not producing results. The increasingly rapid pace of secularization and the variety of religious and non-religious views which have taken the place of the Christian establishment of the 1940s can no longer be denied. Evidence of the extent to which pupils understand and accept Christian doctrine and biblical teaching is discouraging in terms of the old expectations. The gap between the ideal and the reality becomes more and more threatening. Not until the model finally breaks down do you go right back to the drawing-board.

The writings which promoted the very significant changes in religious education during the 1960s dealt with the psychology of the religion of children and young people, and with method.[3] There was little work done on the philosophical and theological theory of the new approaches, except in Roman Catholic circles. Here there has been considerable new and valuable thought,[4] but the impact on the county schools has been understandably slight. It is also indicative of the serious plight of Christian educational theory that such new writing as has appeared has dealt in the main with religious education as a subject of the curriculum and not with the total relationship between religion and education.[5] Indeed, instead of discussion about the place of religion in education as a whole we now have discussion about the place of morals in education as a whole.[6]

Turning then to the more restricted field of the philosophy of religious education as a school subject, mention must first be made of the work of Ninian Smart. *The Teacher and Christian Belief* appeared in 1966 and was followed in 1968 by *Secular Education and the Logic of Religion*. In Professor Smart's writings the secular environment in which any teaching of religion at any level must be carried out is taken with complete seriousness. This was seldom the case in earlier writings. W.R. Niblett's *Christian Education in a Secular Society* (1960) although valuable in many other respects is disappointing on this matter. It pre-dates the discussion of the secular which has been a central theme of theology in the last few years. Ninian Smart, while not accepting the claim, often repeated, that we are heading for a time of no religion, is convinced of the increasing plurality of British society, and the consequent necessity that the state and the official institutions of education should be neutral.

Religious education is thus presented with a dilemma. '. . . Christian education is intrenched in our school system' and yet 'the typical modern institution of higher education is secular – that is, neutralist in regard to religious and ideological commitment'.[7]

Professor Smart's argument is that far from an open, descriptive, comparative and even perhaps neutral approach to religious matters being inappropriate for Christian education the inner nature of the Christian religion leads one to teach it in just such a manner. Christian doctrines cannot be intelligently believed today without attention to the problems of philosophy which the doctrines raise. Christian doctrines overlap with areas of scientific inquiry (for example, the doctrine of creation) and of historical investigation (the trial and death of Jesus). Evaluation of other forms of religious experience and other claims to religious truth is bound to follow from the Christian's meditation on his own experience and his belief in the truth of his own religion. In short, just because Christian truth claims to be universal, and to be all inclusive, and to be internally coherent, it must set up a dialogue with the rest of experience and with other kinds of truth.

This means that Christianity must be taught not as a self-enclosed self-authenticating system of truth, but by discussion, comparison, weighing of arguments, all without prejudice to the final outcome. Religious education therefore, to be true to the very nature of Christianity, must explore the relationship between revelation and modern thought. This dialectic between faith and the world can in principle be set up even before pupils reach intellectual maturity. Movement from contemporary problems to the Bible and back again as a method of religious education is thus seen to have a justification in the very process of religious thinking.[8]

Ninian Smart's two books on this subject are themselves a guide to the sort of religious education their author advocates. Various views are clarified, contrasted, compared, the arguments for and against described, but the search is not brought to a premature end by a hasty or over-forceful disclosure of the teacher's own view. The style is witty, brief, and lively, the argument is presented so as to create discussion rather than close it.

Two problems are discussed which arise from this approach. The first is the problem of doctrine. For, it might be thought, the history of religions may be taught in the objective open way described, but surely doctrine must be left out. Professor Smart's reply is in the form of an analysis of the structure of religions.

It is shown that 'parahistorical' questions (matters of doctrine, myth and ethics) cannot be separated from the historical aspects of a religion (its ritual, its experiential and its social existences). To omit the parahistorical would be to seriously distort the nature of religion. But this aspect of religion must be taught in the same open way. The doctrines must not be taught as if they were true, but in constant tension with the alternatives. Such teaching must have 'the aim of creating certain capacities to understand and think about religion'.[9]

But what about the faith of the teacher? Must he not be a believer to teach religion? Ninian Smart's reply is that he need not be a believer. Some of the best descriptions of religion are provided by outsiders.[10] But the teacher of religion must have a certain kind of relation to his subject if it is to be taught effectively. He must have a point of view which must be reflective and heuristic. Only this 'can put us in a position effectively to engage in the dialogue with those who themselves, in the process of learning, are reaching out towards a point of view.'[11]

The teacher must also be sympathetic towards religion. If he is a humanist, he must be sympathetic towards the value which men have placed upon religion; if a Christian, he must be sympathetic towards doubt. 'The good teacher is not the Christian one or the humanist one. The good teacher is the open one.'[12] The views of the conservative evangelical may be educationally disastrous, because such a position tends to stop questions by imposing a total pattern of belief.

This then provides a basis for a religious education which will be true to itself, which will be educationally appropriate, which will be taught by teams of teachers of various faiths and non-faiths, and which will interlock with other subjects in a fruitful way.

What problems remain? The principles of the teaching of religion ought, says Professor Smart, to be essentially the same at all levels.[13] What then becomes of the common idea of religious education as a contribution to the personal growth of the pupil? For we do not usually think of universities teaching theology in order to meet the needs and promote the growth of students. Or do we? Smart has some valuable suggestions to make about the progressive growth in understanding of pupils, but the question of what role if any religion has in the education of young children remains open. Of course, Smart is writing as a theologian not as a psychologist, and his approach does not exclude other approaches to the teaching of religion, provided his basic requirements are not infringed.

An observation may be made about the basic argument dealing with the educational implications of the nature of religion. If the logic of religion leads towards the open inquiry, conducted by the sympathetic but not necessarily committed teacher, then what should we be doing in the churches? What sort of education ought to be provided in Sunday schools, junior churches and theological colleges? Does the logic drive us towards a similar conclusion about the education offered within the believing community? If so, Professor Smart is suggesting a revolution in Christian education of unparalleled proportion. This possibility must not be ruled out! But if not, then we must ask to what extent the policy he puts forward for religious education in the official institutions of the state is really governed by the logic of religion rather than by sociological considerations such as the increased plurality of beliefs.

The position is, I think, that we must have the type of neutral religious education advocated by Ninian Smart because of the sociological factors, and it so happens ('It is a happy world'[14]) that this approach is *consistent with* the nature of Christian thought. It is probably an overstatement to say that that type of religious education is *required* by the nature of Christian thought. Dialogue and the investigation of relations with other fields of knowledge and experience are indeed demanded by the nature of Christian belief, but it is sociological factors rather than theological inferences which lead to the suggestion that this education may be conducted apart from the premiss of faith. That suggestion, to repeat the point, can only be consistent with Christian faith; it cannot be required by Christian faith.[15]

In 1969 SCM Press published *Religious Education in a Secular Setting* by J.W.D. Smith. The argument of this important study requires close analysis. After a brief review of the current debate about the aims of religious education in state schools, the history and present position of the subject in England, Wales and Scotland is considered. Smith concludes that the decision in the early 1940s to commit the state to a programme of Christian education was already anachronistic, because of the rapid process of secularization already taking place. The 1944 Act has perpetuated the fiction that the church and the state are partners in education.

The main argument begins in chapter three, with a discussion of the nature of religious language. This, since it is no longer meaningful to many pupils, creates a difficulty in communication which is the central problem in religious education today.

The argument is confused at this point by an attempt to illustrate the ineffectiveness of religious language by reference to the linguistic philosophy of Wittgenstein. The trouble is that Smith does not distinguish between Wittgenstein's interest in the logical status of religious language and his own (Smith's) interest in its sociological status as a language used by a shrinking group of people. The blurring of this distinction is seen, for example, in the question, 'Is religious language still meaningful universally ...?'[16] If this refers to the logic of religious language, the word 'universal' is redundant, since logically sound propositions remain so anywhere in the world, whether they are thought to be important or not. But if the question refers to the possibility that fewer people are using religious language, then this is not a matter which concerned Wittgenstein as a philosopher.

On the same page the educational implications of linguistic philosophy are stated in an inadequate way. 'If religious language is no longer meaningful to everybody, it would surely follow that religious education would only be viable within the limited circle of religious believers.' But if, as it seems, the logic of religious language is such that it can be appreciated by understanding the community which uses it, it is by no means impossible nor inappropriate to educate people into the meaning of that language. Pupils can come to know what that community is and what its members say, just as they are initiated into the language games of physics and music. They can understand its logical meaning even if they reject its truth or its importance. Of course, and this may be what Smith intends to say, the religious education given to all in the belief that what religious people say is worth studying will differ from the Christian education given to the religious few in the belief that what religious people say is in fact true.

What linguistic philosophy has to teach us about religious education is, I think, that since the meaning of propositions resides in their use, teachers should show how religious groups actually use their own speech, and what other things they say about religion which are similar to the particular item under discussion. Religious language cannot be understood (its logical status cannot be grasped) in isolation from the living community which uses it. These inferences are based upon the later Wittgenstein, and the argument of chapter three would have been clarified if it had been modified at this stage by the reappraisal of the later Wittgenstein which is referred to later.

The position of the early Wittgenstein is however badly explained, and that is also true of the significance of the later Wittgenstein. For although we now see that a language game, although played by rules of limited application, is intelligible to those who understand the rules, Smith, still remarks on the failure of theology to 'restore traditional religious language to universal currency'.[17] This is not an apt criticism of Ian Ramsey, whose book is being discussed now by J.W.D. Smith, for Ramsey is not trying to establish the objective verifiability of religious language, let alone trying to restore it to universal use, or to make it seem important to everyone, but merely to show that as used by the religious group, religious language is not without an appropriate logical structure. The question of logic is again confused with the various sociological factors which make it hard for many young people to use religious language.

The distinction between a meaningful private language and a language game is never made clear. 'Traditional religious language has become a private language in the modern world because traditional religious commitment is a minority experience.'[18] But in Wittgenstein a minority language differs both from a language game and from a private language. The logical structure of a language is not affected by the number of people who speak it. In the sentence just quoted, a distinction should be made between secularization as a historical process ('has become ...') and secularization as a consequence of logical assertions.

Chapter three then makes an important and valid claim about one difficulty of teaching religion today, but the chapter would have been clearer if some of these distinctions had been listed, or if the claim had been supported by more psychological and sociological observations and the discussion about Wittgenstein and Ramsey either curtailed or left out altogether.

Chapter four, 'Is Moral Education Enough?', presents a surprising contrast. Metaphysics, ruled out previously as being a private language (*sic*), logically meaningless because incapable of verification, is now re-instated. 'We may need to learn a new language in order to discuss age-old themes, but the themes themselves may be valid and meaningful.'[19] Previously however the author seemed to be agreeing with the early Wittgenstein, in saying that metaphysical questions arise out of logical confusion. The concept of the inexpressible showing itself[20] (= age-old themes) is of no use to us in understanding the new claims of this chapter for we cannot know if the expressible is (logically) valid or (logically) meaningful until it is expressed in propositional form. To discover and assess these age-old themes we will need language; whether new or old is indifferent to their logical status.

It is not easy to determine the direction of the argument in this chapter, but the main point is that morals without religion are not enough, since morality, if argued sufficiently deeply, leads to questions about man which are also religious questions, or which may at least be answered by religion. 'This path leads beyond the secure territory of linguistic analysis towards the frontiers of the unknown – the area once cultivated by metaphysicians.'[21]

At this point Martin Heidegger is discussed. Not only is morality rooted in human nature, and is thus 'a game which everyone must play'[22] but now it appears that religion is also rooted in 'the very structure of man's existence as a finite being'.[23] The author thus asserts on the basis of Heidegger what he had refused to allow on the basis of Wittgenstein. It may have been his intention to expose the limitations of the linguistic approach, as is mentioned on page 36, but on the other hand, it is hard to resist the opinion that chapters three and four are not consistent.

The following chapters are interesting and more coherent. It is suggested that in the philosophy of Martin Heidegger an analysis of human existence can be found which may provide a new basis for religious education, acceptable to Christians and humanists alike. The element of mystery in life, particularly that felt in the presence of death, cannot be ignored without damage to the personality, and it is in the area of fostering the growth of loving trust towards life that religious education can contribute to the health of boys and girls.

Just as in the third chapter a problem arose about the earlier and the later Wittgenstein, so here there arises a problem of choice between the early and the later Heidegger. The early Heidegger teaches that authentic existence can be attained by the determined self without outside aid. The later Heidegger is inclined to look, for the possibility of authentic existence, to the gracious power of being itself. Religious education based on the earlier work would tend to be humanistic, but if based on the later work it would tend to include some emphasis on trustful response to the divine grace.

What answer does J.W.D. Smith offer to the educational problem of the two Heideggers? Religious education based on the early Heidegger is rejected. 'Religious education would be impoverished if it were reduced to "religionless" teaching.'[24] The difficulty here is that the dimension of mystery, as expounded by the early Heidegger, had previously[25] been regarded as 'the religious dimension of human life'. But nevertheless, to base a philosophy of education on the early Heidegger would now apparently provide a religionless teaching. It is difficult to avoid the conclusion that the early Heidegger is here rejected for a reason not unlike that which had formerly led to his acceptance, namely, his analysis of the human situation without recourse to the supernatural.

The attempt to base religious education on the work of Heidegger is thus not without its difficulties. But the original and striking feature of this book is that it should have been attempted. In this respect, these pages are full of promise and point the way to a treatment of religion in schools which will deal with basic human problems but not in such a way as to presuppose the truth of Christianity or even, perhaps, the existence of God.

In chapter seven Smith returns to the appraisal of the religious educational scene, and in a most convincing manner it is shown that Christian education, in the sense of education based specifically on presuppositions about the truth of Christianity and aimed at establishing Christian belief, can no longer be given in the state schools. Christian imperialistic aims are no longer appropriate in religious education nor can Christianity any longer expect to provide a framework to restore wholeness to the curriculum.

The function of the religious education given in the schools will be to deepen the sense of existential mystery and to facilitate personal growth towards love by a factual objective study of Christian origins and other subjects. Illustrations are given of the difference between the religious and the specifically Christian use of biblical material. Some penetrating criticisms of the Goldman type of life-theme are offered. Religious and moral education will be carried out by a team of specialists from various religious and non-religious traditions. The personal beliefs of the teachers will not be very important. 'Their personal convictions might be strong, but their professional concern for tolerance and freedom of opinion should be stronger.'[26]

A concealed apology for Christianity however runs through the book. Why, for example, is it said that although bringing pupils to an awareness of the mystery of existence will *begin* to fufil the aims appropriate to religious education today, 'the Christian interpretation of the mystery at the frontiers of human existence' is that which will *'fulfil* these aims'?[27] Christianity, because of its unique emphasis on love in a human life, is particularly well qualified to assist in personal growth towards love. It looks as if the removal of the aims of religious education from the theological and ecclesiastical realms into the educational realm may in fact, because of the rapport between Christianity and educational psychology, be preparing the way for a Christian renaissance.

The works we have been discussing break important new ground in the theory of religious education. They are prophetic in outlining the future basis of religious teaching in the state schools. Much more work needs to be done, and it is greatly to be desired that these stimulating offerings will lead to a renewal of interest in the theology of education.

Notes

1 This is necessarily rather a simplified summary of the position. But the broad picture is confirmed by a study of standard writings of the period such as Reeves, Marjorie and Drewett, John *What is Christian Education?* (1942); Leeson, Spencer, *Christian Education* (1947); Lester Smith, W.O. *The School as a Christian Community* (1954) and almost all the then current Agreed Syllabuses.
2 Davies, Rupert E. (ed.), *An Approach to Christian Education* (1956), pp. 1–18.
3 Daines, J.W., *An Enquiry into the Methods and Effects of Religious Education in Sixth Forms* (1962); *Meaning or Muddle? An Investigation into the Religious Concepts Held by Secondary School Children* (1966); Hyde, K.E., *Religious Learning in Adolescence* (1965); Lee, R.S. *Your Growing Child and Religion* (1956). Note the discussion and 'life situation' methods pioneered by Loukes, Harold, *Teenage Religion* (1961), and Acland, Richard, *We Teach Them Wrong* (1963), and the thematic method advised by Goldman in *Readiness for Religion* (1965). One of the few works dealing with the philosophy of the subject was Cox, Edwin, *Changing Aims in Religious Education* (1966).
4 For example, the influential writings of Gabriel Moran.
5 The situation in the United States is the reverse. There is much work being done on the relationship between religion and education, for example, Sizer, R. Theodore (ed.), *Religion and Public Education* (1967).
6 For example the writings of John Wilson and the essays edited by Chris Macey, *Let's Teach Them Right!* (1969).
7 *Secular Education and the Logic of Religion*, p. 90.
8 *The Teacher and Christian Belief*, p. 192.
9 *Secular Education and the Logic of Religion*, p. 97.
10 See Smart's article in *Let's Teach Them Right!* ed. Macey.
11 *The Teacher and Christian Belief*, p. 7.

12 *Ibid.*, p. 15.
13 *Secular Education* ..., pp. 7, 99, etc.
14 *Ibid.*, p. 106.
15 The comments about the role of commitment (*ibid.*, p. 98) are helpful but the distinction I am making and its implication for the rest of Christian education could do with some discussion.
16 *Religious Education in a Secular Setting*, p. 24.
17 *Ibid.*, p. 31.
18 *Ibid.*, p. 33.
19 *Ibid.*, p. 39.
20 *Ibid.*, p. 25.
21 *Ibid.*, p. 39.
22 *Ibid.*, p. 37.
23 *Ibid.*, p. 39.
24 *Ibid.*, p. 61.
25 *Ibid.*, p. 51.
26 *Ibid.*, p. 102.
27 *Ibid.*, p. 113.

8. *Religious Indoctrination in the Birmingham Agreed Syllabus?**

The Birmingham *Agreed Syllabus of Religious Instruction* was published in May 1975 and was followed in September by a large, loose-leaf volume of suggestions and aids called *Living Together: Teachers' Handbook of Suggestions for Religious Education*. The syllabus is four pages long and is published in the middle of the 24 page booklet. It was produced in accordance with the 1944 Education Act, the fifth schedule of which is printed in full at the end of the booklet along with the other relevant sections of the Act. The Handbook has no statutory force and is not part of the Agreed Syllabus. It can be revised, withdrawn, or added to by the Education Committee of the city, as it thinks fit. Its importance lies not only in the fact that it is a compendious resource manual, but that it is the semi-official interpretation of the Syllabus, being drawn up by the same Conference which created the Syllabus.[1]

The Birmingham Syllabus is noteworthy in that it is the first such document to abandon explicitly the Christianizing intentions of the older religious education, offering instead a sympathetic but thoughtful education concerning a variety of world religions and their secular alternatives. The emphasis is upon religion in the world today, and the approach is descriptive in that no religion or non-religion is selected for special commendation, and existential in that an attempt is made to relate the religions and non-religions to the interests and needs of young people.[2]

The Syllabus has provoked a wide variety of response, drawing criticism both from Christians[3] and humanists. The humanist criticisms are of particular interest because they have led to proposals for new legislation[4] and have been influential in a recent report on the future of Agreed Syllabuses.[5] In what follows, the humanist interpretation of the

---

* This is part of a paper read at Manchester College, Oxford, in March 1976 during a conference on the Birmingham Agreed Syllabus of Religious Instruction.

Birmingham Syllabus will be examined. I shall not be so much concerned with the idea of a 'stance for living', which underlies the present humanist attitude towards religious education,[6] but with the humanist estimation of the significance of the actual Syllabus.

The two versions of the Syllabus

Dr Harry Stopes Roe, the chairman of the British Humanist Association, claims that the Syllabus is 'dominated by religion', represents 'nurture of religion', that 'the material as a whole is slanted in a religious direction' and that it 'establishes religious indoctrination'.[7]

These conclusions arise from a comparison of the published 1975 Syllabus with an earlier version. In 1974 a one-page summary of the main proposals of the approach was drawn up by the Conference. This was intended to be a simple guide to the teaching materials, which had by 1974 become very considerable. If all the teaching suggestions and the lists of resources were to be formally presented to the LEA and adopted as the Agreed Syllabus it would not be possible to replace them and revise them easily, and so, in order both to meet the requirement of the law, and to make for maximum flexibility, it was decided that this simple, rather general, one-page summary should be described as the 'Syllabus', and that this alone should go forward for formal adoption. The Conference was encouraged in this not only by the example of the City of Bath Agreed Syllabus (1970)[8] but also by the previous Birmingham Syllabus, which had been published in the form of a short summary printed in the middle of a book of essays and general comment.

This summary was sent forward to the Education Committee. It included a reference to an 'area of investigation' for the secondary pupil described as 'non-religious stances for living, their basic assumptions and their outworking in personal and social life'. Then it became more widely known that amongst the variety of teachers' suggestions, intended to help them to meet this part of the approach, was a suggested (but optional) course on communism. Attempts were made to prevent the production of this material, and since it had not actually been presented, and no statutory status was being claimed for it, attention was focussed on the little one-page summary. This did not refer to communism, and therefore, in a sense, it did not matter. But it was being put forward for formal approval, and if the whole enterprise was somehow to be stopped or corrected, it had to be done through raising objections to this summary.

Legal opinion was accordingly sought, and the summary, which was headed 'The Agreed Syllabus' was examined to see whether it really could, alone as it now was, fulfil the requirements of the law. Sufficient doubt was thrown on the document to make the LEA pause for thought and towards the end of 1974 the Agreed Syllabus Conference was called together again, and advised that it had not completed its work (that is, the summary needed some expansion). A sub-committee was set up to make the summary sheet more specific, bearing, in mind the legal comments made. A resolution was passed by the Conference re-affirming the principles by which it had worked for four years, to make it absolutely clear that no shift of outlook or change of policy was contemplated. The sub-committee (of which I was a member) met late in 1974 and early in 1975, expanded the little summary sheet by adding various headings, listing things for study which had previously been set out only in the teachers' suggestions, and generally clarifying the outline of the intended approach. This document was then presented to the LEA and was adopted as the official Agreed Syllabus without further challenge. The suggestions for courses and the various resource aids were then published separately as the Handbook. This is the simple and rather trivial story out of which so much has been made, and upon the basis of which it is now being claimed that the 1944 Act cannot be made to work today.

Does the Syllabus intend to nurture faith in religion?

Dr Stopes Roe argues that the 1974 summary page 'was fair and balanced with respect to religious and non-religious views on ultimate questions, and balanced over the range of them'. It was a 'valid education ... nowhere is the discussion slanted in a particular direction'.[9] The villain of the piece is the 1944 Act, appeal to which is thought to have destroyed this fair and objective education. The Conference 'substantially changed the actual educational value of its Original Syllabus'.[10] The Act cannot therefore provide for an educationally valid syllabus, and a new Act is needed.

But is Dr Stopes Roe correct in thinking that the published Syllabus intends or implies the nurture or fostering of faith in religion? The Introduction to the 1975 Syllabus describes the nature of the religious education process as 'informing pupils in a descriptive, critical and experiential manner about what religion is' (p. 4). Whereas the older purpose was to nurture pupils into the Christian faith, by contrast this new Syllabus is 'directed towards developing a critical understanding of the religious and moral dimensions of human experience and away from attempting to foster the claims of particular religious standpoints.' Lest there should be any remaining doubt, the introduction continues 'there can be no question of making it an aim of religious education in schools to convert pupils to any particular religion or ideology' (p. 5).

But, although Dr Stopes Roe agrees that the 1975 statements about openness are actually strengthened against the weaker 1974 version, he thinks that 'in 1975 the claims do not fit the reality'. The first reason he gives is that the 1975 Syllabus has many more references to religion, and that whereas in the discarded version religious education 'was conceived as ranging over stances for living, not just religious stances' the latter Syllabus abandons this symmetrical balance between religions and non-religion. This is a possible interpretation of the two documents, but it is not the only one nor the most reasonable one. It is not quite correct to claim that the 1974 version 'related the religious and the non-religious as "both sides of the coin"'[11] since the Handbook, which was in 1974 as in 1975 the major detailed exposition of the intentions of the Conference, contained then (as it continued to contain) detailed treatment of six religions and only two non-religious. Still, accepting that in 1974 there was an unbiased placing of the non-religions alongside the religions, is this abandoned in 1975? By no means. The introduction to the published Syllabus states 'the City of Birmingham itself now contains sizeable groups of people each loyal to their own particular religious *or non-religious* commitment' (p. 4, italics added). The Birmingham scene is described as one in which Christianity continues to be important, and other great world-faiths are also significantly present. 'In addition, interest is being shown in many of the ideas basic to what have often been described as "secular faiths". The situation is thus a very open one, and the future is unknown (p. 5)'. In arguing for a Syllabus which will contain studies of Christianity and the other major world-faiths, the introduction continues 'Again, *on the same grounds*, other widely held stances for living . . . *require* serious attention in any realistic programme of education for life today' (italics added). Provisions for the study of a variety of religions in the secondary school are set out. Then we read, 'The other provisions [those dealing with the secular stances] are *equally important* for a *properly balanced* programme of work' (p. 6 italics added). Could a position between the religions and the secular stances be stated with greater clarity and objectivity? It is interesting to note that many of the Christians who disagree with the approach recommended by the Syllabus do so on the grounds that the Syllabus presents the very thing Dr Stopes Roe attacks it for failing to present. Some of the Christians say it is *too* objective, *too* balanced, and there is no trace of the religious emphasis left! There can be little doubt that it would not occur to any reader of the final Syllabus that it could ever be accused of being slanted in the direction of religious indoctrination. This interpretation only becomes possible when the bold and clear 1975 version is contrasted with the weak and vague 1974 summary sheet. And even here, as we have said, this is not the most reasonable interpretation.

Is the Syllabus slanted in favour of religion?

Dr Stopes Roe points out that the word 'religion' occurs more often in the 1975 Syllabus and that often religion stands alone, without any compensating reference to the secular ideologies. This is true, but what is its significance? The additional references to the religious subject matter of religious education do not indicate any desire to nurture faith in religion, or to introduce a different kind of syllabus, or to suggest that religions should be studied in some different way or with some different purpose from that envisaged before. The simple fact of the matter is that the 1974 summary was thought by the barristers to be too short and too vague to be described as a syllabus.[12] The legal Opinion obtained by the City of Birmingham Solicitor's Department concerning the 1974 Syllabus dealt with two questions, the first of which was whether the 1974 Syllabus was indeed a syllabus. In the legal Opinion, the suggestions for the ages 3 to 12 years, and for the sixth form in the secondary school, could not be correctly described as a syllabus. Religious education will explore 'themes within the curriculum of the infant school' but nothing is said about what themes, or about the objects of the exploration. The child will discover 'significance and meaning' but the object of this is not identified. So this brief summary was cast in terms which can only be described as 'general'. (I am abstracting from my personal copy of the legal Opinion.)

The second matter which the legal Opinion considered was whether the 1974 document was a syllabus of *religious* instruction. Again, legal criticism was directed towards the vagueness of the 1974 Syllabus. Concerning the material for the age-group 8 to 12 years, the barrister remarked, 'The contents could be wholly achieved without reference to religion.' For example, the 1974 Syllabus suggested 'study of the lives of men and women who have initiated new ways of living'. The barrister asks whether the fact that the heading for the section is 'religious education' might mean that only the lives of men and women who have initiated new *religious* ways of living may be studied. But he is not attracted by this interpretation, for the actual wording does not specify that they are to be religious ways of living.

This then was the situation late in 1974 when the Conference decided to revise its brief Syllabus in order to bring it into conformity with the legal opinion. Dr Stopes Roe finds the objection that the Syllabus was not really a syllabus 'purely technical' and the BHA thinks it a 'mere technicality', adding, 'It would be a trivial task to strengthen the syllabus.'[13] This happens to be the very view the revising sub-committee took. We also considered it a mere technicality, which could be overcome (and was actually overcome) simply by putting in a few references to religion, and by listing rather more indications of religious subject matter. It was, as the humanists indicate, a trivial task, which involved no change whatever of principle, intention or substance. So where the 1974 Syllabus intended a religious something, the 1975 Syllabus calls it religious. When the 1974 Syllabus intended a secular or a humanist something, this again is made specific. So the 1975 Syllabus prescribes a study of 'how Humanists apply their ideals in everyday life', words missing in the early, vague version. It can safely be said that no member of the Conference ever intended the Birmingham Syllabus to be a general treatment of all kinds of secular stances, ideologies of one kind or another and religions. The study of the religions of mankind was always thought of as being central, as the teachers' suggested courses consistently indicate. If the brief and imprecise wording of the 1974 summary failed to make this clear, the fuller 1975 Syllabus restores it.

The place of the non-religions

But whatever the intention of the Syllabus, do the changes in wording have the effect Dr Stopes Roe alleges, namely, of creating a syllabus so slanted in favour of religion that it 'establishes religious indoctrination'? Dr Stopes Roe asks, 'Are the non-religions to be treated for their own sake or only for the advancement of instruction in religion?' The point here is that the vague 1974 version had indicated that during the ages 12 to 16 pupils should study 'Religion as it manifests itself in our own and other societies, and the claims upon which it rests' and then, as a further section, 'Non-religious stances for living, their basic assumptions and their out working in personal and social life.' Legal opinion, in asking if the 1974 Syllabus was a syllabus of *religious* instruction, commented that there was no need to 'find the topic *of itself* (italics added) objectionable,' and there was 'no reason why instruction in religion should not be informed and illuminated by excursions into other areas and disciplines. Indeed, such excursions *are plainly valuable* (italics added). The purpose of the excursions must however always be such as to enable it to be brought within the description "religious instruction", i.e. it must advance progress in religious knowledge. The reference to the non-religions is objectionable in that its topic is expressed as a subject of itself, i.e. that it is to be taught for its own sake. Instruction in "non-religious stances for living" is not . . . religious instruction.'

It seemed to the legal sub-committee of the Conference that this was a perfectly proper point, and one which it could accept without changing any of its previous intentions. Why had the non-religions been included in the first place? Because they were deemed to be relevant to a thoughtful education in religion, and because any understanding of religion would be impaired which did not place the religions in the context of their great secular rivals and alternatives. This was exactly why the 1974 Syllabus spoke not of 'stances for living' but of '*non-religious* (italics added) stances for living'. It was their very non-religiousness, their self-conscious offering of themselves as foils to religion, which made them interesting, relevant and educationally significant in a syllabus of religious instruction. And whereas the 1974 vague summary had only implied this, the fuller 1975 Syllabus made it clear by adding the words 'This course [on the secular ideology] will thus highlight the distinctive features of religious faith' and, in teaching humanism in the Junior school, 'to clarify the distinctive features of religion by comparison and contrast'.

But this is surely not to indoctrinate in religion, or to introduce a bias in favour of religion. To advance religious knowledge is by no means the same as advancing religious faith. To instruct in religion, in the context of contemporary educational practice, is not to instruct or imply that religion is true, but to deepen an understanding of religion. It is a mistake to think that this purely educational principle means that the non-religions are only introduced to create an impression that the religions are superior. After all, the critics from the other side claim that the Syllabus is in error precisely because it does *not* urge the superiority of the religions, and does *not* offer to give any more help to a pupil moving towards faith in religion than it gives to a pupil moving away from faith in religion or towards faith in a non-religion. To 'highlight the distinctive features' of a subject does not mean that these distinctive features, when highlighted, will be more attractive or credible to the pupils, or will elicit their commitment. Indeed, the reverse may sometimes be the case. The Syllabus is simply suggesting an important way in which pupils can gain an understanding of what the issues are. If a syllabus was being designed which dealt mainly with the secular ideologies, a reverse situation could occur, in which religions would be studied in order to highlight the distinctive features of humanism and communism. And in many books on humanism written by humanists, this is exactly what takes place. Religious people, if they are educators, accept this as a sound educational approach. And if Dr Stopes Roe asks whether a syllabus consisting mainly of the study of religions will not give the impression willy-nilly that the religions are more important than the non-religions, the reply is a simple one. We are concerned with the impact upon the pupil of not only one subject, but a subject often presented only in one or two periods a week, in a curriculum mainly taught by secular people in secular ways. Questions of balance must be considered not only within one subject but within the whole curriculum.[14] It should also be pointed out that the claim that a religion or a secular stance should only be studied 'for its own sake' and 'in its own right' is ambiguous. For example, the Introduction to the 1975 Syllabus, in justifying the inclusion of Christianity, remarks that 'education for life in Britain today must include an adequate treatment of Christianity as the faith which has, historically, moulded British life and culture and is still doing so' (p. 5). But is this to teach Christianity 'for its own sake'? Is it not to teach Christianity because of its cultural and historical significance? Indeed, it might be argued that the religions as a whole are not taught for their own sake, since the Syllabus justifies their inclusion on the grounds 'that pupils shall be prepared for the realities of life in the twentieth century "global village"' (p. 4). Everything in a syllabus should be there for some reason, and the reasons will sometimes be intrinsic, sometimes extrinsic. But it is a mistake to conclude that because humanism is taught for certain educational reasons – namely the insights into religion which the study of a secular stance provides – the study of humanism is thereby made unworthy or distorted. Marx is studied in religious education because of the value of his critique of religion. But he is approached with the thought that he may be right and his criticism of religion may be justified. Marx will be studied in his own context, fairly and with integrity. This is supported by examining the courses in the Handbook, in which no-one's faith is described in a manner which he himself would not choose to describe it, and all are approached in exactly the same spirit of critical sympathy. In this way, the religions and the non-religions are on exactly the same footing, none is commended none is attacked, and all are studied *as part of* religious education.

Does the Syllabus indoctrinate the emotions?

Dr Stopes Roe takes particular exception to the expression in the Introduction to the 1975 Syllabus (p. 4) which says that religious education will increase the pupils' sensitivity 'to the areas of experience from which a religious view of life may arise'. Dr Stopes Roe's comment is that 'fundamental emotional forces are taken over by religion'. This seems too alarmist. When one turns to the illustrations (p. 9 of the Syllabus) one finds mention of 'love, trust, acceptance, forgiveness, compassion, care, courage, patience and endeavour'. These are the experiences from which a view of religion may arise They may also be the areas from which a humane secular stance may arise, and the intention in teaching them is specifically *not* that the pupils *shall* come to religious views, but merely that, enriched by such experiences, the religious views will be available for their understanding. Would Dr Stopes Roe wish to *deny* children experiences of love and trust, in order to make sure that religious views *should not* arise?

Is there an unconscious hostility towards religion?

It is difficult to resist the conclusion, when one examines his use of words like 'dominance', 'slant' and 'indoctrination', which are used by him merely to describe the fact that the object of study is a *religious* object of study, that Dr Stopes Roe does not think there can be any study of religion *per se* which could escape the charge of establishing indoctrination. No matter how it is presented – no matter how critically, how descriptively – the mere fact that the subject matter of teaching is world religion is sufficient to create a 'domination by religion'. This remains the case even when a syllabus insists that the religions cannot be well understood without placing them in their secular context and contrasting and comparing them with the non-religions, the latter being taught in exactly the same spirit of critical sympathy and openness. To Dr Stopes Roe, it is still indoctrination.

The Birmingham Syllabus and the law

We have given detailed consideration of the humanist response to the Syllabus because of the claim that the Birmingham experience proves that the 1944 Education Act cannot provide for a religious education suitable for modern conditions and justified by contemporary educational standards. An attempt was made in the spring of 1976 to introduce a Private Member's Bill into the House of Commons which would have replaced religious education by 'Education in Stances for Living'.[15] Now, whatever the merits of this suggestion, it cannot be supported by the claim that the Birmingham Syllabus illustrates the inability of the Act to provide for a sound education in the religious area. For, as has been shown above, the Birmingham experience was not that a 'stances for living' syllabus was turned into a 'religious indoctrination' syllabus by the application of the letter of the 1944 Act, but that a vague and short religious education syllabus was turned into a clearer and slightly longer religious education syllabus which, although it is not faith-nurturing (a possibility which the framers of the Act did not envisage) is a perfectly legal syllabus. So what is proved is that the makers of the 1944 Act were wiser than they knew, and (the worship clauses apart) have created a very flexible and adaptable piece of legislation which can generate and clarify the modern critical and descriptive religious education as successfully as once it generated the nurturing and faith-establishing kind.

Notes

1 For reviews, see E.J.R. Cook in *Faith and Freedom*, 29, autumn 1975, pp. 43–5 and 29, spring 1976, pp. 99f. Note that on 11 June 1976 the Education Committee, now controlled by the Conservative Party, asked Birmingham headteachers to return to the Education Offices the pages in the Handbook dealing with humanism and communism in the secondary school.

2 I have discussed the Birmingham Syllabus in the light of earlier syllabuses, and have pointed out the leading features of it, in 'Agreed Syllabus, past, present and future, in *New Movements in Religious Education*, 1975, pp. 97–119, Horder D. and Smart, N. (eds) in 'Birmingham Agreed Syllabus: its significance explained', *Times Educational Supplement*, 12 December 1975, p. 28, and in the editorial of *Learning for Living*, summer 1976.

3 See Hardy, D.W., 'Teaching religion: a theological critique', *Learning for Living*, 15, (autumn 1975), pp. 10–16 and Taylor, John V., 'Initiation into agnosticism', *Learning for Living*, 15 summer 1976, pp. 129f.

4 British Humanist Association, *Objective, Fair and Balanced, A New Law for Religion in Education*, autumn 1975. This document is referred to below as OFB.

5 Religious Education Council of England and Wales, *What Future for the Agreed Syllabus?*, May 1976.

6 Stopes Roe, H.V., 'The concept of a "life-stance" in education', *Learning for Living* autumn 1976.

7 Stopes Roe, H.V. Education and the law in Birmingham', *Learning for Living*, 15, summer 1976, pp. 133–5. See also the reply by Professor John Hick which follows in the same issue.

8 'Agreed Syllabuses, past, present and future', *op. cit.*, pp. 104ff.

9 This and all the following references to Dr Stopes Roe are to his article mentioned in note 7 above.

10 OFB, p. 7.

11 OFB, p. 8.

12 The humanists realize this but do not seem to appreciate its significance. OFB, p. 7.

13 *Ibid.*

14 See the editorial in *Learning for Living*, 15, spring 1976.

15 See Allen, J.H., in *Faith and Freedom*, 29, spring 1976, pp. 95–8.

9.   The Birmingham Agreed Syllabus

From 1966 to 1968 the Agreed Syllabus (in England) passed through a period of creativity. The Syllabuses of the West Riding (1966), Wiltshire (1967), Northamptonshire, Lancashire and the Inner London Education Authority (all 1968) had a common emphasis on the needs and interests of the child, and suggested new ways of relating everyday life to religious education.

It has been much more difficult to produce new Agreed Syllabuses since 1968. Only three new ones have appeared. Bath's (1970) was remarkable in that it was not a syllabus, but a three-page statement of general policy in religious education, to be followed by occasional papers produced by working groups under the guidance of the Bath Standing Advisory Council for Religious Education (SACRE), although the fifth schedule of the 1944 Act was adhered to in the adoption of this initial policy statement.

The Cornwall Syllabus (1971) can be classed with the 1966–8 group, since, although good of its kind, it represents no significant advance. Bradford produced an important supplement to the 1966 West Riding Syllabus, *Guide to Religious Education in a Multifaith Community* (1974). And now we have the Birmingham Syllabus (May 1975) and the teachers' Handbook (September).

Why have there been so few new Agreed Syllabuses? Because change has been so rapid, because the machinery of the Act is so cumbersome and because a more teacher-centred approach was needed, much curriculum development of religious education has been by-passing the Agreed Syllabus. Most frequently, the SACRE, as a less formal body than an Agreed Syllabus Conference, has been the channel for development. Cambridgeshire were the first Local Education Authority to decide (in 1970) that it preferred not to create a new Agreed Syllabus. Schools Council projects became important influences on the religious education syllabus.

But there are deeper reasons – the Agreed Syllabuses had always been ecumenical documents, in that they represented the agreement of the Anglicans and the Free Churches on the content of the Christian faith. Could they become pluralist documents, suitable for use in multi-faith and deeply secularized teaching? And if so, what was one supposed to agree about? Could Agreed Syllabuses become educational in the modern sense, or must they remain Christian nurture and Christian apologetics, like the famous Syllabuses of 1966–8, which for all their new insights, remained Christianizing syllabuses?

The Birmingham Conference met early in 1970 and took five years to complete its work. At the Conference were representatives of the Hindu, Muslim, Sikh and Jewish communities, as well as Christians, and humanists were co-opted onto the working parties. The result is a syllabus which can be taught by any well-informed and enthusiastic teacher, regardless of his faith or lack of it, to any interested pupil, regardless of *his* faith, or lack of it.

The Syllabus concentrates upon developing a critical, but tolerant, understanding of the religions in their modern secular context, leaving the fostering of faith in particular religions to the churches, mosques, etc. The main religions dealt with are the five already mentioned, with Buddhism in the sixth form only. Humanism is specifically mentioned as a secular alternative. The religions and the alternatives are to be presented in the same spirit of critical tolerance; none is singled out for any special commendation (the recommendation that all pupils shall study Christianity is no exception) or special attack.

The emphasis is on the life of man today, rather than in the past. The approach is descriptive, in that the religions are to be studied as they actually appear today, and existential, in that at each point an attempt is made to relate the material studied to the pupil's life, to help him to form his own sense of meaning in life, whether this be, in the end, religious or not.

The Syllabus, a short document, is accompanied by a much larger volume, in loose-leaf form, *Living Together; Teachers' Handbook of Suggestions for Religious Education.*

Here are details of resources and suggested teaching units. In the secondary section of the Handbook, we find the famous minor optional course on communism. The Syllabus requires that, as well as the courses on religions, 12 to 16-year-olds shall study a minor course in one of the non-religious stances for living. The Syllabus does not specify which secular way of life, and the teacher could offer atheism or the ideas of Freud or Albert Camus.

The Handbook suggests two courses which relate to this requirement – one on humanism, the other on communism, although communism is not mentioned in the Syllabus. These are treated in the same spirit of critical sympathy, or tolerant understanding, as are the religious courses. Representatives of the secular views were consulted just as were representatives of the religious. No-one's belief or outlook will be described except in the way he himself sees it.

The secular courses have stimulated criticism, both from those who think there should be much greater emphasis on them and from those who think they should not be present at all. Those who take the former view claim that the Syllabus still shows some favouritism towards religion. Religions occupy the major place and secular alternatives are included as minor studies and only to heighten a critical understanding of religion by comparison and contrast.

In a syllabus of 'religious' education, it is proper that the central concern should be religion. This indicates no intention to nurture faith in religion. The school should give no more (and no less) help to the pupil moving in the direction of faith in religion than to the pupil moving away from faith in religion. Those who do not accept this kind of study seem to think that no study of religion *per se*, however conducted and for whatever reason, could be educationally valid.

Then there are those who do not think there should be any treatment of the secular outlooks at all. But this is a syllabus of religious 'education'. It is perfectly proper in religious education to make excursions into non-religious areas, provided these are related to the religions in such a way as to advance knowledge and understanding of religion (which is by no means the same as advancing faith in religion).

In forming an evaluation of religion, young people should know not only how religious people evaluate it, but also how, for example, Freud and Marx evaluated it. These secular evaluations should in turn be grasped in the context of the general outlook of Freud and Marx, seen from the inside, as their followers see it, and not presented defensively in a spirit of 'warning young people'.

Some of the comments which this simple and moderate approach to religious education has received indicate a lack of educational insight. Some critics seem to think that, because the Syllabus includes a secular option, the intention is to instruct young people that this ideology is in fact true. The Birmingham approach is not to instruct that communism is true nor to instruct that Christianity is true, but to offer an understanding of religion in its secular context.

Those who defend this approach are getting rather tired of being regarded as leftist infiltrators. The Birmingham approach could not exist in any communist country, nor in any 'Christian Nationalist' state (South Africa) but only in a liberal and pluralist democracy.

Religious education has an important role to play in the preservation of good community relations in Britain. The Birmingham authority is the first to recognize through a completely new Agreed Syllabus that the Local Education Authority is responsible for the religious education not only of the Christian child but also of the Islamic child. When the state offers such education, it should do so to all alike, without discrimination on the grounds of colour or creed. Birmingham is the first to recognize that, in an Agreed Syllabus, the agreement to be sought is not agreement about what is held in common to be true, but about what is held in common to be worth knowing. It is also the first to prove that the classroom provisions of the 1944 Act permit a religious education which is fully educational and entirely appropriate for the conditions of life in this country today. There are good reasons for re-examining the sections of the Act dealing with Agreed Syllabuses, but the claim that the Act will not permit a good modern approach to the subject does not appear to be very plausible.

10. *Christian Nurture, Stances for Living, or Plain RE*

It has been a brisk year for religious education. Seven reports have appeared, mostly in reaction to the humanist document *Objective, Fair and Balanced*, which came out in autumn 1975. All, in one way or another, continue the 1974 and 1975 discussions aroused by the Birmingham Agreed Syllabus.

Three different visions can be discerned of what religious education should be. The first approach emphasizes Christian nurture – the fostering of Christian faith.

The Child in the Church (British Council of Churches) springs from the belief 'that since the l.e.a. school can no longer be expected to carry any more responsibility in principle for Christian nurture than for the nurture of Muslims, Jews or humanists, local churches must accept full responsibility for the Christian nurture of their young'.

The distinction between Christian nurture and religious education is not only accepted but welcomed. 'We recommend that local churches should explore ways of building upon the work done by the l.e.a. school in its provision of an open, descriptive religious education into a variety of religions, realizing that there is no necessary tension between such religious education and the goals of Christian nurture.

The report considers the meaning and practice of Christian nurture in the British churches today in view of the situation in which the county schools are now performing a different task.

Ways Whereby Christian Education in State Schools Should Be Saved (Order of Christian Unity) argues that the county school should be the agent of Christian nurture. Indeed, this document does not betray any awareness of the distinction between fostering Christian devotion and providing an education in religion.

The subject is usually described as 'Christian education' or 'Christian teaching', but no distinction is made between Christianity as the content of teaching and a Christianizing intention in presenting that content. 'The majority of Britain's citizens are still christened, married and buried according to Christian belief and we believe that this majority relies on the retention of the right of school children to study and discuss the life of Christ and His teaching ... Christ said "Suffer little children to come unto me".'

This approach is broadly supported by *Religious Education: Should It Be Taught in Schools?* (Association of Christian Teachers of Wales).

The opposite point of view is that of the British Humanist Association in *Objective, Fair and Balanced*. The humanists are far from satisfied with the Birmingham Syllabus's inclusion of the secular ideologies, because these are subordinate to the study of world religions.

The humanists suggest that the ways of life which respond to 'ultimate questions' should form the subject, and it would then be unfair to give any greater emphasis to the answers given by the religions than to those offered by the non-religions. This would require a new name for the subject, and Education in Stances for Living is being proposed.

This approach has found additional support (although perhaps not independent support, in view of the overlap in the membership of the working parties) in *What Future for the Agreed Syllabus?* (Religious Education Council of England and Wales): '... the subject is essentially a study of belief systems and ... no such system can be arbitrarily excluded. It includes studying systems which have a supernatural referent (and which are usually called religions) as well as those which have not. Some change of name would seem to be indicated but we do not feel it within our brief to suggest what the new name should be.'

The council has not yet adopted the report, presented to it by one of its working parties, and since several of its most influential member organizations have expressed disagreement, it seems unlikely that it will receive even general approval from its parent body.

The central ground – that broadly represented by the Birmingham Syllabus – takes the view that the subject should be religious education, emphasizing both these words. The religions, which continue to be the major content of study, will be presented in order to increase understanding and to encourage personal growth and independent response to living, and will be studied in the context of the secular ways of life.

These are significant alternatives to religion, and knowledge of them leads to a better understanding of religion. This understanding of religion may lead to a more critical attitude towards religion, or to a more sympathetic attitude, as the case may be from pupil to pupil.

This approach has most recently been supported by the Free Church Federal Council in the report *Religious Education in County Schools* and (with some reservations) *Religious Education, a Considered View* (Association of Christian Teachers).

The Free Church report accepts that the Syllabus might well include 'the ideological stances of those unable to accept or practice the tenets of any religious faith'. The mainly conservative ACT agrees that there should be 'an examination of other significant world views' and these will include 'world views which have no overt religious basis'.

Both agree also that the existing law, although needing some minor improvements, has shown itself quite capable of sustaining this kind of religious education.

More conservative is *Religious Education in State Schools* (Professional Association of Teachers) which, 'while recognizing that non-religious philosophies of life are valid subjects for study in school, would deplore their inclusion in syllabuses of Religious Education'. Even the teaching of world religions 'will only lead to further confusion and total rejection' and as for areas of immigrant population, the PAT report remarks merely that it does not see 'value in teaching elements of common understanding between faiths'.

The main question during the coming year will be whether the descriptive, wide-ranging kind of religious education which attempts to take pluralism seriously and yet to retain a firm grasp upon the proper central content of the subject will find more sympathy from the right (the OCU, the ACT of Wales and PAT) and the left (the BHA and the working party of the RE Council).

The case for the centre is a strong one, and is supported not only by the FCFC and the ACT but also by the Church of England (in the great *Durham Report* of 1970) and the largest of the voluntary RE groups, the Christian Education Movement. It would be a further valuable support for this approach if during 1977 or 1978 the Birmingham Syllabus were to be adopted by several other authorities.

The debate is a serious one, involving social and educational issues which go far beyond the classroom confines of this little subject. The activity of the past year indicates the immense symbolic significance which religious education in schools continues to have.

Another encouraging feature of these many reports is that almost all of them realize that there is little point in discussing which ball Cinderella is to go to, and which of them is to be fairy godmother, if in the meantime the poor thing dies of starvation. Resources, timetable provisions, and the supply and training of teachers are increasingly being seen as crucial for religious education.

Readiness to take practical steps to improve actual conditions will be the best proof during the coming year of the sincerity of the many friends religious education seem to enjoy.

PART III

Methods in Teaching Religion

11. *The Theology of Themes**

When in the 1920s and 1930s the first Agreed Syllabuses of religious education were being devised, the main drive behind their formulation was theology. There was of course some recognition given to the need to adapt materials for the various ages of the pupils, but the main inspiration was theological not psychological. The hesitancy created by biblical criticism was giving way to a new confidence that the idea of God's progressive revelation of himself was the key to understanding the Bible. The new Syllabuses were organized around this belief; God had spoken, and the task of religious education was to convey to pupils the drama of the divine unfolding, in the history of Israel, in the person of Jesus Christ, and on through the history of his people, the church.

The situation in religious education in this country at present offers a striking contrast. We are again in a period when new syllabuses are appearing, and the whole nature and content of religious education is undergoing considerable change. But the impetus behind the developments comes now not from theology but from child psychology. The new teaching materials are coming out of a new awareness of the nature of children's religion, and of the nature of their thinking and believing about religious matters.

These developments are, in the secondary school, increased emphasis on the problem-centred discussion method and the inclusion of a wide variety of material dealing with current affairs such as studies of the plight of the developing countries and the work of charitable organizations like Oxfam, Christian Aid and Shelter; and, in the junior school, the appearance of the life-theme, or as it is now more generally called, the theme.

* This paper was read to the Churches of Christ national conference at Chester on 16 August 1970 as the Albert Leavesley Memorial Lecture. The Christian Education Committee of the Churches of Christ kindly agreed to its publication (in 1972).

But the switch to subjects and methods of this kind, whether carried out because the findings of child psychology seem to indicate that that is the better way to present religious truth, or whether adopted because of pressure from pupils, or simply because the older manner of concentrating upon the drama of biblical salvation is proving increasingly difficult to teach in practice, is certainly creating a number of problems. Of these the most serious are not those concerned with technique or with the supply of teaching materials but those which concern matters of theology. Indeed, the various publishing houses and teaching agencies are producing material of the new type much more rapidly than teachers can theologically assimilate them.

The theological questions which are raised vary widely. What is the place of the Bible not only in teaching the Christian faith to young people but in the general structure of Christian belief? Is study of what God is believed to be doing today just as legitimate as study of what God is declared to have done ages ago? In what sense is Jesus Christ central? Previously he was taught, in the older Agreed Syllabuses, as the fulfiller of the Old Testament and as the climax of the story of God's dealings with his people. If we are to abandon the systematic presentation of that story, in what context is Jesus to be presented? Is he to be held up as a saviour figure and a benefactor not like Moses, Elijah and all the prophets but like Bonhoeffer, Martin Luther King and all the revolutionaries? What does all this imply about revelation? Does God speak directly to each child in his own life, through his own life situations and ethical dilemmas or does the revelation of God take place only or mainly in the slice of so-called sacred history, extending like a wedge through history from Abraham to the story of modern church missions?

These are some of the problems which the new approaches are raising for the thoughtful teacher. They are serious because many teachers find that they are unable to make a satisfactory alliance between the structure of the Christian faith as they understand it themselves and the picture of the Christian faith which they are presenting to pupils. They do not know why they are teaching what they are teaching, that is, they cannot give a religious or theological account of what they are doing. The result is confusion and lack of integrity in teaching.

Let us then look a little more closely at themes in religious education and particularly at what this way of teaching implies about the Christian faith.

Teaching through themes has become popular in the last five or six years, since the method was suggested by Ronald Goldman.[1] The method was adopted by the first of the new generation of Agreed Syllabuses, the West Riding Syllabus, in 1966[2] and has been prominent in all of the several official Syllabuses which have appeared since then.[3] The syllabuses prepared for use in the education given to children by churches on Sundays are also making steady use of themes.[4]

What is a theme?

A theme is a unit of work organized around a topic which is known to the child from first-hand experience.[5] I think the word 'theme' is used because 'subject' means a school subject such as history or mathematics, while 'topic' is probably thought to suggest something rather more narrow, exact and limited than 'theme'. The word 'theme' suggests that the work will be something which crops up at various points of a child's experience, so that it is a constant theme of his life, or that it will be work treated from several different angles, so that while the work includes history, geography, religion and so on, what holds it all together is the theme running through it all. In this latter sense there is not much difference between a theme in a junior school and an integrated subject in a secondary school, except that, as used in religious education, it is essential that the theme should spring from the actual experience of the child. It was to emphasize this that Goldman called them 'life-themes'. So a teacher might devise a theme on homes, on food, or on holidays, friends, hands and feet, water, presents, and so on.

The advantages of using themes are usually said to be that, since the chosen theme will spring from the experience of the child, the religious aspects of it can be made relevant to his experience and appropriate to his understanding. Since the theme will perhaps present distinctively religious material alongside everyday materials, religion will not be thought of as estranged from ordinary life, and this impression will be reinforced by the fact that religion will no longer be taught as a separate subject of the timetable but will be seen as part and parcel of the united world of knowledge.

Abuse of themes

Although with wise and disciplined use, thematic teaching can be excellent, there is some evidence that the method is running to seed. A recent textbook contains details of a theme called 'All work and no play' which consists of 32 topics, ranging from the advantages of midweek travel, through places Jesus visited, to holiday in space, and including how to avoid travel sickness, words which have entered the English language from other languages, a map of Palestine 200 years ago, how people celebrate Christmas, the earth's atmosphere, the Egyptian myth of the creation of the world, Darwinian evolution, horoscopes, bank holidays and how to make an electric map of Palestine complete with wiring diagram. Here the conception of the theme has become a vast assortment of associated ideas. The association is sometimes based on etymology (as when school holidays are linked to the Church's calendar through the derivation of holiday from holy day), sometimes based on pressure of current events (travel to the moon), sometimes on the teacher's desire to include something for every subject (sunshine graphs for the mathematics, Drake's voyage for the history, fossils for the nature study, the people of Israel and Jordan for RE), and sometimes merely on random association (the introduction of ancient Palestine seems to have led to the thought of holidays in the future and this to the idea of the extreme past and this to the Sky God Svarog). It is impossible to discuss the theological implications of this sort of thing, since it represents no disciplined interrogation of a theme. A theme which is consistent with almost anything contains almost nothing.

How to stop a theme from going wild

A theme can be tamed by giving careful consideration to the implication for Christian faith of both the method of constructing a theme and also the implications of the content of the theme. The implications of the method need to be carefully distinguished from the implications of the content. If, for example, you teach a theme on symbols, which includes practice in interpreting symbols and study of specific Christian symbols, the conclusion that symbols and symbolic thinking are important in the understanding of Christianity follows from the nature of the content. This is actually *what* you are teaching. But let us look at *how* you are teaching. What is your method? A theme is a method of arranging and presenting materials to children. What are the implications of doing it in this way rather than in some other way, such as by direct study of parts of the Bible?

Themes and the relationship between the sacred and the secular

Some themes are mainly concerned to familiarize pupils with biblical metaphors,[6] but in the case of those which seek to help the pupil to explore and interpret aspects of his own experience, important problems about the sacred and the secular arise.

To what extent is a child's religious experience specific? It is sometimes said that there is no specificity in children's experiences of religion, but that a religious experience is to be seen as an ordinary, an everyday, a normal experience understood in a certain way.[7] Eating food together, for example, will be seen as having relationships with the people who are sharing the meal, so that the food represents the giving of care and loving attention, or it represents the giving of the labour of the father to the children, or it represents the dependence of human life upon the fruitfulness of the earth and thus upon the graciousness of God. Or eating together may be seen as fellowship, as sharing a common life, since the same food is eaten, the same loaf sliced, and so the food is seen as a physical and metaphysical bond between the participants. Eating may even be regarded as symbolic of the oneness of all humanity, and this, taken together with the ideas of interdependence and mutual dependence on nature, may quickly become a religious view of the status of mankind. Some of the aspects may be studied with younger secondary pupils in the way food is sometimes treated in the television commercials.

These ways of thinking about food and eating it together are rooted very deeply in the ancient experience of the race. Most primitive religions involve food ceremonies, often in the form of sacrifice, and some modern religions retain this conception. The Bible is full of food symbolism; the notion of a bond established between God and his people by means of a food ceremony is prominent in the Old Testament and is taken up by Christianity in the idea of the Lord's Supper. The ability of the teacher to teach in such a way as to bring out for children the symbolism of eating together depends upon the teacher's own awareness of this traditional religious attitude towards food.

But another point of view about the nature of religious experience in children stresses that religious experiences are specific.[8] They are not simply ordinary experiences seen in a certain way, but are special experiences unlike other experiences. They might, for example, be characterized by some specific emotion such as reverence, awe, wonder[9] of a kind not normally experienced in relation to ordinary things and normal situations, or they might include a sort of awareness such as a sense of being a creature, being finite, being sinful, or again religious experiences might include feeling the presence of God, experiencing God's forgiveness, or the experience of worshipping God.[10]

The relation between the two views, the view that religious experience is ordinary experience seen in a certain way but lacking anything specifically religious, and the view that, on the contrary, religious experiences are quite distinct and unlike other experiences, is complex and religious educators urgently need help from philosophers of religion at this point.[11] Would those who think that religious experience is ordinary experience understood in depth agree that when it is understood at such depth the resulting experience is so much *more* profound, or even ecstatic, or that it offers such a unifying vision of life, that the resulting experience (now described as 'religious') is different *in kind* as well as *in degree*, from ordinary experience? If it is agreed that the experience is indeed different in kind from ordinary experience, there would not seem to be very much difference between the two views, since those who stress 'ordinary experience at depth' would then be agreeing that religious experience is really specific, but that it is arrived at by a certain method, namely, the contemplation of ordinary life. The issue between the two emphases would then be about the manner in which religious experience is best induced.

If, however, the 'ordinary experience at depth' view is that the difference between (a) ordinary experience and (b) ordinary experience understood in depth is one of degree only and not of kind, then the question arises, how deep is deep? For it is agreed that ordinary experience in itself, at face value, is not religious. Or at least, it is agreed that it is only *experienced* as religious when it is contemplated and interpreted in depth. So at what point does the experience become sufficiently deep to be called religious? This question can, I think, only be answered by setting up criteria for calling an experience religious, and I imagine that this list of criteria would not differ very much from the list of criteria which would be offered when defining a specifically religious experience. So again the difference between the two views might tend to be minimized.

A conflict between belief and method?

Of these two views about the nature of religious experience, the popular traditional one is that religious experience is specific. This is probably the view accepted by the vast majority of religious education teachers. Probably most teachers believe, for example, that partaking in the Lord's Supper is a religious experience not because it is the ordinary experience of eating understood in depth, but because it is a sacred institution of Christ which conveys the merits of his death and resurrection and is thus a means of grace in a manner which ordinary meals are not.

This is why when teaching a theme many teachers become concerned about how to bring in religion. A sample of the specifically religious must be introduced. So journeys turn into journeys in Palestine, and sheep turn into the Good Shepherd and families turn into the Holy Family at Nazareth, and the theme becomes simply a means of catching the attention and interest of the class before the real meat of the religious lesson begins.[12] The artificiality of this is often uncomfortably obvious to both teacher and class. Not only so, but the purpose and nature of thematic teaching is distorted and then lost.

The notion of a theme, based as it is upon the idea of introducing the child to religious experience by means of his examination and discovery of the meaning of his own experience, *as a method* commits the teacher to the view that religious experience is not specific.[13] In spite of the fact that the relation between the two views of religious experience is very confused, the general tendency of the theme is in this direction. The teacher finds then that the tendency and the logic of the method he has adopted may be at odds with his own assumptions about the nature of religious experience. It is then that the theme begins to go wild.

Indeed, when material about the child's normal experience and contemplation of it is made a preface to material of a specifically religious nature drawn, for example, from the Bible and specially from the life of Jesus, the real belief of the teacher, that it is the latter part of the course which is really religious, can come out so strongly that the class is left with the impression that religion and life are very different. The end result is thus the exact opposite of the intention and inner logic of teaching in a truly thematic way.[14] It is easy to accept the superficialities of the method; it is more difficult to accept the philosophy of the method and integrate it with one's own philosophy of religion.

Themes and revelation

Thinking about the sacred and the secular in themes raises another but related subject. What conception of divine revelation does the thematic method presuppose? How does the logic of a theme lead us to expect that God will communicate with young people?

It might be thought at first sight that whereas teaching directly from the Bible supposes that God is the giver of revelation and that his self-disclosure comes unaided by human effort and independently of human inquiry, in the theme the emphasis is upon human efforts to discover God. After all, a theme is intended to be a way of pupils discovering for themselves the implications of their own experiences.

Thematic teaching might therefore be taken as rather a Pelagian method of teaching.

But this is to oversimplify the situation. It is to misunderstand the difference between theme teaching and direct specifically religious teaching. Pupils can after all be invited to discover for themselves what is in the Bible just as they can be invited to discover for themselves what is in their own lives now. The pupil-discovery method is not unique to theme teaching and on the other hand, both themes and Bible stories could be taught in a dogmatic and factual manner through a teacher's lectures. Moreover, although in a theme the pupil, if taught correctly, will be invited to discover for himself, this does not mean that what he discovers will be created by him or will in itself be the product of his own efforts. People do not make death, nor is the need for friendship created by discussing it. Loneliness, love, and the need to see significance in life are in a way part of what is given in human experience, and here, as well as in meditating upon the Bible, the Christian may be surprised by joy and believe that joy to be the grace of God.

The distinction then is not between human effort and God's self-giving. Both methods are agreed that only God can reveal God. The difference is rather in what area of human life God does in fact offer himself. Does God come to men only in their meditation upon his dealings with the people of Israel and with Jesus Christ his son? Or may he also speak something of himself in meditation upon the natural world and the world of contemporary human life? We can now see that the problem resolves itself into the same distinctions about revelation as previously we were making about religious experience. Is God's revelation specific, that is, contained or communicated in specific history and specific lives, or it is *also* general, so that all history and all lives may communicate something of him?

It is easy to see that teaching by themes involves the latter belief.[15] If a theme is being taught according to its own assumptions and not just as an introduction to something else, it clearly rests upon the supposition that however else God may speak, he can also speak to pupils through their understanding of the moral, personal and distinctively human aspects of their lives.

This view is not repugnant to Christian orthodoxy, provided it is not maintained that this is the only or the main way in which the divine comes to men. From this we can conclude that although religious education might perhaps be conducted entirely through themes, which would heighten sensitivity to the basic religious quest of man and show the roots of human experience from which religion springs, themes cannot be the whole content of Christian education. Here, they may only legitimately be a part. The part they will play may be a sort of preliminary preparation by way of showing the things about religion we have mentioned, but this education to become Christian must ultimately seek to interpret human experience not only in the light of the hopes and fears of men but in the light of the death and resurrection of Jesus Christ.

Themes and the Bible

I have tried to show that themes, although they may contain biblical material, are probably more faithful to themselves and less prone to turn into something else if they do not contain biblical material. I have also argued that a Christian education, as distinct from a religious one, will be compelled to introduce biblical material in some other way. A theme-based religious education may also use biblical material in other ways, but it will not be compelled by its nature to do so.

This raises for the Christian religious educator a question about the relation between thematic teaching and the Bible. If it is better on the whole for themes not to contain material from the Bible, then what is the connexion between the theme and the Bible?

The central message of the Bible includes the teaching that the God of Israel acts in history. He is not a nature deity nor a local or tribal god but one whose acts concern all mankind, and one who declares himself primarily in the national and international crises of the age. The prophetic view was that Israel's history, if examined closely in the light of faith, revealed truth about God and man. This is to say that the biblical God reveals himself in the lives of men, since history is the history of human lives.

So it is that when the idea of the personal becomes located in the individual as well as in the group, the dealings of God with men are found in a series of individuals, men who in reflection upon their experience, their vocation, their relationships with their wives and friends, their reactions in the presence of sickness and death, declared the nature of God. Hosea, Jeremiah, Ezekiel and Jesus are the outstanding representatives of this tradition.

The Christian church inherited this. Although it cannot be denied that there are New Testament writers who see the dealings between God and man primarily in the specifically religious (Luke is the outstanding example, with his divine dreams, angels, and special outpourings of Spirit), the idea of discovering the will and nature of God in meditation upon the ordinary was not lost. The parables of Jesus (as used of Jesus) come to mind, and it must not be forgotten that to see a crucifixion was for the Palestinian Jew of the first century rather an ordinary experience.

It must not be overlooked that throughout the whole Bible man is the main symbol of the divine. This is seen in the creation account where man is the divine image, and reaches a climax in Jesus who is declared to be the image and representation of God.

By developing observations of this sort it would be possible to show that the idea of a theme is compatible with biblical theology. It is probably because of this inner connection between the theory of a theme and the nature of biblical theology as it is now understood that the theme as one method of Christian education has emerged and been so rapidly and easily accepted in Christian circles. The connection has however been implicit and has seldom been explicated.[16] It may be that further exploration of the connection would clarify the minds of Christian teachers using this approach and help them to use a theme in its own right without a feeling of disloyalty to the Bible.

Notes

1 Goldman, Ronald *Readiness for Religion* Routledge and Kegan Paul, 1965.

2 *Suggestions for Religious Education: West Riding Agreed Syllabus*, 1966. The suggested content for each age group is headed 'Themes and Activities'.

3 For example, *Religion and Life: The Agreed Syllabus: Lancashire Education Committee*, 1968. The work for children aged 3–7 is described as 'themes' (pp. 23–33) but that for older children is described as 'topics'. It is not clear if this change is significant. *Learning for Life: Agreed Syllabus of the Inner London Education Authority*, 1968, particularly pp. 33ff and 41ff. This syllabus is certainly the most specific on the question of teaching through themes.

4 For example, *Alive in God's World* Church Information Office, 1968, 4 books; *Experience and Faith*, compiled by the British Lessons Council, Religious Education Press, 1968.

5 '... teaching by means of themes, based upon the real life experience of the children. I have called this teaching by life-themes.... A life-theme can take any area of a child's life, of which he has first-hand knowledge' (Goldman, *op. cit.*, pp. 110ff). 'A life-theme is where we begin with the real life experience of children, and through this lead them to see its religious significance. This is quite the opposite of beginning with religious stories or ideas then seeking to illustrate them from life' (*Readiness for Religion* series, ed. Ronald Goldman, *Notes for the Teacher*, Rupert Hart-Davis, 1966).

6 Holm, Jean L., 'Life-themes: What are they?', *Learning for Living*, November 1969, p. 15.

7 In this group may be placed Jeffreys, M.V.C. *Glaucon*; Goldman Ronald, *Religious Thinking from Child to Adolescence*, 1964; Lee, R.S. *Your Growing Child and Religion*, 1965. Allport, Gordon, *The Individual and his Religion, 1951*, holds that the religious sentiment is general rather than specific. See also Lee, Dorothy, 'The religious dimension of human experience' in *Personality and Religion*, W.A. Sadler (ed.) 1970, pp. 33–46.

8 Lewis, Eve, *Children and their Religion*, 1962 and *The Psychology of Family Religion*, 1968; Bovet, Pierre, *The Child's Religion* 1928; Harms, E. 'The development of

religious experience in children', *American Journal of Sociology*, 50, 1944, pp. 112–22. See, for the problem, discussion by Carrier, Herve, *The Sociology of Religious Belonging*, 1965, pp. 31f and 43–8.

9 Fahs, S.B.L. 'Beginnings of mysticism in children's growth', *Religious Education*, 45, 1950, pp. 139–47; Fukuyama, Y. 'Wonder Letters: An experimental study of the religious sensitivities of the child', *Religious Education*, 58, 1953, pp. 377–83.

10 Interesting accounts of childhood experiences of this sort appear in Bovet, *op. cit.*

11 Burnheim, John, in 'The concept of religious experience', *Sophia*, 6, 2, July 1967, pp. 15–30 remarks on the need for clarification of the ideas.

12 Although containing many good examples of themes, the work offered in *A Handbook of Thematic Material* prepared for the Kent Council of Religious Education (Kent Education Committee, 1968) sometimes suffers from this fault.

13 Smith, J.W.D. *Religious Education in a Secular Setting*, 1969, p. 40, suggests that life-themes are the product of a secularized Christianity. Goldman remarks (*Readiness for Religion*, 1965, p. 117) that the religious significance of the theme of home and family is 'much deeper' than any specifically religious material which might also be used. Compare the ILEA syllabus, *op. cit.*, p. 42: 'This method is fundamentally an exploration of the meaning of human relationships as means of understanding the divine-human relationship.'

14 Holm, Jean L., *op. cit.*, p. 16.

15 *Alive in God's World, op. cit.*, Vol. I, p. vii. It is argued that the ubiquity of the divine creativity prohibits selection of some material as being more religiously significant than other material.

16 Compare Hubery, D.S., *The Experiential Approach to Christian Education*, National Sunday School Union, 1960, pp. 16–20.

12. *Theme Teaching as a Method of Religious Education*

The origins of thematic teaching

Thematic teaching is the result of many years of change in religious education. By the late nineteenth century the deficiencies of an education which sought to convey information without affecting the deep life of the child were widely recognized. 'There can be no doubt that the older forms of orthodox religion, and of the accompanying ecclesiastical training, overwrought upon the capacity of the child, to the marring and degrading of his religious experience.'[1] These words, written in 1905, were typical of the new interest in the relation between religious teaching and the actual experience of children.

A powerful impetus was provided by the Edinburgh World Missionary Conference of 1910. Christian educators from many countries reported that Christian converts in other cultures tended to memorize biblical teaching and Christian doctrine but that the imported faith failed to touch the deeper layers of their thinking or to affect the social relationships of the people. Education in Britain had been 'regarded largely as the imparting of useful information. The intelligence and memory of the child were the faculties chiefly appealed to and relied upon ... we carried this fundamental error with us to foreign countries.'[2]

The principle of child-centred education was taken up by Christian educators in the churches in Britain under the leadership of the National Sunday School Union (now the National Council for Christian Education). G.H. Archibald, one of the most influential leaders of the new methods, wrote in 1926 that the popular view in the past had been that 'all religious education must begin with the Bible; but the point of view at the present day is that all religious education must begin with the child.'[3] J.W.D. Smith has briefly traced the growth of life-centred religious education from the 1928 Jerusalem Conference of the International Missionary Council to its incorporation into religious education in the state schools in the 1930s.[4]

The emphasis upon the life and experience of the child was however incomplete. Not enough was known of the religion of children. The important study by Pierre Bovet did not appear in English translation until 1928[5] and although during the thirties there was a widespread realization of the need for more scientific study of *children's religion*[6] little empirical work was done, least of all in Britain, until the 1950s and 1960s. In the meantime religious education tended to be controlled by theological belief rather than by any detailed understanding of what the child was able to grasp.

A new emphasis was placed on the experience of the child in the period which began about 1960. The description used was 'experiential religious education.' The life theme, as we know it today, grew out of this.

Experiential religious education

Experiential religious education seeks to make the Christian faith[7] real to children by showing them that it springs from their own experiences and that it helps to make sense of experience. Douglas Hubery speaking from within the Christian faith described it as being concerned 'to provide the right kind of environment and situations through which the children will interpret their experiences as God Himself intends.'[8] The experiential approach will mean that 'the appeal of any particular lesson should be directed to the experiences of the boys and girls.'[9] This is contrasted with the presentation of facts taken from the Bible but not related to the lives of pupils. So, Hubery explains, a teacher using the experiential approach would not teach the temptations of Christ by simply giving the reported details of Christ's own victory over temptation, but would ask what experience of temptation his pupils had had and seek to relate the biblical story to the moral dilemmas of the class.

The experiential approach will also mean that boys and girls will be involved as much as possible in the lesson.[10] Involvement will not only be a prelude to the lesson but will continue throughout the period and will help children to discover for themselves by studying their own environment.

The teacher may use the actual experience of the class and of himself, or the lesson may centre upon imagined experience, or a planned attempt may be made 'to confront pupils with a situation or an experience which may evoke certain desired responses.'[11] This last type of experience is described, perhaps rather unfortunately, by Douglas Hubery as 'contrived experience'.

Experiential religious education was developed at Westhill College in Birmingham by a group which included Douglas Hubery and Ronald Goldman. The first materials for teachers were published in 1963 in two series, *Experience and Worship* and *Living and Praising*.[12] The group had been impressed not only with the need to include the child much more fully in the activity of teaching but also by the fact that so often teachers who presented the biblical stories only highlighted the *differences* between the biblical world and the world of the children. 'By so much of our teaching we stress the extraordinary until the children, weary of looking for the same in their lives and not finding it, are neither brought into the presence of God, nor lead to hear God speaking His truth to them.'[13] Rather than the abnormality, the normality of religious experience should be shown. Many aspects of religious truth 'are revealed in more normal experiences.'[14]

The appearance of the life-theme

The lessons in the 1963 series we have been discussing were already described as 'themes'. But the word was not used in the later almost technical sense. The 'themes' the Westhill experimenters considered were not only those connected with ordinary life but also 'themes less obviously connected with everyday experience',[15] that is, the themes of the revelation of God through the Bible, through Jesus Christ and through worship.

It was Ronald Goldman who carried the thinking of the group further, and, no doubt because the word 'theme' had already been used in the previous publications to indicate *biblical* material, coined the expression 'life-theme' to indicate the kind of teaching he wished to emphasize. When Goldman distinguishes life-themes from religious themes[16] the latter indicate a content specifically religious, whether from the Bible, from the church or from Christian life and belief. In his *Readiness for Religion* (1965) and in the textbook series of the same general title which Goldman edited (1966–8) the approach to teaching religion through life-themes was for the first time set out and publicized in a manner which caught the attention of religious education teachers throughout Britain and brought thematic teaching to the centre of experiment and controversy.

Since 1965 life-themes have occupied a prominent place in every official Agreed Syllabus and in every handbook of suggestions issued from semi-official sources in Britain. Numerous textbooks based on the thematic method have appeared, and although in the past three or four years interest has to some extent moved to more factual areas connected with teaching world religions, the life-theme remains a major new contribution to the method of teaching religion.

The differences between experiential religious education and life-theme religious education[17]

We are dealing here with ideas which have grown gradually over more than a decade. The authors of the early life-themes did not realize, as far as can be ascertained from the literature, into what new and unexplored regions their suggestions were leading. The life-theme is still evolving and only recently has it emerged almost completely free of its origin in the experiential approach.[18] Nevertheless there are important differences and it is possible to discover fairly stable lines of development.

1   Whereas experiential religious education seeks to relate the ordinary experience of the child with the experiences recorded within the religious tradition, the life theme is concerned to explore the religious significance of the pupil's experiences as such.

The experiential method is essentially a method of correlation in which the revelation recorded in the Bible and the experience of the men and women which was enlightened by the revelation and which in turn became revelatory to those who followed is placed beside the experience of young people today. In this way the experience of the pupils is enriched as they are enabled to understand it in the light of the biblical faith and the Bible comes alive since it is seen as a book about experiences similar to those which the pupils have had themselves. 'We must look first,' say the authors of 'The Wonder of the Body' scheme, 'for something in their experience of which they may be reminded or made aware, with enjoyment; then we must link this fact of their experience with the fact of Jesus Christ.'[19] So the class may begin holding their breath, by seeing how flexibly the wrist may move or by trying to feel each other's pulse. After discussion of the wonder of the body the story of St Christopher who used his bodily strength to serve Christ is told and prayers in thanksgiving for bodily strength are used.

Living and Praising is an experiential series for the adolescent in which 'the awareness of change and growing powers is linked with God, so that He is not remote from life, but seen to share life with the boys and girls.'[20] The second course, 'which is concerned with the Bible, links itself equally naturally, with the questing spirit, the enquiring mind.'[21] Course three gives 'significance to those aspects of Christ's life which correspond to the relevant needs of young adolescents.'[22] In this series, for example, a variety of pictures of Christ are exhibited and discussed for their qualities. The qualities themselves are discussed and the nature of their attractive power is considered. Passages from the gospels which illustrate similar qualities perceived by the apostles in the character of Christ are read.

Commenting on these lessons and on the life situations suggested by Harold Loukes in his *Teenage Religion* (1961) Douglas Hubery remarks, 'These were deliberate attempts to use life situations in order to communicate the relevance and the challenge of one or other aspect of the Christian religion.'[23] Through discussion of their home life, young people could 'recognize emphatically the challenge of Christian standards of relationships.'[24] In following the experiential approach with older young people current events, both local and international, 'need to be put alongside the realities of the Christian faith.'[25] An example offered by Douglas Hubery is that of teaching the significance of worship. The experiential approach might begin with an understanding of worship as offer and response. Consideration can then be given to the idea of offer and response as it appears in ordinary life, in advertisements, in a song, in a situation at home. Then a hymn is examined to see what God offers and how man is invited to respond or Isaiah 6 may be read as an example of God's offer and man's response. In this way the correlational logic of the method is strictly followed; through placing religion and life beside each other the two will interpenetrate, and become one.

One of the clearest examples of the experiential method is the syllabus drawn up by the British Lessons Council published under the title *Experience and Faith*. In 1963 the Council, prompted by the Birmingham work of Kenneth Hyde, Douglas Hubery and Ronald Goldman, had begun work on the production of this new syllabus for use in the Free Churches. The work based on the syllabus has been appearing under the title *Partners in Learning. Experience and Faith*, the foundation booklet for the syllabus, exhibits clearly the correlational method of experiential religious education, not only in its title (the titles of the other experiential courses we have been discussing indicate this feature as well) but in its setting out. Sections dealing with the characteristics of boys and girls at various stages of their lives are set against theological ideas and biblical passages which may be related. There is little attempt to examine the experience of the children for its own sake, but rather to show that 'the educational approach to these great biblical and theological ideas must develop through the ideas and interests of the boys and girls themselves.'[26]

'Anyone using this syllabus or the courses based upon it will lose immeasurably if he fails to relate his teaching to the theological concepts outlined....'[27] Thus when teaching the idea that God is trustworthy, the lesson will begin with discussion about people in whom the children might place unquestioned trust, such as a parent, a teacher, or the school-crossing patrol man. Stories of people who have trusted God and found him trustworthy are then told.[28]

But theme teaching is concerned to explore the religious experience innate within the ordinary experience of the child. Norman J. Bull says, 'Their purpose is to expose the symbolism in these common features of everyday life, and *thus* [my italics] to lead children to see their religious significance.'[29] So 'it is in the actual experiences of *daily* [author's italics] life [not what is usually thought of as 'religious life'] that the encounter between God and the children will take place. The role of the teacher in this case is to encourage the children to explore these daily experiences....'[30] Jennifer Ferguson explains that the purpose of theme teaching is to 'start with life and explore it at depth; it is in this process of exploration that we encounter the activity of God' and that one should 'take a "secular" subject and see the religious significance within it.'[31]

When a life-theme deals with the idea of bodily growth, the object of the teacher is to show that 'it is a religious experience *in itself* [my emphasis] for a child to use and enjoy his powers' and 'to help boys and girls to enjoy their growing powers and developing interests and *in so doing* [my emphasis] to become aware of themselves as children of God.'[32]

The 1968 ILEA Agreed Syllabus points with sound insight into the true nature of theme teaching in contrast to the correlational method of the experiential approach when it remarks, 'This method is fundamentally the exploration of the meaning of human relationships as a means of understanding the divine-human relationship.'[33] We thus conclude that whereas experiential teaching is a form of biblical hermeneutics, theme teaching is a form of existential analysis.

> 2   Life-themes are less committed to the Bible as an ingredient in the pupil's work.

This is consistent with and follows from the first distinction. The whole of the experiential approach to Christian education can be considered as a method of understanding and interpreting the Bible. It is an educational theory based on a hermeneutical theory. The clue to the whole approach,' writes Douglas Hubery, 'may be given quite simply by saying that there is no experience, whether of the individual or of society, which cannot find its parallel in the Scriptures. The task of the educator . . . is to place the present situation in whatever form it reflects itself alongside the parallel situation discernible in Bible study.'[34] The experiential method of teaching demands a corresponding experiential approach to Bible study. 'We need to examine the reality of experience under review and find that portion of Scripture which reflects a similar reality of experience.'[35] The place of the Bible is thus 'to confirm and interpret experience'[36] and the reason why the Bible can carry out this task is because it is itself a book grounded in human experiences. Through the methods of experiential education, 'teachers can recapture those realities of experience; then the theological or Biblical phrases can have significance in their own right and as a means of articulating and interpreting the experience.'[37]

The authority and centrality of the Bible thus remain unchallenged in the experiential approach to Christian education.[38] Indeed, the experiential approach is often commended precisely because it is thought to be consistent with the biblical pattern of revelation. 'Both we and they learn to look at normal experiences in such a way that God is enabled to speak through them and in them. Such a way of looking at life is essentially the Biblical way of looking. Jeremiah, for example, may look at an almond tree and see within it and through it the truth of God. . . .'[39] 'A concern for an experiential approach to Christian education,' writes Douglas Hubery, 'does not arise merely from theory. It rises much more from an awareness that it is precisely in this experiential way that God Himself has chosen to communicate to the world of men.'[40] The influence of C.H. Dodd's *The Authority of the Bible* is evident here, and is not infrequently referred to, as showing that the authority of the Bible rests upon the fact that it is a confirmation of experience.

The life-theme however has a different approach to the Bible. Certainly, most themes include biblical material, but they do so very often at the cost of their own integrity and for reasons which we will consider later. More interesting is the way in which Ronald Goldman replies to the criticism that in life-themes there is not enough material of a religious kind. His reply is in two parts. First, he points out that references to the Bible and also to hymns, prayers and churches can be 'used in abundance in the context of the child's experience'[41] and many illustrations are provided. Secondly, and significantly, in connection with the theme 'Home,' he remarks, 'The religious significance of this theme is, of course, much deeper than the use of "religions" material. The nature of the home as a place of mutual help is explored, the physical

141

environment is only the setting for the love which binds a home together, and a concern for those who need our help, as well as thanksgiving for homes in a final festival of worship, are all religious in a broader and deeper sense.'[42] The London Syllabus, in warning that the mere addition of biblical material is often fruitless and may not necessarily contribute to the religious depth of a theme, remarks 'The teacher . . . will look for the underlying religious theme to which the educational theme points.'[43] The way to deepen a theme on animals is not to study the Bible zoo but to draw out the sense of wonder for the animal world and man's responsibility for it; the way to deepen a theme on hearing is not to study the musical instruments of the Bible but to discover the experiences of reverence and exaltation which great music can convey.

For various reasons, few published themes have so far managed to treat the Bible consistently but it is interesting to see that by far the greater number of themes suggested by the Cambridgeshire Religious Education Advisory Council in its 1970 handbook are entirely without biblical reference or suggestion. The theme is slowly coming to maturity.

3   There is a sense in which themes may be thought of as preparation for and preliminary to experiential Christian education.

Parallel with this is the observation that life-themes are usually recommended for young children and religious themes for somewhat older children. In Ronald Goldman's own suggestions for a developmental religious education, the period of early childhood (5–7 years), described by Goldman as pre-religious, is characterized by use of life-themes which are intended to enrich general experience and create a readiness for the later specifically religious materials.[44]

It is very important to realize that when Goldman refers to a sub-religious stage he means a pre-Christian stage. The sub-religious stage is from about 7 to 11. 'I have characterized this period,' explains Goldman, 'as the sub-religious stage intellectually, since the more spiritual truths of Christianity are frequently reduced to pre-Christian concepts. I use the term sub-religious as synonymous with pre-Christian.'[45]

The same is true of Goldman's use of pre-religious to denote the earlier stage of childhood. Goldman certainly does not mean to suggest that children are not capable of religion in some senses during these early years. On the contrary, he thinks that with young children, 'There appears to be a natural sense of the numinous, the mysterious and awesome, nature of God as the child sees him.'[46] But the young child cannot think religiously in any coherent way and for this reason he cannot grasp the abstract spiritual and moral nature of the main

Christian beliefs about God, the world, and history. 'This is why,' he continues, 'I have characterized early childhood as pre-religious.'[47]

It is because young children are not capable of grasping intellectually the doctrines of Christianity that life-themes rather than specifically religious themes or experiential methods are more suited to them. The limits are such that 'the emphasis should be placed more and more upon using the natural experience of children so that the religious nature of that experience shall be known and placed alongside the experience of others, both in the past and the present.'[48] A certain amount of 'placing alongside' is possible even in early childhood, but as the child grows older, the number of religious themes will increase and the number of life-themes will in Goldman's view decrease.

The use of life-themes is sometimes described by Goldman as religious education rather than as Christian education and sometimes life-themes are described as preparatory religious education.[49] 'We are trying to make children spiritually sensitive to the religious nature of their lives in a general sense, as preparation for their later encounter, in terms of their own experience, with the Christian faith.'[50]

In the case of children having no home background in religion the preparatory stage may be prolonged into later childhood and adolescence. This is why life-themes have been found so relevant in many state schools, where teachers are seeking to create a minimal awareness of religious attitudes to life and to equip pupils with at least some vocabulary to express the emotional sensitivity and the symbolic richness of religious responses.

These then are the main differences which have gradually emerged between experiential Christian education and thematic religious education. The differences are not found absolutely in any of the works discussed. Indications of the approach of the later life-theme are to be found in the earliest examples of experiential lessons and most of the life-themes which have been published in the last few years continue to carry traces of the experiential approach. This is natural and probably inevitable. But the main tendencies of the two methods are discernible and one can safely predict that the two approaches will increasingly diverge as time goes by. But it is worth asking ourselves why it is that so many themes have been inconsistent or have gone to seed in various ways.

Inconsistent themes

The difficulties arise when one begins to enquire as to the manner in which the daily normal experience of the child can be explored so as to reveal its religious significance. Where themes are used as part of a programme of specifically Christian education, it is often said that the task of the teacher is that of interpreting the children's experiences in the light of the Christian faith. 'As children grow older they need to be helped to interpret their experiences and the knowledge they gain. Teachers of religious education have the responsible task of helping their pupils to understand a Christian interpretation of these.'[51] Sometimes the Christian interpretation requires the extension of the theme. The Northamptonshire Agreed Syllabus explains that 'children are encouraged to explore their experience of life, at home and at school, and then enabled to deepen and to extend that experience so that they gain some Christian understanding of the nature and purpose of life ... a theme may be begun at any stage and then developed to include a Christian understanding of that theme.'[52] In practice this usually means that biblical or ecclesiastical material is included in the later stages of the theme.

Inclusion of biblical material is certainly the most popular way of helping a child to explore his experience in depth. Themes are indeed sometimes set out with secular material on the left and the biblical references on the right of the page. So we find 'the work of the family' on the left with 'the family cares for its members' as the main aspect of experience to be explored. 'Jesus helped a sick mother' (Luke 4: 38–41) is suggested as a possible final stage of the section before the practical activities begin.[53] The appearance of such pages is not unlike that of the pages of the syllabuses for use in county and diocesan schools produced 70 years ago, except that they would have begun by reading the passage from the gospel, then gone on to consider what it taught us about family responsibilities. At first sight, it is far from clear that there is much to choose between what profess to be two methods.

Yet the *Readiness for Religion* series tells us that the life-theme method 'is quite the opposite of beginning with religious stories or ideas then seeking to illustrate them from life' and we can be sure that what is intended is something much more profound than a mere inversion of the traditional relation between Bible passages and what used to be called their application. We have seen that while some use of biblical passages need not be inimical to the conception of a theme, the purpose of theme teaching is to explore the religious dimension of life itself and this can be done it is suggested without reference to biblical passages or to anything specifically within the ecclesiastical tradition. But this aspect of theme teaching, although it is the central and most original which theme teaching presents, has often been misunderstood.

There are at least two reasons for this failure to grasp the inner intention of theme teaching. In the first place Ronald Goldman did not sufficiently elaborate the conception, either in *Readiness for Religion* or in the life-theme textbooks which he edited. Secondly, probably as a result of this factor, the actual theme textbooks are often confused about what they are doing. Since these textbooks and pupils' work cards tend to be liberal in tone, offering themselves as suggestions only and inviting the teacher to construct his own examples, it is not surprising that the confusion has spread.

The ambiguity of the *Readiness for Religion* series can be seen, for example, in the *Notes for the Teacher* booklet accompanying *The Importance of Bread*. It is pointed out that 'children's experiences connected with discovering the wonder and importance of bread can be of more than passing interest and, in fact, of religious value'[54] and that the theme is intended to be an exploration of 'the religious significance of quite ordinary events.'[55] But then, almost as an afterthought, we are told that 'the work cards also show how children can explore the Christian tradition associated with bread.' The theme thus tries to do two things at once. The same feature could be illustrated many times.

The *Sheep and Shepherds* work cards have as their general aim 'to help children to explore imaginatively the work and life of sheep and shepherds . . . and then to develop these feelings and ideas and transfer them imaginatively to Palestine.'[56] This last phrase is surely not appropriate in a true life-theme.

Perhaps the authors were worried about the possibility of bringing out the religious implications of ordinary life unless some specifically religious material was added. It is also possible that the problem which these booklets are dealing with is, in spite of the protestations of their compilers, not that of the religious significance of ordinary life but the problem of the meaning in a secularized society of religious language. They seek to introduce children to the special way Christians use certain words. The *Notes* on the *Bread* theme remark, 'If in our generation of the Western world we are to understand the force of what Jesus was saying . . .' and the *Notes* on the *Sheep* theme express a hope that 'the children will be able to feel their way into a greater understanding of many biblical metaphors.'

It is a pity that these, and some of the others in the *Readiness for Religion* series, were described as life-themes in the first place. They should have been described as aids to understanding things Jesus said or biblical figures of speech. It is easy however to be wise in retrospect, and these comments although critical are not intended to imply that the series could have been done better at the time. Religious education will continue to be grateful to the experimenters who produced these exciting new books. Only when looking back after some years is it possible to see that the inner conception of the life-theme was so undeveloped.

Nevertheless the result was that in the hands of those less expert than the authors of the *Readiness for Religion* series the theme method inevitably deteriorated. The examination of life tended in some cases to be little more than an interesting but long and elaborate introduction to the essential religious lesson. Themes were chosen not because they represented any particularly vivid or significant segment of the lives of the children but because they offered easy or apparently natural biblical connections. Nothing else can account for the disproportionate representation in themes on daily work and workers given to fishermen, shepherds and bakers.[57]

Without some conceptual clarity and some degree of theological insight, themes can run to seed in rather a frightening way. Their exuberant growth presses through every part of the curriculum, here parasitic on other sturdy growths, there creating new and deviant mutations, so that the very birds of the air can hardly find room to take up abode in their luxurious branches.[58]

Themes can be tamed by giving careful consideration to the implications for Christian faith or for any other religion as the case may be of both the method of constructing the theme and also of the content of the theme. The implications of the method need to be distinguished from the implications of the content. If you teach a theme on symbols including practice in interpreting symbols and study of specifically religious symbols the conclusion that symbols and symbolic thinking are important for an understanding of Christianity follows from the content. This is actually what you are teaching. But let us look at how you are teaching. What is your method? The way you do it carries its own distinct implications about the nature of Christianity.[59] A theme is a method of arranging and presenting certain chosen materials to children. We must understand why we do it in this way rather than in some other way.[60]

Notes

1 Stephens, Thomas, (ed.), *The Child and Religion*, Williams and Norgate, 1905, p. 128.
2 *Education in Relation to the Christianization of National Life: Report of Commission III*, World Missionary Conference 1910, p. 246.
3 Archibald, Geo. H., *The Modern Sunday School*, The Pilgrim Press, n.d., p. 9.
4 Smith, J.W.D., *Religious Education in a Secular Setting*, SCM Press, 1969, pp. 64–67.
5 Bovet, Pierre, *The Child's Religion*, 1928.

6 For example, Hartshorne, H., 'Need for fresh study of childhood religion', *Religious Education*, 34, 1939 pp. 8–10; Sister I.H.M. Mary and Hughes, Margaret, 'The moral and religious development of the pre-school child,' *Studies in Psychology and Psychiatry*, IV, Catholic University of America, Washington D.C., 1936.

7 Experiential approaches have not been used very much as yet in Britain for the teaching of non-Christian religions.

8 Hubery, Douglas S., *The Experiential Approach to Christian Education*, The National Sunday School Union, 1960, p. 23. This was the first publication which used the expression 'experiential' in the modern British context.

9 *Ibid.*, p. 28.

10 *Ibid.*, p. 29.

11 Hubery Douglas S., *Teaching the Christian Faith Today*, National Sunday School Union, 1965, p. 63.

12 Both published by Religious Education Press.

13 Westhill College staff, *Experience and Worship*, REP, 1963, p. 8.

14 *Ibid.*, p. 7.

15 *Ibid.*, p. 9.

16 For example, Goldman, Ronald, *Readiness for Religion*, Routledge, 1965, pp. 145 and 205.

17 In the previous chapter, I defined the nature of a theme as understood by the Christian educators of the sixties.

18 Cambridgeshire and Isle of Ely Education Committee, *Religious Education, Suggestions for Teachers*, 1970, contains some rather mature life-themes.

19 *Experience and Worship, op. cit.*, p. 11.

20 Westhill College Staff, *Living and Praising*, REP, 1963, p. 14.

21 *Ibid.*, p. 14.

22 *Ibid.*

23 *Teaching the Christian Faith Today, op. cit.*, p. 59.

24 *Ibid.*

25 *Ibid.*

26 British Lessons Council, *Experience and Faith: A Christian Education Syllabus*, REP, 1968, p. 8.

27 *Ibid.*, p. 11.

28 *Ibid.*, p. 36.

29 Bull, Norman J., *Symbols: Notes for the Teacher*, Ronald Goldman (ed.), Rupert Hart-Davis, 1966, p. 5.

30 Hughes, Margaret E., *The Importance of Bread: Notes for the Teacher*, Ronald Goldman (ed.), Rupert Hart-Davis, 1966, p. 4.

31 Ferguson, Jennifer A., *To Do and to Know*, REP, 1968, pp. 27 and 40.

32 Parker, Constance M. *About Myself: Notes for the Teacher*, Ronald Goldman (ed.) Rupert Hart-Davis, 1967.

33 *Learning for Life: Agreed Syllabus of Religious Education*, Inner London Education Authority, 1968, p. 42.

34 *Teaching the Christian Faith Today, op. cit.*, pp. 97f.

35 *Ibid.*, p. 98.

36 *Ibid.*, p. 39.

37 *Ibid.*, p. 35.

38 In spite of the repeated insistence upon this point, experiential syllabuses and textbooks are still accused of neglecting the Bible. For examples of the insistence upon the place of the Bible, see *Experience and Worship, op. cit.*, p. 37 and *Experience and Faith, op. cit.*, pp. 6f.

39 *Experience and Worship, op. cit.*, p. 7.

40 *The Experiential Approach . . ., op. cit.*, p. 16.

41 *Readiness for Religion, op. cit.*, p. 117.

42 *Ibid.*
43 *Learning for Life, op. cit.*, p. 42.
44 See the chart on p. 196 of *Readiness for Religion, op. cit.*
45 *Ibid.*, pp. 47f.
46 *Ibid.*, p. 81.
47 *Ibid.*, p. 80. The often repeated remark that Goldman did not believe that children are capable of religion at all before the age of 11 cannot be confirmed from his writings. On the other hand, it is a pity that Goldman used words like 'pre-religious' and 'sub-religious' which do encourage this misconception about his intention.
48 *Ibid.*, p. 39.
49 *Ibid.*, p. 220.
50 *Ibid.*, p. 221.
51 Hyde, Kenneth, (ed.) *Topic Books*, Lutterworth, 1970; in the 'General Introduction'.
52 Northampton Education Committee, *Fullness of Life: Agreed Syllabus of Religious Education* (Primary Section), 1968, pp. 9f.
53 Lancashire Education Committee, *Religion and Life: Agreed Syllabus of Religious Education*, 1968, p. 37.
54 Hughes, Margaret, *op. cit.*
55 *Ibid.*, p. 5.
56 Dingwall, Ronald, *Sheep and Shepherds: Notes for the Teacher*, Ronald Goldman (ed.), Rupert Hart-Davis, 1968, p. 6.
57 Kent Education Committee, *A Handbook of Thematic Material*, 1968.
58 Smith, Kenneth N., *Themes in Religious Education for the Nine to Thirteens*, Macmillan, 1969. Although afflicted by the defect I describe, the book has many lively ideas which would stimulate religious teaching.
59 This is discussed on p. 128 above.
60 Since this study was written, in 1973, Michael Grimmitt's *What Can I Do in R.E.?* (Mayhew-McCrimmon) has been published. The distinctions made by Grimmitt fulfil the expectation that theme teaching is slowly maturing.

13. *History, Experience and Theme in Religious Education*

One of the most perplexing problems in teaching life-themes is whether or not biblical material should be introduced and, if it is, what the practical and the theological relationships between the thematic and the biblical materials should be. Different forms of these relationships constitute different methods of religious education and should therefore be distinguished as carefully as possible. So, for example, we have on the one hand, experiential Christian (or, for that matter, experiential Muslim) education, which, since it is essentially a technique for interpreting explicit religious material, must necessarily at some point contain such explicit religious material. On the other hand, we have thematic teaching which, although preparing for the reception of specific religious material, does not propose to do this directly, being more concerned with a religious interpretation of the child's ordinary experience. Inclusion of biblical material, therefore, is not essential to the nature of thematic teaching. Biblical material may actually distort or obscure the particular functions of theme teaching.

In the English state schools, and for mainly historical reasons, the problem of the use of specific religious materials has amounted to the problem of the use of the Bible. In the discussion which follows, the Bible is taken simply as the main case to hand of this broader tension within religious education, the tension between the received tradition and the actual experience of the present.[1]

If we were to label the left-hand side of a page 'all biblical and no experiential' and the right-hand side of the page 'all experiential and no biblical', as in Figure 1, the emphasis on the experiential increases as one moves across the page to the right. The life-theme is at the right-hand extremity. Over on the left extremity, we find a kind of teaching which some secondary schools regard as praiseworthy because 'it is academic' and represented by the sort of textbooks full of pictures of piles of stones labelled 'remains of X' and maps. Since the approach is purely historical, with emphasis on quantity of facts, this kind of teaching is judged to be successful if, at the end of it, pupils can recall the facts. A sufficient number of facts must be presented, hence the teacher's emphasis is on 'getting through the syllabus' and characterized by such comments as, 'It's already half way through term and we're not up to chapter ten.' We could call this approach the biblical-archaeological method.

All biblical and no experiential	All experiential and no biblical

Figure 1

It would be a mistake to suppose that on the continuum pupils' activity necessarily increases as we move towards the right. Materials on the extreme left, purely biblical study, can be taught by child activity methods. These procedures need not take the form (still alas astonishingly common) of pupils reading a passage followed by the teacher offering exegetical and historical remarks about it, nor need it be taught in the exclusively factual way indicated above and falsely called 'academic'. There can be plenty of emphasis on principles and problems of Bible study in such teaching – upon the methods of the biblical historians, upon the types of literature they present and on the methods of modern scholars and archaeologists. Indeed, the teaching could proceed by means of pupil discovery, projects, work cards, group work and so on.

Some meanings of 'child-centred'

'Child-centred' religious education can, in the first place, be a method of teaching in which the child's activities are encouraged, his participation aroused, and in which the child is encouraged to find things out for himself instead of simply being told by the teacher. Such a way of teaching religion might be termed a 'discovery method'.

But 'child-centred' religious education can also refer to ways of teaching in which the experience of the child is related, whether by 'discovery methods' or in some other way, to the explicit religious material so that the one illuminates the other. This is 'experiential Christian education'.[2] It would certainly be rather odd if experiential Christian education were carried on by anything but discovery methods, but it might perhaps sometimes be done. As for the purely biblical content, it is also probably taught better by discovery methods, even when unrelated to the pupils' experience, not only because the biblical content would be less compatible with a more teacher directed approach, but simply because children learn better, whatever the content, when they are finding out for themselves.

Our continuum therefore is not simply a page of method, in which teacher directed methods must always be on the left with the purely biblical material and pupil-centred discovery methods must be on the right with the thematic and the existential. The diagram is a listing of objectives in religious education in so far as these are reflected in biblical or experiential content. There is obviously a stage at which the objectives with their related content must be applied in a method, and there are methods which are more and less appropriate to each of the various objectives, but the relationship between the objectives and their content on the one hand and methods (seen in terms of teacher directed through to child discovery) on the other is not such that more Bible necessarily means less pupil discovery.

A final point about the extreme left-hand side of the diagram must be made: the extreme position, dealing with the Bible but with no experiential application at all, may be a perfectly worthwhile form of teaching. It is not necessarily any the worse for not being experientially related to the pupil; that is, for not being child-centred in the second sense. The criterion depends on the teacher's objectives. Teaching the Bible in an exclusively historical and exegetical manner may be a useful prelude to Christian studies and, in so doing, form part of religious education, provided that the goals are not too dominated by merely factual requirements, for it is necessary to include insights and understandings of a historical and exegetical kind to make biblical interpretation possible. Although such teaching has a worthwhile role, it is necessary to stress that it is only a prelude. This prefatory role is made clear if in answer to the question, 'In what way does this study illuminate the life of the pupil?' the answer received is, 'In no way'. Such a non-religious study of the Bible and its background is more properly regarded as part of history or literature.

The same judgement is true of materials at the other end of the continuum, the existential materials without any specifically religious content, which in the example we are discussing would be biblical material. Such material is also a prelude to religious education, and an important prelude, perhaps more vital than the historical study of the Bible, but it is not in itself part of the religious education of the child. Again, the prefatory role emerges when in answer to the question, 'In what way is the life of the pupil here illuminated by the specifically religious?' the answer continues to be, 'In no way'.

Only in the centre of the page, where the objectives and corresponding content include both the specifically religious and the experiential illumination, can we say that religious education is taking place.

Making doctrine together

Taking a closer look at a mid-point on the continuum, we come to the area which includes both the specifically religious and the personal illuminatory materials, and we may thus describe this situation as being constitutive of religious education.

There is a sense in which the different relationships in this central area might be thought of as nothing but a matter of the order of the content. The syllabuses of 70 or 100 years ago offered the 'application' after the biblical passage whereas some forms of apparently experiential biblical teaching simply offer the application first. This sketchy summary might convey a misunderstanding of the nature of contemporary religious education. The application which the religious educator of 100 years ago drew from his biblical material was mainly a moral one, dealing with the duty of the pupil to develop the Christian virtues, to quell the vices, and to observe the religious duties. To some extent this was due to the fear in the state schools that discussion of doctrines, as opposed to ethical precepts, might take the teacher into forbidden areas of denominational controversy. No way had been found whereby the specifically religious aspects of the Bible could be presented without infringement of the Cowper-Temple clause. Another and perhaps deeper reason was that Schleiermacher had not been applied to religious education in Britain and Kierkegaard had not even been discovered. Put another way, the stress on anthropology and existentialism dominant in twentieth-century religious thinking was lacking, and revealed doctrines were taught without an adequate understanding of either the nature of revelation or the nature of a doctrine.

There is a difference between understanding the *history* of a doctrine and understanding a *meaning* of a doctrine. The religious educator of today is not only concerned with the former but with the latter as well. If you teach, directly or indirectly, what Paul said about it, or what Luther said about it, or Tillich, you are teaching the history of the doctrine, that is, the story of some of the various meanings which have been perceived and which can be objectively demonstrated by reading what people have said and written. This is what the older teachers were doing. The doctrine was objectively given, handed down from the past, in the form of articles, creeds and texts. This fixed teaching was passed on to the pupils. The history of the doctrine was thus mistakenly identified with the meaning of the doctrine, and all that remained was for the doctrine to be applied. This was where the second half of the lesson began: 'What lessons can we draw from this? What, from this message or teaching, is the duty of the Christian?'

The modern teacher's conception of the relation between doctrine and life or, for that matter, between history and faith, is quite different. For example, a meaning of the doctrine of redemption will be found in the concept of freedom today. Indeed, the doctrine will have as many meanings as there are different concepts of freedom. So it is no longer helpful to speak of the doctrine of redemption as if there were only one. There are many, and there always have been many. Even, or perhaps most of all, in the New Testament, there are many kinds of freedom and several types of doctrines of redemption. We ought rather to speak of a cluster of redemption meanings, gathered around the aspiration for freedom. Discovering the meaning of freedom to me and discovering the meaning of redemption are interconnected parts of the same activity.

To take another example, a contemporary meaning of the death of Jesus cannot be learned from the New Testament unless a view of people today towards death happened to be the same as a view towards death held in the first century. But if death has today taken on a new cluster of meanings, one can no longer discover anything but a historical meaning for the death of Jesus by examining the New Testament. The meaning of the death of Jesus is part of the meaning of death, and although a Christian believes that Jesus has in fact given a new meaning to death, the significance of this statement is lost unless one knows what a new meaning means. To say, for example, that Christ's death puts an end to sacrifice by being the eternal sacrifice was once a radically new meaning of death and of sacrifice, a new meaning given by the death of Jesus and the reflection on death it gave rise to. But this idea was new by comparison with the other ideas about death and sacrifice current in the culture of Judaism. Such an idea today would not be a new meaning for to most modern people it is without meaning at all. We need then to do always again but with greater deliberation what the New Testament writers and preachers did. We need to examine the meanings of death in the culture around us, in religion, in law and punishment, in illness, as reflected in literature and the arts, and ask ourselves what new meaning the death of Jesus throws upon these meanings. The result will be a meaning of the death of Jesus, that is, a small part of the doctrine, the cluster of significance, gathered around the ideas of death and of Jesus.

Now what does this mean in the classroom? When the teacher about to take a lesson on redemption begins with the experiences and attitudes of his pupils towards freedom, he is not merely placing the application first. There is more to this than a reversal of order of presentation. He is not simply creating an attention catching opening, nor merely trying to establish relevance or motivation. He is beginning with his pupils a process of discovery (which may also be a process of revelation) of meaning which he does not yet know any more than the class yet knows it. He is beginning to explore what the doctrine means, what it is, and not simply introducing his pupils to what it was. The teacher and the class are making doctrine together. They are taking part in an enormous ongoing movement whereby in discussion, in study, in reflection and in all the aspects of living, the meaning of religion is being reborn. It is not being passed on only, it is being remade. This is what we mean when we say that experiential Christian education is a method of parallelism, in which the experience of the pupils is placed against the scripture, so that each illuminates the other, and so that the experience of the teacher and the pupil becomes a principle of interpretation. Interpretation here means *re*-interpretation, the conferring of new insights, the discovery of new meaning. It is not simply a technique for making the old meaning alive and relevant, though this may well happen in certain circumstances, but since that which is re-interpreted takes on new meaning, such teaching is in fact a contribution to the development of doctrine.

Bible-centred teaching

On this central part of the continuum, the emphasis upon the experience of the pupil increases, as we have noticed, as we go further to the right. Moving to the left, the lessons become more and more Bible-centred, with the expression 'Bible-centred' referring to the objectives of the lesson, not to the order of presentation. A teacher might, for example, begin a lesson by introducing some material from the Bible, but move on from this to deal with various points at which the material touched the actual lives and interests of his pupils, or stimulated them to reflect about their lives and values in certain ways. If indeed, this was in fact his objective, and he was using the Bible as a stimulus, moving from it onto his real purposes, the situation would be the reverse of that in which the pupils' lives are used to provide a point of interest in order to move on to the real business, the study of the Bible.

The character of Bible-centred teaching can be considered in the light of an interesting lesson a student teacher recently gave to a class of intelligent first-form girls in a secondary school. The lesson was about the choice of Rebeccah as the wife of Isaac. At three points in this story, questions relating to their own lives and interests were raised by the girls themselves. The first was the right age for a girl to marry. The second was the matter of arranged marriages (even if God arranged them!) and finally somebody, whose mind had admittedly been wandering a bit, asked what God looked like – the sort of question which does often arise when the mind begins to wander during a Bible-centred lesson. Each of these three questions was greeted in this lively and eager class of 12-year-olds by a buzz of interest and a forest of hands. The teacher however dealt with each question in the briefest way only, taking no more than three or four of the many comments, and then returning to the board where she was drawing a Bedouin tent which she had asked the girls to copy into their books. When reproached afterwards by a saddened tutor, the student defended herself by saying that she wanted to get on with the lesson!

Such a lesson was truly Bible-centred in the 'archaeological' sense for the teacher's objectives were all connected with the historical study of the bible, and any attention paid to the religious, ethical and other personal concerns of the pupils was an aside. I do not use the expression 'Bible-centred' here in a derogatory sense. There is a place for such teaching; such objectives, as we have seen, may be a legitimate preparation for religious education. Their justification in a religious education lesson however is exactly that they are so useful as preliminaries. In a lesson which was outstandingly successful (considered in this way), since the biblical material immediately raised three questions of religious and ethical concern, it was a shame to see the teacher rejecting the parts of the lesson which were most powerfully religiously educational by insisting that the class be confined to the preliminaries. Although it might perhaps have been adequate for an historian or someone dealing with the geography or anthropology of the middle-east, her notion of the lesson was too limited for a religious educator.

It might be thought that the term 'Bible-centred' is being used in rather a strict and narrow sense, for there are other senses of this expression which we might usefully observe. So far, 'Bible-centred' refers to the lesson in which the objective is to study the Bible itself for its own sake in its own period and culture and without reference to the personal concerns of the pupils. We need now to ask to what extent this kind of lesson, in spite of the teacher's declared intention, is in fact being true to the nature of the Bible itself. There is, for example, in the biblical tradition, almost no interest shown in the past for its own sake but only in the past as offering a dynamic for the present and a hope for the future. The God who brought Israel out of Egypt remained the God of the living not of the dead, and the remembrance of the Passover was not a brooding over the past in isolation from the present but a renewal of the daily covenant between God and his people. Time and time again the memories clustered around the exodus were renewed to interpret contemporary events as, for example, in thinking about the exile and the return from Babylon, and again in the New Testament to interpret the redemption won by Jesus for his people. Similarly, we may well wonder whether the many lessons which concentrate on the historical background to the life of Jesus are as truly biblical as they appear to be. Paul claimed to know Jesus according to the flesh no longer, but to be caught up in the new creation where Christ made all things new. Because it is always the intention of the biblical writings to confront man in his present moment with the demands of God and of his neighbour, we may well conclude that teachers who restrict their teaching to historical exegesis of the Bible are not being truly Bible-centred.

Let us therefore distinguish these two senses of 'Bible-centred'. First, we have Bible-centred-historical (study of the past) and, second, we have Bible-centred-religious in which the Bible is allowed to be itself, speaking to the present moment of both teacher and pupil. Bible-centred-religious would be appropriate for a religious education lesson, but Bible-centred-historical would only be appropriate for a preface to religious education.

We are now in a position to arrange the various kinds of teaching we are discussing to amend our first figure. Beginning at the left-hand side, where the teaching can now be described as 'Bible-centred-historical', we may locate the following:

1 Bible-centred-historical teaching. No attempt made to illuminate the life of the pupil.
2 Bible-centred-religious teaching. The Bible is used to illuminate the life of the pupil.
3 Experiential Christian teaching.
4 Life-themes.

Bible-centred- historical	Bible-centred- religious	Experiential Christian	Life-themes

Figure 2

The difference between *Bible-centred* religious teaching and *experiential* Christian teaching is partly a question of emphasis. In the former, the syllabus is controlled by the contents of the Bible, part of the teacher's purpose being to give some insight into the historical nature of the Bible. One may, for example, be dealing with the life of Jesus, in which the order of presentation will to some extent be determined by anything we may happen to know of the order of the main events in his life, or we may simply decide to accept one of the various gospel orders. But our teaching will always admit criticism from the question, 'To what extent did the lesson throw any light on the life of the pupil?'

With experiential Christian education or experiential Bible teaching or whatever the explicit religious content may be, the life of the pupil is taken much more consistently as the control in the selection of material and the biblical order is in the main ignored, although lessons might be gathered around a certain biblical area or theme. For example, the teacher might decide to take a number of concerns of pupils, such as the use of money, the question of violent retaliation, friendship, courage and work, which would perhaps be linked together by the fact that in every case the biblical material would be from the teaching of Jesus. The Bible, however, is used as a religious source book, as a resource for interpretation, and as a store of illustration, the content of the lessons themselves being controlled all the time by the pupils' interests and experiences. A second difference is that the modern human experience is taken much more seriously, radically and creatively, as a principle of biblical interpretation.

Ways of teaching the Joseph saga

Let us take the Joseph saga and see how it would look if taught according to each of the four patterns we have distinguished.

1 A Bible-centred-historical approach

The Joseph stories make ideal material for this approach with the best place to begin probably ancient Egypt itself. Pages cut by pupils in the shape of the sphinx or a pyramid can be tied together inside a cardboard cover decorated by pupils with hieroglyphic motifs. Travel posters, newspaper headlines and pictures of Tutankhamen's treasure from the colour supplements are displayed. Joseph's life is recreated against this background with some examination of the different strands which have come together in the extant biblical traditions.

2 A Bible-centred-religious approach

While the Joseph story is ideal for historical treatment, it is also rich in human material. The teacher committed to the historical approach will often find, as the young teacher dealing with Rebeccah found, that the material keeps slipping out of its context in the past and coming alive in the interest of the pupils today. That this should happen becomes an important objective of the teacher if he is dealing with it in this Bible-centred-religious approach. In addition to the material from ancient Egypt, the teacher sets work which encourages his pupils to enter imaginatively into the mind of Joseph and encourages the discussion to flow freely on such questions as family favourites, jealousy between brothers, revenge, slavery, ambition, and the meaning of dreams.

3 An experiential-Bible-teaching approach

If the third method is being followed, the lesson will not intend to be a lesson principally about Joseph at all. It will be about, say, dreams. The lesson might be one of a series dealing with various aspects of human psychology, with the overall aim of giving pupils more insight into themselves and helping them to understand some religious ideas in psychological terms. A subsidiary objective would be to convey a sense of the depth of meaning to be found in parts of the Bible. So one might have dealt in such a series with memory, conscience, childhood, sleep and death, before coming to the topic of dreams. As part of his resources for the lesson, the teacher has the texts or pictures of some biblical dreams such as Jacob's ladder and Joseph's dream of the stars. These are passed around at an appropriate time, read and discussed. The question, 'How do religious people think God speaks to men today?' is perhaps the crucial enquiry which might emerge.

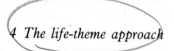

4 The life-theme approach

It is essential that in the third method the pupils' experience is placed against the material from the religious tradition whether biblical or not. This laying side by side is of the essence of the method. In the fourth approach this is no longer the case, for the life-theme, although it may be enriched and at other times distorted by the inclusion of biblical material, does not have to have such biblical material. The life-theme has an integrity of its own for a theme on dreams could be devised which made little or no specific reference to biblical or religious dreams. In such a situation we have come to the area which cannot be called religious education in a full and rich sense, but only a preliminary or a subsequent to it. The objective of such a life-theme on dreams would be to open up the mysterious nature of the subconscious mind, to encourage a critical understanding of the dream life and the dream work, to see that there are various theories about dreams, to see something of the use of the dream in music and art and literature, and thus to prepare for the use of dream motifs in world religions. It is a preparation without which Joseph's dreams will never be understood, but for all that it is still only a preparation.

Life-themes and integrated teaching

The integration of the various subject disciplines around a common topic must be distinguished from religious theme teaching whether explicit or preliminary. An integrated topic may or may not contain an overt or covert religious element. This will depend upon the extent to which the religious aspect of the common theme is important in it. Religious aspects could hardly be left out of a theme on 'Service' or 'Beauty' or 'The Arabs' but a theme on 'Transport' can be dealt with quite adequately without any treatment of religion. Teachers of religion are sometimes so concerned to stress that religion is to do with all life that it becomes difficult for them to admit there might be a theme without an essential religious aspect. We must however distinguish between a general sense in which religious beliefs and values might enrich the life of a bus driver and religious motivation might make the planning of a city's bus routes more compassionate, and the specific sense in which the integrated study attempts to bring together various disciplines including the study of religion. There is nothing about the origins, organizations and techniques of transport itself which requires the introduction of religious ways of thinking. If we move into an area such as the motive for transporting oneself or other people and so come to pilgrimages, we have moved away from the study of transport itself. Religion is an important motive in moving about and so is desire to see one's relatives, but the study of religion is no more relevant to a study of transport than is a study of relatives. Integrated teaching loses in integrity if these distinctions are not observed and becomes simply a random association of ideas.

Even when an integrated topic requires a religious aspect for its adequate treatment, this religious aspect may not be of an experiential kind, let alone of a thematic kind. For example, a theme on Norman castles would presumably have to deal with the fact that every Norman castle had a chapel and that many of the remains of Norman life are of a religious kind. But although a study of the religious life of the Normans could easily be carried out by discovery methods – visiting the chapel of a castle, gathering photographs of illuminated manuscripts of the Bible, writing eleventh-century prayers for victory and so on – this would all come under the first of the four kinds of teaching we discussed. It would all be religious-historical, and none the worse for that provided its religious education limitations were understood. There could also be examples of integrated studies in which a religious sector was of an experiential or even a thematic kind or could be dealt with in one of those ways. The Goldman *Readiness for Religion* textbooks are, for example, integrated studies containing a religious segment which is treated generally in an experiential or a thematic way – *Light* and *About Myself* as examples.

On the other hand, there may be an integrated study of which the whole is so pregnant with religious values or has been so deeply affected by religion that it can all be thought of as religiously thematic. A theme on 'Human Rights' with older pupils so quickly brings one to fundamental questions of the nature, dignity and future of man that even although it can usefully be tackled by the politician, the historian, the lawyer, the artist and the scientist, it can nevertheless be looked upon as a whole as providing an anthropological basis for an understanding of religion.

There are thus many relationships between integrated studies and thematic religious work. An integrated study need not necessarily have any religious work. Even if it has, this need not be of a thematic or experiential kind. But it may include a thematic or experiential religious segment, or it may even be possible to consider the whole study, whatever disciplines happen to be dealing with it, that is, in all of its various 'subject' segments, as thematically religious. Note that a whole integrated study could hardly be experientially religious since this would involve constant reference to specific religious materials at every point (to preserve the parallelism of experiential work). This might be the case only if something like 'The Bible' or 'The Church' was actually chosen by a religiously minded school as a topic for integrated study. But an integrated study could be considered religious-thematic as a whole if it dealt with a subject which was essentially preliminary to religious understanding or if it was absolutely shot through with religious implications. Integrated studies on subjects like 'Death', 'Service' and 'Love' might be examples of this.

Notes

1 The problems of method discussed in this article arise whatever sacred literature is being presented but the theological problems discussed are those which arise particularly within Christian faith.
2 Since experiential methods always require an explicit religious content, it is more exact to speak of experiential Christian education (that is, teaching, the content of which is Christian studies) or experiential Islamic education (Muslim Studies) etc., rather than to speak in a general way of experiential religious education.

14. *Perennial Symbols: Preparing to Teach Religion through Life-Themes*

There are certain areas of human life which have in world religions and in all ages been found especially suitable for the conveying of religious meaning. To find what they are we look at the actual religions of the world. Here we find the great perennial symbols, such as fire and air, earth and water, which have always had this mysterious transparency. These provide the content for our life-themes.

In this way we can discriminate between content suitable for life-themes and content not suitable. A life-theme on animals and plants would be appropriate because the divine has often been pictured in animal and plant form. Think of the idea of the sacred tree (the burning bush and the cross of Christ as a tree) and the current realization that human life depends upon the tree.[1] Food and eating is one of the great religious themes.[2] We could also include the senses, especially hearing and seeing, the mountain, the cloud, light and darkness, motherhood and fatherhood, almost everything connected with sex, and birth and death. But a subject like books is probably not suitable for such treatment. This subject is often used to introduce the Bible,[3] and it may be an excellent way to do this, but it would not be a life-theme in the sense under discussion, since the idea of a book is not one of the great aspects of human life which has always been thought of as having religious meaning.

The type of theme suggested here springs from the observation that while all life may be religious, some aspects of life are more religious than others. This is not to deny that the religious person does indeed interpret all his experience in the light of his faith, so that whether he eats or drinks or whatever he does he does all for the glory of God. But it is to claim that there are certain aspects of the human experience which have an uncanny power about them, certain experiences which lead us more quickly to a depth of meaning, some which reverberate more loudly to the divine than others. The task of the specific life-theme is to explore these subjects and reawaken for the modern person their ancient meaning.

Preparation through television

It is impossible for adults to prepare to teach such themes by reading children's school textbooks. We need first to awaken our own awareness of them. For we are all so deeply secularized today that we do not find it easy any longer to respond to the sacred world around us. One of the best ways to start our own preparation is by watching the advertisements on independent television. Get a notebook and perhaps a tape recorder and sit down in front of the television set for a couple of weeks. Ignore the programmes. Watch the commercials. It will be an ordeal, but it will be worth it. Ask yourself, 'What is the meaning, the emotional significance, the symbolism of water, of food, of the domestic hearth, of the countryside and the soil, and of fire in the advertisements?'

In life-theme teaching we can only open the eyes of children to what they already know. If, for example, the meaning of eating together has gone dead for a child, because the family so seldom does eat together, then there is little the teacher can do. If the child has bread and jam when he comes in from school, letting himself in with his own key because his parents are both still at work, and if mum only cooks with a tin opener and dad sends you round the corner for chips and curry sauce (which are eaten in front of the television), then the meaning of food as representing the mother's love and father's toil will hardly survive. Of course, a good deal of it is probably already lost. Even in the case of church-going families, only the most devout say grace any longer, and certainly the kind of family meal when father carved and the children dared not be late and had to ask permission to leave the table is now only found with Sunday lunch, if then.

Yet the meaning of food lingers on. The head of a special school told me that time and again children would run away from the residential wing, where they slept between clean sheets and were fed on good, wholesome food, back to home, where home is a dilapidated terrace house with the paper peeling off the walls, and dad is in gaol and mum makes beans on toast. It doesn't matter, it's still mum's food, and mum's food is best. But if the cultural experiences which give meaning to food were lacking, it would be no good visiting a bakery and making bread in the classroom.[4]

The most vivid evidence of the surviving power of food symbolism is to be found on television. A recent advertisement praising baked beans sprang right out of the Oedipus complex. A little boy of 4 (he began by telling you he was 4 years old) is seen, saying, 'I've just realized Mummy loves Daddy more than me because she gives him more Heinz beans.' Here we have the rivalry between the father and the son for the mother's love as expressed in her giving of food. The mother is being persuaded to distribute her love fairly, to give herself equally to her husband and her son. Such emotions go back to the mother's breast, when the mother's milk is the mother's love.

Food has an astonishing power to create unity, to build people up into one body. One of the most attractive beans posters show a football team of grubby, cheerful, tough-looking little boys above the caption 'Teams means Heinz'. The Oedipus advertisement just referred to should be compared with the commercial film showing a mother serving up the meal. In comes her husband and her son, a boy of about 8 to 10, from the garden where they have apparently been mending cars or chopping down trees. As they sit down, the song is heard, 'There are two men in my life. . . .' Another advertisement has the theme. 'These are the things a woman builds: strength in her man, energy in her sons, love in her home. She builds with . . .' (a breakfast food).

The meanings of eating cannot be grasped by studying a chart of the digestive organs. Eating has always been more than stuffing food through a hole in your head. Look at the huge drinking mugs with two handles and think of the use of food and drink in celebrating. In the sporting trophy we have a relic of the communal celebration after victory. The Welsh lover gave his beloved a loving spoon, elaborately carved, often with several bowls and interwined handles. Sharing food is a symbol of sexual life – 'bed and board'. When a couple are married, we eat and drink with them, when a baby is baptized, champagne is drunk and cigars handed around: when someone dies, a funeral tea is still offered in some parts of the country. An advertisement for a cooker shows an attractive woman presenting her dinner with the caption 'Some men like it hot'. An old Russian proverb says, 'Woman marries for meat, man for soup', which refers to the economic agreement about the provision and the preparation of food which is the basis of the marriage contract.

The unifying power of food lies behind the idea of religious sacrifice. To be united with the gods men ate with them. The gods' part was burned, going up in smoke, or poured on the ground, or offered in a temple to a representative of the god. Fellowship was made, restored, heightened. Christians are one body in Christ.

Many of the television advertisements deal with domesticity and the meaning of the hearth. The typical film shows the family hurrying through the stormy night towards their home. The wind whistles through the black, threatening trees; they stumble through the mud; the father picks up the child and carries her under his great-coat, muttering to himself, 'Hot drinking chocolate'. Now in the distance the silhouette of the house is seen, the lights go on, and the camera closes on to the window. Inside we see the family now happily laughing, bouncing each other on their respective knees. Keep your family warm this winter. Install double glazing. Get central heating. Buy a radiant smokeless coal burner. To make a home, to protect the family, to provide security and warmth for his dependants, these basic needs have driven man ever since the cave and the fire were his only protection against the hostile night.

Since the advertisements are all trying to sell something, a certain trivialization is inevitable. But a great symbol can be given a half-serious or even a fully serious application to a quite trivial subject and yet retain some of its native power. Only when the symbol itself is made fun of does fragmentation take place. Take, for example, symbols of time and eternity in the advertisements. One for long-lasting carpets shows a beautiful hourglass in a wooden frame lying broken on its side on a fine expanse of golden carpet. The sand from the broken glass has trickled out on to the carpet. The caption reads 'Brand X announces the conquest of time'. Another shows a view of an impressive carpet leading up to a manager's desk, all seen from ground level through the outline of a shapely pair of female legs. The caption says, 'Every time your secretary comes to your desk, your carpet dies a little.' In spite of the rather trivial question of how long your carpets will last, the symbols of shattered glass, sand, sex and death are here used with some skill and power.

The importance of sexual symbolism can hardly be exaggerated. We need to distinguish between advertisements where the female figure is used merely as an eyecatcher and those where sex is expressed through one of the other basic themes or is itself shown as a basic aspect of the life of man. A classic case of the latter is the now famous Fisons advertisement which occupied a full page of *The Times* in 1970. A young woman was shown, naked, kneeling with her arms half extended in an attitude of supplication. She was extremely beautiful, but the pose was not explicitly provocative. She was kneeling on the ground and the caption simply stated the name of the sponsoring firm, Fisons Fertilizers. One of the indignant letters which subsequently appeared in the correspondence columns claimed that the most objectionable feature of this advertisement was that the girl had nothing to do with the product. The student who showed me the letter he had sent to *The Times* (which was not published) had come much nearer to the point. 'Dear Sir,' he wrote, 'I will fertilize your product with pleasure.' Behind the Fisons advertisement we have the ancient connection between woman and the soil. In tribal life, the women often carry out the agriculture, particularly the sowing of the fields. There is a sympathetic connection between woman and the soil. Both are productive, both are fertile, both receive seed, and the rituals of fertility in the ancient Near East and in many tribal customs today act out the similarity and ensure the coming harvest. The religious form is taken more specifically by the religions of the Great Earth Mother, and expressed in Cybele and Demeter.

The aspiring life-theme teacher will soon make his own collection, for his own meditation, even if not for use in the classroom, of materials of this sort. He will find the symbolism of locks and keys, of dreams, of the sea and of fish, of clothes, of flowers, of animal and plant life, of bed and table, window and door, roof and hearth, of the road and the journey, of the city and the machine, of the heart and the lungs, the hands and the mouth, of hair and feet, of the darkness, the moon, the sun and the rain, all these and many other symbols, as old as poetry and literature, as old as religion, still living in the advertisements. But they are all used in the service of industry and commerce. His task is to use them to re-awaken an understanding of religion.

Preparation through stories

There are many other ways in which the teacher who wishes to prepare himself to teach life-themes can do so. He can read fairy-stories. 'It was in fairy-stories,' writes J.R.R. Tolkien, 'that I first divined the potency of the words, and the wonder of the things, such as stone, and wood and iron; trees and grass; house and fire; bread and wine.'[5] One can indeed hardly do better than read Tolkien's own masterpiece, *Lord of the Rings*, noticing the way in which the tree and the forest, the oath and the covenant, the prohibition, the mountain and the cave, the brand, the wand, the torch, the stairway, the city and the sword are used to carry mystical meaning and to radiate the hopes and fears of the characters. Such stories as *The Lion, the Witch and the Wardrobe*, by C.S. Lewis, are also helpful, but the richest stories are to be found in traditional lore and in collections such as those by the Grimm brothers and Andrew Lang. Use of a dictionary of motifs in folklore, such as the great one by Thompson,[6] will uncover masses of material, which will often have the most surprising links with current proverbs, plots in television dramas, even the lyrics of popular songs.

Moving on from folklore, these great themes of which we are speaking can be explored by the adult in poetry and literature. T.S.

Eliot's *Four Quartets*, the writing of Dylan Thomas, e. e. Cummings, W.B. Yeats, the novels by Kafka (especially *The Tower*), William Golding (*The Spire*), and the figure of the artist Kondrashov, working away in the attic of the special prison at Mavrino, with his pictures of the chilled book waiting for the clutch of the ice, the huge oak clinging to the fact of the precipice suspended over the abyss, and the search of the solitary horseman for the castle of the Holy Grail,[7] all these will serve to stimulate the imagination and to awaken in the would-be teacher the ancient power of the images he wishes to convey. Study of the paintings of Chagall, Salvador Dali or Kandinsky will reward the student in the same way.[8]

Another approach may be made through depth psychology, both through C.G. Jung (especially his *Archetypes of the Collective Unconscious*) and through certain psycho-analytical writers, but not particularly through Freud himself. The *Psychoanalysis of Fire*[9] is essential reading, and *The Psychology of Clothes*[10] and *Thrills and Regressions*[11] are good examples of the sort of enrichment which may be obtained by the cautious student.

We must never, however, lose sight of the fact that our fundamental criterion for the selection of these religious life-themes is that they are motifs which have in fact been taken up into the great religions of the world. An equally useful place to start the quest, and a necessary control over all the rest, is provided by the study of the actual symbolism of world religions. This can then be supported by study of some of the extensive literature in contemporary Christian theology dealing with topics which from our present point of view could be called life-themes.[12] Harvey Cox's *Festival of Fools* is a study in the religious symbolism of festivity and celebration, and Walter Ong's *The Presence of the Word* deals with the ear and the voice.

It will by now be clear that preparation for teaching life-themes is not a simple matter of making a few work cards and buying a set of new textbooks. The actual construction of a scheme of work is the final stage of what must necessarily be a long period of meditation. To teach a life-theme one must be something of a pagan, in the classical sense of Roman and Greek paganism – one for whom the world is alive with divinity. It is a question of acquiring that point of view.

Notes on a life-theme: The ear[13]

It can say 'Goodnight'. The caption is from an advertisement for the telephone and shows a little girl, smiling and cuddling her teddy bear, with the telephone pressed close to her ear. What the camera did for the eye the telephone did for the ear; the tape recorder and the record are the reply of the ear to the printed book. Marshall McLuhan has pointed out that most of the inventions can be considered as extensions of the senses, and that with the multiplication of electronic communications the ear is coming into its own again. McLuhan's vivid phrase 'The Global Village' sums up his view that with the instantaneous communication offered by radio, television, telephone, and so on, modern life is again taking on the intimate immediacy of village culture.[14]

It is only when we consider the role of the ear and of hearing in human life that we can begin to see why this sense has more than any other come to express the relationship between God and man. All the senses are used in religious thought, of course, and it would be an interesting task to study the way they are used in the Bible. 'O taste and see that the Lord is good.' . . . 'blessed are the pure in heart for they shall see God'; . . . 'that which we have touched and our hands have handled'. . . . But sight and hearing are by far the most common of the senses used in religious language, and of the two, talk based on the ear is the most important. To hear the word of God, to know that God listens when I call, to speak with God as a man with his friend, these are fundamental conceptions in Christianity and Judaism and in Islam to go no further afield. Why should this be so? For we might imagine creatures who have no ears, or who live in an atmosphere not capable of transmitting sound waves who, if they had a religion, would not use such expressions. For such creatures, the whole of what we call prayer would be something different, since the imagery of prayer (but not its meaning) is controlled by the contingency of aural evolution. Our speech about prayer is based on metaphors of hearing.

What then does it mean for the nature of human life that things are as they are? That we do in fact live in air which carries sound waves, and that we have in fact evolved these extraordinary apertures in the sides of our heads which pick up these vibrations? If we contrast the ear with the eye, we can see that in one sense the eye is vastly superior in the sheer quantity of information it can convey. Even when only a fraction of sight is left, perhaps only a little of the central field of one eye, an enormous amount of information can still be conveyed to the brain about the environment. A similar fraction of hearing left would be rather useless. And the eye is a logical sense, laying things out in front of the seer and revealing the special relationships between things. Although it has a general directional sense, the ear cannot pinpoint a thing in space the way the eye can. Part of the problem of educating the blind child and of devising instruments to take the place of sight is just this overwhelming superiority of the eye as far as information input goes.

The striking thing about the ear is not the quantity of the information input but the quality. And here we notice some remarkable things about hearing. Seeing is in some ways a remote sense. Seeing requires distance. You stand back from a picture; you can't read if the page is too close; the attractive appearance of many things (like the human skin) is marred if it is inspected too closely. In this way, sight does not involve the watcher but puts him at a distance and separates him from the object of his inquiry.

It is otherwise with hearing. This is a sense of great intimacy. You put your lips to the ear of a friend; we draw our chairs closer together to have a good talk; I press the watch as close to my ear as possible to listen carefully to the ticking; and I lean against the breast of a friend to hear his heart beat. Think of the significance of whispering galleries – you are surprised at how close you seem to be to the whisperer, when sight tells you that he is some distance away. But he is not! Sound brings people closer. 'It can say "Goodnight".'

A 'good likeness' in a photo, although having a power of its own to recreate the presence of the one depicted, does not make you feel 'he could have *been* in the next room', the way you feel after a particularly clear telephone conversation with someone far away. It was hearing, or overhearing, the snatches of conversation between the two walkers on the moon which brought the viewer of the Apollo landings right into the drama. The detailed pictures, published a day or two later, had their own fascination, but they did not draw you into the actual scene. Notice also that in the most intimate of human embraces hearing is placed midway between the excitement of seeing and the final bliss of feeling. You don't normally kiss with your eyes open. In the darkness, or in candlelight or firelight, the murmuring of lovers, the linking through hearing, is the way each is intimately present to the other. Only touch is more intimate.

Another interesting aspect of hearing, and this is why it is so intimate, is that it tells you what is going on inside something. Sight in a way is so crude. To see the core of an apple you must break the apple in two; to inspect a flower you pull the leaves off, and although with visual probes medical technology is making progress in extending the scope of the eye, it is not so in nature. There, to see the heart you must cut. But the doctor puts a stethoscope against your chest or your back; to find out what the inside of the moon is like, you bounce something off it; the sound of a drum tells you about its shape, as do the sounds of all musical instruments. It is sound which tells you what is going on inside a person – the noise tells you someone is in the next room; his exclamation tells you you are hurting him. Sight links the exteriors but sound links the interiors. So to express the relation between God and man, the sense of sight has to be stretched – the Lord looketh not as man looketh, for man looketh upon the outward but the Lord upon the inward heart.' It is at this point that it becomes necessary to say 'the Lord hears me.'

The tragedy of the sightless is to be cut off from contact with other minds, through the loss of the human face (not for nothing is the eye called the window of the soul). The tragedy of the deaf is to be cut off from the inner life of the persons around them, and to be left with the outward husks, the shells of people. The blind are helpless but the deaf are lonely.

Notice, by the way, that the ear possesses two other characteristics of intimacy. First, it cannot be closed. You can shut your eyes but not your ears. True, you can learn not to listen; you only notice the ticking of the clock when it stops, but you cannot decide not to hear the clock, you can only decide not to listen to it, that is, to pay no attention to it. The ear needs external help to resist the information which comes to it – you put your fingers in your ears, or shout so you can't hear what is being said, or you use ear-plugs. The eye needs no such help. We have eyelids but not earlids. The ear is thus symbolic of the fact that we are meant for each other. The openness of the ear corresponds to the openness which each man should have towards his neighbour. And the ear operates 24 hours a day. You wake a person by speaking to him; you only pull his eyelids apart when you begin to think he might be dead. Darkness and light are both alike to the ear.

Finally, because of the openness of the ear, sounds go into you in a way that sights do not. Men can be driven mad by the use of a high-pitched sound. You don't feel the physical impact of the images on your retina, but your head does actually reverberate with sound. 'It made my head ring.' Sound not only surrounds you, envelopes you in itself, blankets you, and 'seems to come from everywhere', but it links you with the environment so that the sound is in you as well. When you listen to a stereo record with headphones the sound seems to come from within. Is this why teenagers are seldom content to listen to Radio One with an earphone? By placing the sound in this way entirely within the head, the linking of the self with other selves and with the surroundings, the power of music to unite people, is broken.

All these aspects of sound, speech and hearing lie in the religious use of the sense. The word of God is that which comes from within God, when I listen (and the word is sharper than a two-edged sword, penetrating to the very marrow), I am intimately linked with God. With the idea of speech we have rationality. The word of God is not a noise. The ear picks up the grinding of boulders, the crash of the waves, but it is in the miracle of speech that the most distinctively human aspect of hearing is found.

God's word (in Christian faith) is Jesus Christ. He is thought of as the rational expression of the divine intimacy, springing from within the bosom of the Father, telling us what is going on inside God. The sound of his word tells us the shape of God. We cannot fail to hear that word, for its sound is gone out to the end of the world. But we can fail to listen. The word leaps the barrier between man and God, bringing the two into unity.[15]

This kind of life-theme may thus be thought of as an exploration of the physical basis of analogical language. It suggests that theology is, at least in part, biology, transformed by a vision of unity.

This then is how we might prepare to teach religious life-themes. The approach presents many problems in psychology and in theology[16] but it can result in rich and vibrant classroom work which will help children to have a deeper understanding of what it is like to be religious.

Notes

1 James, E.O., *The Tree of Life, an Archeological Study*, Studies in the History of Religions, supplements to Numen, XI, Leiden, 1966.
2 For textbooks, see Penguin Primary Project, Food, Barrett, M. (ed.) Penguin, 1973, and Deverson, H.J., *The Story of Bread*. Puffin Picture Book 119, Penguin, 1973, and Taylor, Dorothy, *Food* (Topic Books), Lutterworth Educational, 1971.
3 Humphrey, Robert, *Books* (Topic Books), Lutterworth Educational, 1971.
4 Smith, J.W.D., *Religious Education in a Secular Setting*, SCM Press, 1969, p. 86.
5 Tolkien, J.R.R., *Tree and Leaf*, 1964, p. 53. See also Eliade, Mircea, 'Myths and fairy tales', in *Myth and Reality*, 1963, pp. 195–202.
6 Stith Thompson (ed.), *Motif-Index of Folk Literature*, 1955–8, 6 vols.
7 Solzhenitsyn, A., *The First Circle*, Chapter 42. Fontana, 1968.
8 Chagall, M., *The Jerusalem Windows*, 1968, and Kandinsky, W., *Concerning the Spiritual in Art and Painting in Particular*, 1972.
9 Bachelard, G., *The Psychoanalysis of Fire*, 1964.
10 Flugel, J.C., *The Psychology of Clothes*, 1950.
11 Balint, Michael, *Thrills and Regressions*, 1959.
12 Eliade, M. *Images and Symbols, Studies in Religious Symbolism*, 1961, and Cirlot, Juan E., *A Dictionary of Symbols*, 1972.
13 For a pupils' textbook, see Taylor, Dorothy, *The Senses* (Topic Books), Lutterworth Educational, 1970.
14 McLuhan, M. and Flore, Q. *The Medium is the Massage*, 1971.
15 Ong, W.J. *The Presence of the Word*, Yale University Press, 1967. Ong offers the best theological reflection on the significance of listening and speaking in religious awareness, and I am indebted to him for some of my reflections on this subject.
16 C.f. this book p. 123. See my 'Theology of themes', *Scottish Journal of Theology*, 25, 1972, pp. 20–31.

PART IV

Religious Education and Christian Commitment

15. *Open Minds and Empty Hearts?*
Convergent and Divergent Teaching of Religion

It is often taken for granted that a religious person will want to pass on his faith to others. In the case of teachers of religion who are themselves religious, the assumption is that they will be obliged by their faith to try to pass their own religion on to their pupils in their religious education lessons. This assumption is perhaps stronger when we think of the great missionary religions like Islam and Christianity. But even with religions such as Hinduism and Judaism which are for various reasons not usually regarded as being so obviously committed to universal evangelization, it remains odd to many people that a member of such a faith should be happy and at ease, with no sense of hypocrisy or unfaithfulness to his own commitment, when he is teaching some other religion. But is this widespread assumption justified? Is there indeed something about commitment to a religion which logically and psychologically compels a believer always to seek to convert others to this faith? Or might it be the case that there are at least some religions or some types of religious commitment in which the believer, if he is an RE teacher, will be compelled to encourage a variety of responses to a variety of religions from his pupils? In the following pages we will discuss these two types of teacher, calling them either 'convergent' in their approach or 'divergent'.

Convergence and divergence

Some teachers of religious education simply teach what they believe. This one, for example, believes that the Bible is the Word of God, teaches that it is the Word of God, and hopes and intends that his pupils will form the same view. Another teacher believes that Islam is the most noble faith, teaches this, and hopes and intends that her pupils will come to see this. We may describe this situation as one of convergence, since the personal faith of the teacher converges with the content of his lessons and with his hopes for the pupils. Convergence may take a negative form, as when a teacher believes that the Bible is not the Word of God, teaches this, and expects his pupils to form the same conclusion. Convergence should be regarded as a general pattern of identity between faith-commitment, classroom work and teaching aims, which may not be apparent in every scheme of work. A convergent teacher, say a Catholic teacher in a Catholic school teaching Catholic pupils, may teach a course on world religions, having a content which he may see as diverging from his own commitment to Catholicism. His pattern of convergence may be shown in that he may treat the world religions objectively and from the outside, while Catholic teachings are taught from the inside and with the assumption of faith in his pupils. It may also sometimes happen that a convergent teacher is not very consistent, being, perhaps, naively convergent rather than self-consciously and deliberately convergent.

We may find another teacher who is a Christian but is teaching Islam as part of the worthwhile educational experience of the pupils, intending neither to deepen their faith in Islam nor to discourage it. Similarly, when this teacher teaches Christianity, although his or her faith and the lesson content do now in fact converge, the religion is similarly taught only for its educational value, without the intention of either fostering Christian faith or making it more difficult. In situations like these, the personal faith of the teacher diverges from the content and the aims of the teaching. Like convergence, divergence is a pattern which will be sharper or less sharp according to the particular syllabus, the pupils, and so on. It is a divergence in principle, which will actually appear more or less frequently. Divergent teachers, like their convergent colleagues, may be inconsistent or naive, and there may be some teachers of religion to whom questions like these have never occurred, and who could not be clearly diagnosed.

Convergence is a simpler situation than divergence. This is an immediate and obvious unity of life and work. Simple descriptions, however, can be oversimplifications, and before we can understand what is at stake between convergent and divergent teachers we must distinguish several kinds of teaching, and see that convergence occurs only in certain *kinds* of teaching. For the nature of teaching itself changes when viewed from converging and diverging perspectives.

A group of convergent teaching processes: nurture, evangelism and indoctrination

Religious nurture, the teaching activity which intends to foster or deepen the commitment of those who are already believers or already inside the religious community, is clearly a convergent process. Only a Muslim can nurture a child within Islam. The faith of the nurturer, the content, and the goal of his nurture are identical. This unity finds expression in a unified religious community, and nurture is a domestic activity of that community, taking place within the home, the church, mosque, synagogue or temple. Because it is specific to a community of faith, we should speak of *Christian* nurture, *Hindu* nurture and so on, and the theory and practice of religious upbringing will vary from one religion to another. Not only can nurture be offered only by a teacher whose own faith is also being nurtured in the same process, but it can be received only by a child or adult already inside that faith. The Christian nurturer deals only with children being brought up by their parents as Christians. Moreover, the goal of the nurture process is identical with the content and the learners – the Sikh teacher nurturing faith in the Sikh religion fails as a nurturer if his Sikh pupil forsakes Sikhism.

We can distinguish religious nurture from general encouragement. A Christian pupil may be encouraged by the understanding attitude of any patient and wise teacher who treats Christianity with respect although not himself a Christian believer. Indeed, teachers should encourage all noble commitments which their pupils possess, just as they should encourage virtue and discourage vice. This is quite different from the active process of Islamic upbringing, or the definite practice of Christian child-rearing.

The convergence of personal commitment on the part of the teacher with his lesson content and his teaching aims is seen still more clearly when we turn to evangelism and indoctrination. You do not sincerely evangelize someone with beliefs you do not hold yourself. There are cases where professional public relations firms are engaged to spread religious and political opinions, but they are merely agents of the evangelists and not evangelists themselves. In a similar way we might think of a teacher who imagines himself employed to teach religion in order to persuade children to go to church, and who might conscientiously do his best in that direction, although not a church-goer himself. But leaving such cases on one side, evangelism seems a pretty clear case of a convergent style of teaching. Of course, it differs from religious nurture in that it is addressed to anyone. Far from being confined to the existing members of the religion, it is usually directed towards non-adherents. But like religious nurture, it certainly seeks to establish convergence, in that the evangelist is not successful unless at least some of his hearers commit themselves to his message. He might not have failed in his *duty* if they do not respond. Nevertheless, his hope and intention is that some at least and all if possible shall respond. We can see then that the evangelist tries to establish the unity of convergence and the nurturer tries to deepen it.

The indoctrinator is prepared to sacrifice almost everything for the sake of convergence. Divergence and the freedom and variety of opinion which it entails are repellent to him. He does not want his pupils or subjects to think or choose for themselves but wants them to conform to his own likeness. Indoctrination can be offered both to those already committed and to those uncommitted, and in this sense it straddles nurture and evangelism, but it differs in that it is an assault upon the person of the hearer. Instead of displaying the reasons for choice, as happens in good evangelism, reasons are concealed and reason is bypassed. Differences between religious nurture and religious indoctrination will be more subtle, and will vary widely from religion to religion, but it is enough for our present purposes to say that there are certainly some religious child-rearing patterns in which to indoctrinate would be to deny the very ideal of life into which the child is being nurtured. Be that as it may, the central point is that in indoctrination a particularly rigorous or even ruthless attempt is made to secure convergence.

Education and divergence

The remarkable thing about education, and the feature which distinguishes it most vividly from the other teaching processes we have been considering, is that this convergence of the commitment of the teacher, the content of the teaching, and the commitment or desired commitment of the pupils, does not exist. A teacher can educate a pupil with respect to Islam whether he (the teacher) is a Muslim or not. Such education may be good or bad, sensitive or insensitive, skilful or crude. Such an education will not necessarily deepen the Islamic faith of the pupil (should he be a Muslim) although it certainly should not discourage him; it will not seek to convert him, although what will actually take place in the heart and mind of any pupil can never be known for sure beforehand by any teacher; it will certainly not indoctrinate him. But if it is good and successful it will educate him.

Moreover, just as good teachers can educate pupils in a religion whether they themselves are believers in that religion or not, so pupils can receive and benefit by such education whether they are members of the religion or not.

The reason why the 1975 *City of Birmingham Agreed Syllabus* was such an important landmark in the development of religious teaching in

Britain was because this was the first new Agreed Syllabus which was addressed to divergent teachers. It is a syllabus which can be taught by any well-trained and well-informed teacher, regardless of his faith, to any pupil whose interest can be caught, regardless of his faith. But the move from convergency to divergency which this implied became a thorny problem for many teachers, for the idea that they should teach something which was not identical with their own personal faith came as a shock to the naive convergent teacher and as a challenge to the shrewd one. The simple link between faith, content and aims was broken, for, to take an example, a successful piece of education about the resurrection of Jesus is not necessarily one after which the pupils come to believe that Jesus did indeed rise from the dead (that is, their commitment becomes identical with the obvious content of the less); it is, rather, a lesson after which the pupils come to know the accounts, stories and traditions of the resurrection, have a degree of insight into the ideas, feelings and actions inspired by these accounts, and have acquired some skills in studying and evaluating them from various points of view. Such evaluation might result in the pupil's forming the judgment that Jesus did, after all, rise from the dead, although it would not be in the formation of that judgment *per se* that his education would lie. He might, on the other hand, evaluate the stories as probably unreliable, but again, his education would lie in the way this judgment was reached and not in the opinion itself. Education does not seek or assume convergence. Any convergence there might be is the result of accident or individual psychology and not a matter of principle or intention. But with religious nurture, evangelism and indoctrination, divergence, if it occurs, is exceptional and accidental while convergence is assumed or sought as the pattern and the norm. For the convergent teacher, a divergent pupil represents a failure, but for the divergent teacher a convergent pupil does not necessarily represent a failure, for being educated is not simply a matter of what views are held but has to do with the way in which views are formed.

Must RE teachers have empty hearts?

If we were to see a lesson on the joy of Lord Krishna as he played his flute in the forest, and we knew that it was intended to be an evangelistic lesson (perhaps the teacher had told us so), we would then know what was in the heart of the teacher, assuming his sincerity: the joy of Krishna. And if we saw a lesson on Jesus as Lord given as part of a programme of Christian nurture in a Christian church or school, then also we would know what was in the heart of the teacher: Jesus as Lord. But if we saw an educational lesson on Lord Krishna or Lord Jesus or both, and knew that it was intended to be an educational experience, then, no matter how seriously we believed in the sincerity of the educator, we would not have an obvious way of knowing what, if anything, was in his heart. So we come to our central question. Is divergence a situation without commitment? Or (to put the same point more vividly) must RE teachers, in having open minds, also have empty hearts?

It is *possible* that the teacher who seeks to be a true educator *will* have an empty heart as far as any religious commitment is concerned. It is possible that such a teacher may be able to teach several religions without any problem of religious commitment simply because he is equally indifferent to all of them as concerning his personal faith. Where there is no commitment of a specifically religious kind, there can be no convergence of religious commitment and lesson content, and such teaching will meet the bare requirement of divergency. That will be sufficient to mark it off from religious nurture and evangelism. But there is, as we have seen, both good and bad education. It is perfectly possible that children would be able to learn more (let us think now of children learning rather than adults teaching) from sincere and interesting evangelism than from such bad education. This would not justify school evangelism; it would point to the need for improved education.

Heartless or uncommitted education, education in which the heart of the educator remains a mystery, has been a particular problem for the RE teacher in recent years in Britain. Part of the blame must lie with the false distinction between confessional and non-confessional teaching of religion, a distinction made popular by the 1971 Schools Council Working Paper 36, *Religious Education in Secondary Schools.*[1] Confessional or neo-confessional teaching was that teaching which sprang from the teacher's personal confession of faith whilst its opposite was that teaching which did not spring from personal faith but was professional. This shallow and harmful distinction has led to the view that there is and should be a gulf between having a personal faith and being a professional teacher of religion, suggesting that personal religious faith does not and could not illuminate good educational practice. The Working Paper was right in regarding *what it called* confessionalism as being other than education, but wrong in *calling it* confessionalism in the first place. Good education can be *as confessional* as good religious nurture and good evangelism, and the belief that it cannot leads to the teacher with the open mind and empty heart.

So far we have spoken of the teacher without a heart as the one whose lack of religious commitment made him a mystery to his pupils, or the one who felt that his duty required him to ignore his own religious commitment because of the assumption that religious commitment can lead only to convergence. There is another sense in which we might think of a teacher without a heart, namely, one who not only lacked a religious commitment but who also thought that being a good teacher was possible without deep commitment of any kind. The teacher who lacks religious commitment may still be a perfectly adequate RE teacher and even an excellent one, but it is hard to see how the teacher who does not see that teaching itself demands beliefs, values and commitments could be a successfully divergent teacher.

The reason why teachers with empty hearts in this second sense are likely to be bad educators is that divergence is itself a value, or a bundle of values. If divergence is to be expressed in good education in the classroom, it must be realized that it springs from commitments as deep as the commitment which is expressed in convergence.

Education and passion

The values expressed in divergent teaching are easy to identify. First, this truly educational teaching is directed to all pupils alike, since no distinction is made in divergent education between Christian pupils, Jewish pupils and pupils of no religious affiliation. This value is unique to the teacher who is an educator. The Christian nurture teacher is only dealing with his Christian pupils. The teacher who is an evangelist is speaking to all his pupils *except* those of his own faith, and in this way, the nurturer deals with one section of the class and the evangelist with the other. But who is to teach *all* the children? Moreover, although the teacher as evangelist is concerned with all the pupils except those who share his own faith, he is not concerned with them *as* Hindus, Jews or as secular young people. If he is a Christian evangelist he is concerned with them as *non*-Christian, as those who do *not* follow his way. They are, to him, the unconverted. Far from offering them encouragement in their own commitments, he would see his task as to win them to his own.

This availability of the teacher who is a true educator to all his pupils is part of what is meant by the neutrality of education. It does not mean that the teacher does not care but that he cares for them all, accepting them as they are. It does not mean that he is not committed, but that he is committed to them all. He recognizes his responsibility as a teacher to give equal support to all. It means that each child has the right, just because he is in the school and in the charge of the teacher, to expect that the teacher shall be *his* teacher. The teacher as religious nurturer *per se* cannot consistently express this value. His convergence prevents him from doing so. Possession of this value, availability to all, is the first mark of the superiority, in the pluralist schools of a democratic society, of education over all the other teaching processes. The others may be superior in other situations for which they are intended (for example, the church or in the media) but education rules in the county school.

But this availability of the teacher to all his pupils is a belief which must be felt in the heart, a conviction which must illuminate classroom practice, which makes education warm, personal and self-giving. When teaching in schools where potential divisions along social, ethnic or religious lines appear, the teacher as educator, committed to every child, must possess this commitment as a passion.

Second, the teacher as educator seeks certain kinds of lives for his pupils. His divergence does not mean that he does not have ideals for them. He wants them to learn to think for themselves. In this also he is unusual. The instructed pupil thinks what he is told to think. The socialized pupil thinks what others think. The evangelized pupil comes to think what the evangelist thinks. The indoctrinated pupil does not think at all, but merely conforms or echoes. The educated pupil thinks for himself.

But thinking for yourself is a value. It is difficult to attain, difficult to maintain. It is precious. It involves respect for the personality of the pupil. It requires great patience on the part of the teacher, and his constant vigilance. The teacher who teaches in this way must believe that the autonomous man or woman possesses a greater value than the merely pleasure-seeking man or woman, or the person fitted for life in the consumer society, or the one merely trained for the needs of industry. In a society where group pressures, consumer delights, and the daily appeal of a mindless acquisitiveness are all around us, belief in the dignity and value of the person who thinks for himself must be held with passion if it is not to be swallowed up.

The third value of divergence is inquiry. The teacher as religious nurturer, the evangelist and the indoctrinator seek to create or deepen their pupils' commitment to the content of their lessons, but the teacher as educator seeks to make his pupils critical of the content of his lessons. He asks many questions. It is not true that he gives no answers; he gives many answers, and more questions spring from every answer. There is no end to this process; indeed, one of the purposes of this teacher is that his pupils shall not cease their education simply because their schooling is over. They are to go on asking questions and finding answers which lead to more questions all their lives.

But is this not confusing for children? Yes, it is confusing, and not only for children. Choice is confusing. Democracy is more confusing than dictatorship and thinking for yourself is more confusing than being told what to think. Nothing could be more secure and simple than accepting indoctrination. This is why the teacher as educator takes an interest in developmental psychology, and in the idea of 'readiness' for various kinds and levels of educational content and method. Children, like all people, must be prepared for education, educated into education. Education is dangerous, but the danger and the confusion are acceptable not only because of the skill and the patience of teachers who handle them so as to benefit children, but because without them the values of independent thought and inquiry might never be found by the growing child. If we are teaching in schools where the value of inquiry is subordinate to the idea that we learn mainly in order to pass examinations or mainly to get a better job, then belief in the value of asking questions can only be maintained by the teacher for whom it has become a passion.

Divergence as a theological problem

These then are some examples of the commitment which lies in the heart of the teacher as true educator. The divergent quality of religious education is only a symptom of these deeper causes. But many teachers of religion will need to press deeper yet. What is the relation between *religious* commitment and commitment to the values which lead to divergence? Unlike the simple, convergent situation of the religious nurturer and the evangelist, the religious beliefs of the divergent teacher are mediated *through* the intervening values, and are not intruded directly into the teaching content and aims. Now it is easy to see that a religiously committed person would want to evangelize. But why would he *on religious grounds* want to educate? So it is that divergence, which stands between religious faith and the lesson content and aim, becomes a problem in theology.

But this is only a *possible* situation. The theological problem *need* not arise. It is quite possible for a teacher to educate his pupils in religion, expressing through divergence the educational values discussed above but combining these with his own non-religious outlook. A humanist, a non-religious existentialist or a secular liberal democrat might well have such values (although such teachers may be equally tempted to adopt convergent styles), and passionate possession of such humane and educational values expressed through divergence is not only necessary but sufficient for educational work in religious teaching as far as the question of commitment is concerned. Still, it is possible in theory and probable in practice that the religious educator may and will in fact possess religious faith.

Let us then consider the situation of these two kinds of teachers of religion, both kinds having religious faith, leaving aside the equally good teachers who lack religious faith. First, we have the religious nurturers, the evangelists and the indoctrinators. Their problem is that their commitment to convergence prevents them from becoming educators. Second, we have the religiously committed religious *educators*. Their problem is to see whether (and if so how) their religious beliefs support and even generate their educational work, that is, how to be confessionalist and (for that very reason) divergent and thus educational. The problem of the first group of teachers has no solution. They must simply resign themselves to not being true educators. They may find other teaching work. In the case of the religious indoctrinators, this will be other bad teaching work. In the case of the religious nurturers and evangelists, this will probably be other good teaching work, if what they are nurturing and evangelizing into is itself good.

For the second group, the religiously committed religious *educators*, the problem seems to be soluble in at least some cases. Finding the solution will depend on the kind of religious beliefs to which the teacher is committed, and we may suppose that within each of the major world religions there will be some varieties of religious belief which will hinder divergence and others which will facilitate it. The essential questions are: Does my religion help me to think for myself or does it require me to submit without question to authority? Does my religious commitment cause me to discover questions and do the answers provided by my religion lead me to further questions? Is this how being religious actually makes me live? And if the answer is yes, is this for merely psychological reasons connected with my temperament or is it a result of the beliefs themselves? Are the ideas of learning, autonomy and inquiry actually an integral part of my theological system?

There are religious systems, theologies, which meet the test of these questions, and which actually give rise to such questions. Religiously committed teachers who want to be religious educators must find such theologies. If they do not, they need not, like the convergent group, abandon their teaching since they will still be educators. But they may become those with open minds and empty hearts, unable to connect their deepest religious values with their work. Those on the other hand whose educational work is richest because their hearts are full, who are committed to divergence on religious grouds, will probably be those from whom young people will have most to learn about the life which is both open and passionate.

Notes

1 Schools Council Working Paper 36, *Religious Education in Secondary Schools* Evans/ Methuen, 1971.

Further reading

For an influential (and fully justified) attack upon 'confessionalism', see Schools Council Working Paper 36, *Religious Education in Secondary Schools*, Evans/Methuen Educational, 1971, pp. 30ff. Chapter 13 of the Working Paper, 'The Christian as RE teacher', pp. 92ff, is quite unsatisfactory in that it merely highlights the problem, offering no Christian reasons for the Christian's participation in teaching faiths other than his own. Professor Paul Hirst rejected the idea of an education springing from religious belief in his article 'Christian education: contradiction in terms', *Learning for Living*, 11, 4, 1972, pp. 6–11, and I have attempted to discuss his claims in 'Christian theology and educational theory: Can there be connections?', *British Journal of Educational Studies*, 24, 2, June 1976, pp. 127–43. The position of the Christian Education Movement on a Christian rationale for participation in a critical, exploring religious education was discussed in the Editorial, 'Are you a Christian?', *Learning for Living*, 16, 4, Summer 1977, pp. 146ff, and for an interesting denial of this possibility ('a Christian can *only* seek the cause of his own party'), see the letter from John Herbert in *Learning for Living*, 17, 2, Winter 1977, p. 97. More recently, Richard Wilkins has discussed the convergent/divergent distinction in his letter to the *British Journal of Religious Education*, 3, 3, Spring 1981, p. 108, and I have tried to show how Christian believers are required by their faith to enter into critical inquiry in my article, 'Christian nurture and critical openness', *Scottish Journal of Theology*, 1981 (reprinted in this volume).

16. *The Divergent Teacher, the Plural Society and the Christian Faith*

Two views of pluralist education

In a country inhabited by various ethnic, religious and cultural groups, there will be various views of education. There may be a Catholic view, a Quaker view, Islamic, Jewish and other religious views, alongside various secular understandings as well – education being seen as existential, vocational, national, etc. In so far as all these are truly views of education, we may speak of a plurality within education. Of course, some of these views might claim to be the only 'true' ones, the others being either false or not views of education at all but of something else like indoctrination. In that case, although we might not have a plurality *within* education, we would at least have plurality *about* education.

In addition to thinking of education or different views of education as springing *from* plurality, we may think of education as *leading* to pluralism. We might think of education as a liberal, enquiring, cultivating sort of activity, such that the ideal of being an educated person could *include* being an educated Christian person or an educated secular person and so on. We would then be saying that the nature and goals of education are compatible with being Christian, Jewish or secular but do not *require* any such specific religious or non-religious outcome in order to *be* education. We might go further and claim that in a society which contains a plurality of views within or about education, one task of education should be precisely to uncover that plurality, raise the distinctions to the conscious and critical level, and enable young people and adults from the various religious and secular communities to discover their vocation in that identity. On this view, education would tolerate or comprehend the plurality, whilst having cultural aims of its own (we may call this the weak sense of this view) or education might actively promote pluralism, fostering an informed, tolerant and intelligent pluralism (this may be called the strong sense of this view).

Of course, this view of education in which education actively promoted pluralism, whether in its weak or strong sense, is itself one of the views of education which were referred to in the first paragraph. Indeed, it is sometimes claimed that it is as deeply ideological as any of the other views in the first paragraph, springing (it is said) from liberal humanism and in that sense being a rival to the various Christian and other religious views. It is sometimes claimed that this view of education (that is, education as including or promoting pluralism) sees itself as possessing a kind of superior, neutral character by means of which it can judge or discriminate between the other, more obvious partisan views. Having described it as professing this kind of supreme impartiality, the opponents of this view go on to 'expose' it, showing that it really does have as much of a value system as the others.

In this hostile description of the view that education should itself include and promote pluralism there is, I think, some clarity and some confusion. The clarity lies in the perception that this view of education is indeed only a view which must be argued for like any other. The critics are correct in pointing out that this view springs from values which are characteristic of it and these values need to be made critically conscious. It may be true that some advocates of this pluralist view have described it as if it had some kind of innate authority, as if it were analytically true that education must be like this, and there have even been some attempts to claim the word 'education' for this view alone, consigning all the other pretending views to the realms of 'tribal instruction'. But generally, I think, exponents of the view that education should promote pluralism have seen quite clearly that this is certainly a value-laden position and not an objective, value-free height from which the 'lesser' and more 'partial' views of education could be assessed, itself free of assessment.

The confusion lies in the critic's belief that the view of education as promoting pluralism must be placed *alongside* the various Christian, Jewish and other views or should be seen as being placed *above* them, in some unconnected, alternative, or even judicial role. It seems to me that this is a possible interpretation of the relationship between the view of education as promoting pluralism and the Christian faith but not a necessary one. The plausibility of the opinion that it should be placed alongside in a position of rivalry would largely depend upon the type of Christian education with which it was being contrasted. One could certainly imagine certain views of Christian education, which would be evangelistic, instructional, or convergent in the sense that Christian education was seen as promoting nothing but Christianity and this view would certainly be in opposition with education seen as promoting not Christianity alone but pluralism. But has a convergent view of Christian education any greater claim upon the title 'Christian' than a divergent view? Since it is agreed that the view of education as promoting pluralism rests upon values and beliefs, might not these include Christian values and Christian beliefs? Might not Christian faith *generate* such a view of divergent education, education as fostering pluralism? Might not the relationship between Christian faith and such divergent education be that of a foundation to a superstructure, roots to a tree, rather than the relationship being that of disconnected and mutually judgmental rivals?

It is significant in discussing this relationship that one speaks of Christian faith as providing *a* foundation, not *the* foundation. Christian faith cannot possibly claim to be *the only possible* or actual foundation for an education which seeks to comprehend and foster pluralism. Such education may also be generated by the ideals of other religions and, for all I know, by secular humanism as well. Whether that situation should be regarded by Christians as an embarrassment is a moot point. Must Christians pursue only those goals which are not pursued by anyone else? Can exorcisms not be performed by those who 'follow not with us'? Seldom, if ever, are the signs of the Kingdom free from ambiguity, and education which promotes pluralism, a divergent education (which I believe to be one of the signs of the Kingdom) does have an in-built ambiguity in that it *may* be related to Christian faith and should be, but others will also contribute to it.

I have discussed two senses in which education may be pluralist, in that education may merely express or actively promote pluralism. Although different, these two views are related. It could be argued that education should be divergent even in societies which were not pluralist, since controversy and the presentation of critical alternatives might well be thought to be an important part of any worthwhile education. The second view, however, does take on much more obvious point and urgency in societies where there is plurality. In that case, the view that education should promote pluralism springs *from* pluralism as well as tending to encourage it.

Convergent and divergent teachers

We have already spoken of a 'convergent' Christian faith – that which seeks only its self-promulgation – and we have referred to education as being 'divergent' meaning that education is able to tolerate and even to promote a variety of religious and secular outcomes.[1] Elsewhere, I have applied this distinction to the religious education teacher, my purpose being partly to break down the false distinction between the 'confessional' teacher and the 'professional' teacher of religious education, where the classroom work of the former was inspired by his Christian faith. My view is that Christian faith may generate both convergent and divergent styles of teaching, and that there is an important sense in which the divergent teacher may be as confessionalist as the convergent teacher, if confessionalist means that one's teaching springs directly out of one's Christian faith. The ambiguity of pluralism which is reflected in the work of the divergent teacher may well spring from his Christian faith, it may equally well spring from his Jewish faith (if he possesses the necessary kind of Jewish faith) or he may be quite effectively divergent without having this supported by a religious faith of any kind. It is particularly important today to realize that although the work of the divergent teacher *need* not spring from any Christian faith, it *may* spring from such a faith.

It is perfectly possible that the same Christian faith should strengthen the Christian teacher in his convergent teaching in one situation (church, Sunday school) while strengthening his divergent teaching in another situation (teaching religious education in the state school). It is the connection between Christian faith and divergent teaching which people often find rather curious. One can see why a Christian would want to teach his faith so as to share it with others but why would he want to teach somebody else's faith? Why would a Christian, on Christian grounds and not merely as part of his professional work, want to teach Islam and Hinduism?

The divergent way of teaching is related to such values as openness, enquiry, dialogue and criticism. We must ask, therefore, whether when the Christian possesses such values it is *because of* religious faith or *in spite of* it. A crucial factor in determining the relationship between criticism and religious faith is the nature of the sacred literature which commands the obedience of the believer. It is not mere coincidence that Protestant Christianity with its emphasis on Biblical authority was probably the first modern tradition to establish a critical approach towards the Bible, for the Bible is a book which demands historical, documentary, textual and theological criticism. It would be wrong to see this criticism as hostile to faith or even independent of faith. It is a product of faith, because it is *demanded* by faith. The criticism of Protestantism, which has been 'commanded' by the Bible can be compared with the other kinds of criticism which are found in Orthodoxy, with its theology of iconography, and Catholicism, where, because of the papal and conciliar forms of authority, it has been expressed in questions about the development of doctrine and the relative weight of various centres of ecclesiastical authority. One can also contrast these forms of Christian criticism with the role of criticism in religious traditions where the sacred writings are not so complex. One thinks of the relative unimportance of textual criticism in Islam where there can be no possible doubt about the location of God's Word while in Christianity it is not only the interpretation which is prone to hermeneutical problems but, because of the multiplicity of texts and versions, the very location is perplexing. In the case of Protestant Christianity one had sacred scriptures, the complexity of which became more apparent as study continued. There could never be any question of restraining the constant flow of new translations, which were demanded by the very nature of Protestantism. The fact that the doctrine of progressive revelation, when it did come along in the late eighteenth and nineteenth centuries, was inspired by biological, historical or philosophical models and could not be enshrined in any single ecclesiastical custodian meant that the critical spirit of Christianity, always latent, now had the widest possible scope. Something of this can be seen in such Protestant educators as Friedrich Schleiermacher, Horace Bushnell and F.D. Maurice. These can be contrasted with Catholic educators such as John Henry Newman and Paulo Freire who are most certainly no less critical but whose criticism is of a different type.

The many types of Christian criticism have a common root in the critical attitude of the New Testament church. Once again, one could think of the sense in which there was a pluralism *within* Christianity[2] (that of Matthew and James, of Paul and Mark and of the Johannine circle) and of the sense in which there was a Christianity which fostered pluralism through awareness of ambiguities, through seeking to distinguish true from false within those ambiguities and through a simple acceptance of the ambiguities where their implications or inner meanings could not be reliably seen. So the wheat and the tares grew side by side. Let us look a little more closely at the kinds of criticism and openness which developed in the early Christian character as a result of exposure to this ambiguity and this plurality.

In Peter 1: 10–11 we read, 'the prophets who prophesised of the grace which was to be yours searched and enquired about this salvation – they enquired what person or time was indicated by the Spirit of Christ within them.' This type of enquiring and searching is certainly some way removed from the enquiring spirit which modern education seeks to impart to its pupils. The prophets are not thought of as examining the evidence to see whether the foretold was credible or not. Rather, they are thought of as conducting a spiritual search into the inner meaning of the prophecy, to discover what was certainly already there to be discovered, the truths hidden there. The sense is similar in John 5: 39, where the

Jews are spoken of as searching the scriptures. The Beroean Jews (Acts 17: 11) did display a spirit of enquiry somewhat closer to that which we meet today when they 'received the word with all eagerness, examining the Scriptures daily to see if these things were so'. But generally when the Spirit of God or Christ is described as searching, the reference is to a searching out or a bringing to light of what is already known, probing or testing, as when Christ searches the minds and hearts of men (Rev. 2: 23) or 'the Spirit searches everything even the depths of God' (1 Cor. 2: 10). But when this searching Spirit dwells in the hearts of believers, he enables them to search out what they did *not* know before, giving them spiritual insight and discerning power. So 'the spiritual man judges all things but is himself to be judged by no-one' (1 Cor. 2: 15). The penetrating power of the Spirit is spoken of in Rom. 8: 26-7, where human ignorance of what to pray for is overcome by the searching knowledge of the Spirit, too deep for words. This power of penetrating enquiry is to be turned outwards, as when Christians are advised to 'test the spirits to see whether they are of God' (1 John 4: 1), and inwards, as when the Corinthian Christians were told 'examine yourselves, to see whether you are holding to your faith, test yourselves' (2 Cor. 13: 5). The gift of discrimination follows from the knowledge of God's discrimination, his judgment between people. 'If we judged ourselves truly, we should not be judged. When we are judged by the Lord, we are chastened so that we may not be condemned along with the world' (1 Cor. 11: 31f). It is because the judgment of the Lord is expressed through his giving of himself in the bread and the wine (1 Cor. 11: 27) that Christians are not only to examine themselves before they partake, but also to discern the body of the Lord (vv. 28ff). We can see that the critical and discriminating spirit of the early church sprang not only from the Old Testament doctrine of the all-searching eye of God, but also from the peculiar tension of the early Christian community, poised between a given salvation and a not yet given vindication. It is this situation of being balanced on the edge of a great crisis, of being granted complete certainty yet enjoying it in uncertainty which gave the early Christian critical spirit its essential flavour. On the one hand, 'there is no condemnation' (Rom. 8: 1) and, on the other hand, 'the time has come for judgement to begin with the household of God' (1 Pet. 4: 17). Certainly there are times when this critical spirit of testing is to be suspended. When the Corinthian Christians sit down to dinner they are not to ask questions about the food set before them just for conscience's sake (1 Cor. 10: 25) and Paul acknowledges the limits of self-knowledge and self-criticism. 'It is a very small thing that I should be judged by you or by any human court. I do not even judge myself' (1 Cor. 4: 3).

The thought is that it is ultimately God who is the supreme tester and validator of hearts. 'It is the Lord who judges me' (1 Cor. 4: 4)

This enquiring spirit of the early church may be called eschatological criticism. It springs from the knowledge that the goal has not yet been grasped (Phil. 3: 12). The future not yet known (1 John 3: 2), the true and false grow side by side (Matt. 13: 30). Everything therefore was to be tested and that which survived the test to be held fast. 'You judge according to the flesh; I judge no-one, yet even if I do judge, my judgement is true, for it is not I alone that judge, but I and he that sent me' (John 8: 15f). The opposing poles of human error and divine insight are both found in the church which is in the world and therefore cannot assess, but which is also in the Spirit and therefore assesses everything. The criticism which we have seen to be so marked a feature of the early Christian existence sprang from the ambiguities which this situation posed. Were the prophets true or false? (1 John 4: 5). Were the miracles those of Christ or Anti-Christ? (Thess. 2: 9–12). Satan himself appears as an angel of light. One must always be vigilant, always watchful, ready for constant examination (Luke 12: 35–40).

The emphasis upon this critical, testing attitude was not a mere appendage to the Christian life but was part of the 'instruction of the Lord' and part of his chastening, which made the whole Christian life an experience of being in the School of Christ (Matt. 11: 29; 13: 52). In some senses, as we have seen, there were definite limits to this criticism. The question was, 'which *was* the wheat and which *were* the tares?', not whether there was any wheat! It was a matter of when and where Christ would come, not whether. And yet, in another sense, there were no limits to the spirit of criticism, for the situation was one from which only the End would bring any escape (1 Thess. 5: 1–11). Until the day when the perfect one came, the believer just had to go on peering into the dark mirror (1 Cor. 13: 12). This criticism was radical in that the tension between the old age and the new age was absolute. But the doubt and the criticism certainly belonged to the new kingdom, it was an aspect of the 'seed growing secretly' (Mark 4: 26–9). The critical doubt was an expression of life in the kingdom (Luke 12: 54–9), since it sprang out of the perception that the kingdom was, and yet was not. The critical testing of all things was thus a demand of Christian obedience (Mark 13: 5–6). It was directed towards the uncertainties but it sprang from the certainties. It was limited in that one knew there was wheat – it was unlimited in that one did not know *which* was wheat, and therefore the criticism was genuine, open and radical. Any child or young person growing up into this kingdom would have to grow up into that spirit of testing criticism, being examined and learning to examine. This was however an easy task because of the curious critical nature of the child himself, and because of the very nature of the kingdom. For unless the kingdom was received as a little child, it could not be entered (Mark 10: 15). For the child, such learning is natural, and it is the nature of the kingdom to consist of such critical, curious learners.[3]

I have not attempted to claim that the enquiring spirit of modern religious education as taught by the divergent teacher can be thought of as a simple product of New Testament Christianity. The nature of autonomy, the stages of personal development, the nature of the pluralism which surrounds it and our attitudes towards it, the nature and scope of reason and of secularity – all these are modern features of the situation, and have been created by a blending of ancient and modern, secular and religious ideas. But I do think that enough has been said to show that at least some of the seeds of the modern critical attitude may be found in New Testament Christianity, and enough has been said about the nature of Christian existence to see that there are sufficient similarities between the ambiguities which the early Christian faced and those which the modern teacher of religion in the secular, pluralist classroom faces. This teacher, if he is a Christian, is also a person placed between two worlds – the world of assured Christian belief and conviction which has nurtured him, and the world of open ideological and religious conflict within which his work as a teacher of religion is set.

I have tried to show that the relation between these two worlds is not one of conflict or opposition, as if the Christian teacher should leave his faith behind him when he enters that world of open enquiring teaching, but rather that his entry into that critical world is demanded by his Christian commitment. It is through his thoughtful, honest, well-informed and probing teaching of Islam, Hinduism and other religions that his Christian existence as a teacher will be demonstrated, and exactly the same spirit will be manifest in his teaching when the subject of his teaching happens to be Christianity itself. Everything is to be tested; we must examine ourselves and others.

The argument from a critical Christian existence through the work of the divergent teacher to the realization of a critical religious education dealing with world religions is central for the task of establishing guidelines for Christian education in a pluralist world. The only possible alternative to it would be one where the Christian convergent teacher taught his own faith beside teachers committed to other religious views who similarly took a convergent view of their teaching. This would lead to a situation which could be described as 'parallel religious nurture' but it would offer no rationale for a Christian conception of the religious education teacher as a professional educator in a plural situation. The approach outlined above combines Christian commitment with a professional role in education for the RE teacher, without seeking to absorb or control that role, yet seeking to show that the Christian participates fully in it not in spite of but because of his Christian commitment.

Notes

1 'Open minds and empty hearts: Commitment and the religious education teacher', in Jackson, R. (ed.) *Approaching World Religions*, John Murray, 1982.
2 Compare the idea of pluralism within Christianity with the idea of pluralism within education, as described in the opening paragraph of this study. On the other hand, Christianity and education, whether *containing* pluralism or not, may lead to or promote the development of pluralism.
3 These paragraphs on the biblical basis of Christian criticism were originally included in a paper submitted to a Working Party of the British Council of Churches and have since been published in *Understanding Christian Nurture*, BCC, 1981.

17. *Christian Faith and the Open Approach to Religious Education*

First, a word of explanation: I use the words 'open approach' because that is the expression which I have heard religious educators in Newfoundland using.* I think that I would prefer simply to speak of religious education, contrasting it with religious nurture or religious instruction, the implication being that just as education is necessarily open so religious education is necessarily open. If this were conceded, then the use of the word 'open' would become unnecessary. I also dislike the word 'open' because it suggests that the other kind of religious education is closed. 'Closed' seems to carry with it a pejorative connotation. The suggestion seems to be that 'open' is better than 'closed'. My own belief is that we are dealing here not with a good process and a bad process but with two different processes, each one of which is good in its proper situation. I refer, of course, to religious education and to Christian nurture. Christian nurture is a convergent activity and perhaps in some senses it may therefore be thought of as being closed, in the sense that the Christian nurturer certainly intends and hopes that the outcome of his work will be Christians and no other; but it would be wrong to describe this as if it were in some way inferior to a critical and exploratory religious education.

I do not regard these two processes as being inferior or superior the one to the other, and I think we should avoid such emotive expressions as 'open' or 'closed' or 'confessional' when used as a derogative title, and try instead to find simple descriptive labels like Christian nurture or religious education which describe the processes without evaluating them over against each other.

My intention here is to discuss the relationship of Christian faith to religious education. The latter is conceived of as an open, critical process of learning in the religious area which is fully part of the total educational

* This is the edited version of a lecture given at a colloquium held in Newfoundland.

experience of the young person and is to be distinguished from Christian nurture in that the latter process is addressed by Christians to Christians in the attempt to foster and deepen Christian faith whereas the former is offered by teachers who may or may not be Christians to people who may or may not be Christians in the attempt to deepen their education in the religious area and to promote their personal development with respect to religion, without, however, prescribing that this development will necessarily lead them away from or towards religious ways of life.

In speaking about the relationship of Christian faith to such religious education I do not imply that the relationship is a necessary one. It would be equally possible to discuss the relationship between a humanist (atheist) view of life and religious education or between Judaism and religious education. The point is that each teacher offering religion, whatever his values and way of life, must find some way of reconciling these values and beliefs with his professional work as a teacher. He must find some way of coming to terms with the content of his classroom work and with his professional objections. I believe that any or all of these commitments (humanist, Jewish, Christian, etc.) are *possible* for the teacher of religious education. I am concerned with those persons who take what seem to me to be extreme positions – on the one hand those who claim that it is *necessary* for a religious education teacher to be a Christian, and on the other hand those who argue that it is impossible for a religious education teacher to derive his professional inspiration from the Christian faith. My own belief is that it is not necessary or impossible. It is simply possible! But how can that possibility be understood? Why do some people think that it is a non-Christian activity to engage in the kind of religious education with which we are concerned?

Another approach to the question is to ask whether a Christian can be an educated person. For if a Christian cannot be a religious educator, that will be for the very same reasons which will make it difficult if not impossible for the Christian to be educated himself. The difficulty lies, for those who feel it, in the fact (as it is sometimes thought to be) that Christianity is based upon authority while education is based upon inquiry. Christianity is thought to be a finished product, given by God in a form finally determined, whilst education is committed to a life-long process of growth, development, and change. Christianity is thought of as given in revelation, a revelation absolute in its demand and towards which the recipient makes no contribution but remains in a state of mere acceptance, whilst education is conceived of as having largely (although, of course, not exclusively) to do with human rationality. The Christian person, we might sometimes think, believes what he is taught to believe, thinks what he is told to think, whether it be church, Bible, or tradition, whereas the educated person thinks for himself. But how can a Christian think for himself? Is not the Christian supposed to take into himself the mind of Christ? Is it not a case of no longer I but Christ? Are we not to cast down every proud thought and to bring human reason into captivity? Do we not see in education an example of human reason exalting itself against the revelation of God? Do we not see in education an example of the pride and self-sufficiency of man which seeks to achieve adequacy in itself without recourse to God?

It cannot be denied that there are such conceptions of Christian faith, and that there are forms of Christian faith which can only flow into instruction (an authoritative or authoritarian transmission of a fixed body of truth) just as there are forms of Christian faith which naturally yield indoctrination, others which generate theologies of Christian growth and others which support the understanding of education and consequently of religious education which we have been considering. I believe that the situation regarding Christian faith and what I shall call critical openness, looking upon that quality as the heart of the religious education enterprise, is such that far from Christian faith being at odds with this view of religious education, it in fact impells the Christian believer towards it. I believe consequently that the form of religious education which we are discussing here is the product of Christian faith, not that it may never proceed from anything but Christian faith, but that it is not only fully consistent with but may for the Christian believer actually be drawn from his Christian faith. I shall illustrate this by reference to several examples.

First example: textual criticism

It is interesting to contrast the nature of the Islamic and the Christian obedience to sacred scriptures. In the case of the Moslem, his obedience to scripture is rather a straightforward matter, not only because the Koran itself is a briefer and relatively more homogeneous book, written by one man within a fairly short space of years, but because there is very little dispute within Islam as to the exact text of the Koran. This means that the one who wishes to submit himself to the Koran may do so in unambiguous confidence that he knows exactly what he is submitting himself to because he has it there in front of him word by word, letter by letter. In the case of the Christian, the situation is very different. There exist hundreds and thousands of copies of the text of the Old and New Testaments, many of them in the ancient libraries of Europe, not even edited or published. There is hardly a verse or a sentence in the Bible for which there does not already exist literally dozens of variants, and almost every year as new texts are recovered and edited further variants come to light. Admittedly most of these variants are of a trivial nature but many are not, and in any case the principle is the important thing. Whereas the Moslem has one text of the Koran which stays the same from generation to generation, the Christian must look for a new Greek and Hebrew text of the Bible in every generation. We see, of course, innumerable examples of Christians who close their hearts and minds to this truth about the nature of the word of God to which they profess obedience, fixing their entire devotion and intellectual life upon the Bible as produced by one particular generation of Christians in the past, and failing to realize that this obedience of theirs can be nothing but disobedience, since they are neglecting the manner in which it has pleased God, according to Christian faith, to make known to men and women his word. The implication, which makes the science of textual criticism a necessity demanded by faith itself, is that in giving his obedience to the word of God in the Bible the Christian does not know with final and detailed certainty what he is giving his obedience to. His obedience drives him towards inquiry. Just as a lover is driven by his love towards a lifetime of loving inquiry into the nature and needs of his beloved, who for him will never remain static but will always be a growing and deepening wonder because he or she is a growing person, who can never be finally and absolutely fixed and held like a dead butterfly on a pin, so it is in the relationship between the lover of God and the Bible. He does not critically inquire into the Bible in spite of his love. His love leaves him no options. His love cannot be expressed in any way other than by such critical inquiry because that inquiry is a demand created by the nature of the thing itself which is loved, namely, the Bible expressed as it is in all of these hundreds of thousands of texts. There is no conceivable end to this process. Even if the number of new manuscripts and the process of textual collation began to decline there would still be absolutely no security against the possibility not only that errors had been made in the reconstruction of the text from the existing documents but that one further document might someday be found in some isolated monastery which would raise again questions which had been thought to be closed long since. The Christian believer is therefore cast by the nature of his faith into a lifetime of faithful intellectual pilgrimage. This is the nature of Christian existence before the word of God. And this is surely why it can be claimed that one of the glories of Christian faith is its spirit of criticism, and of self-criticism; surely it is thus no accident that education as we know it in the West has emerged in conjunction with the

Greek spirit in Christian lands. It is the same spirit of criticism which is part of the logic of Christian faith which has encouraged if not actually created the critical spirit of the West in science, history or geography, in religion and in education.

Second example: The biblical roots of Christian criticism

It is sometimes claimed that the spirit of critical openness is a modern creation. The fact is that it is central in New Testament Christianity. If you carefully look through the New Testament books, particularly the Epistles, you will find numerous examples of exhortations and appeals to Christians to maintain an alert, watchful, vigilant, inquiring and discriminating spirit. We are to test the spirits because many false spirits have gone out into the world. Is it a true Messiah or a false Messiah? A true or a false prophet? There are false miracles which could perhaps deceive even the elect, and Satan himself is transformed into an angel of light. We are to examine ourselves whether we are in faith, and we are told, when we approach the Lord's table, to judge ourselves lest we be judged by the Lord, making sure that we discern the Lord's body. In the synoptic gospels Jesus also continually challenges the assumptions of his heirs, his parables being a method of raising as many questions as the answers they gave. We are to look out for the signs of his coming, being on our guard lest we fall asleep at night, for the day comes like a thief in the night, we are sent out as sheep in the midst of wolves, therefore, being as wise as serpents.

This situation is created for the New Testament church by the fact that it is a church of the apocalyptic period, a people of God living on after the coming of Messiah but before his final coming. The church knew that the kingdom had come and yet it was still to come. In this in-between age nothing was clear and sharp. Tares and wheat were sown together. One knew that both were there but no-one had such certainty about which were which that the process of weeding could begin. The good and the bad fish were together in the net. We see in a glass darkly but only then as we are ourselves seen by God. It is this in-between age which is the essence of the Christian critical, inquiring attitude both internally, towards the church, and towards the outside world. The Christian who does not live like this has abandoned a significant feature of New Testament Christianity.

Third example: The Christian view of man

Education is based upon the notion that human beings grow, learn and develop. In Christian faith, man is similarly thought of as being unfinished. Our humanity is incomplete. The image of God in Christ is being daily renewed in us but we know that we have not attained nor are yet made perfect, that we run in order that we may obtain. When Paul remarks that when as a child he thought like a child but when he became a man he put away childish things, he does not mean to suggest that now he is a man! The thought is rather that he is still a child. This is clearly shown by the context in which seeing in a glass darkly is paralleled by 'when I was a child'. The manhood is still to come, just as the perfect knowledge will one day transcend the partial knowledge. In 1 John 3: 1–2 the apostle writes about the Christian view of man, remarking that we know that now we are the children of God but we do not know what we will become, except that we shall be like him for we shall see him as he is. This again expresses the idea of Christian man as unfinished man. We may note also that education as a process can never be finished. The instruction process has a beginning, a middle, and an end. It is complete when the skill or the knowledge which it conveys is acquired. There is a logical maximum of instruction beyond which instruction can go no further. The same is true of education when it is conceived of as socialization which is finished when one's behaviour conforms thoroughly to that of one's surroundings, or to schooling, which is complete when one leaves the institution. But education as such can never be complete, because it has to do with the achievement of personhood, and that is a life-long task. We see thus that Christian anthropology and a developmental view of human personhood go hand in hand.

Fourth example: God and authority

Let us distinguish between two concepts of authority, first the authoritarian and second the authoritative. The authoritarian is an authority without criteria, which offers no reasons either for rejecting or accepting it. The authoritarian official is right because he holds the office; the authoritarian book is true because it says so. The authoritative person has his authority because of certain reasons. His authority is criteria-referenced. He is right because of his experience or his wisdom or his legitimate elected office. The authoritative report is full of authority because of the breadth of research which lies behind it or because of the quality of its argument. Again, this is authority with criteria.

Is the authority of God to be conceived of as authoritative or as authoritarian? Augustine thought that there were reasons for God's predestination of the elect and for his failing to elect the mass of mankind, but we are ignorant of the reasons. Calvin thought that there were no reasons. God predestines some and reprobates others according to his will alone. There are no criteria. But if there are no criteria there is no way whereby faith can be distinguished from credulity. Consequently, there is no way for faith to purge itself, no way for faith to become more faithful.

We all know how baffling the authoritarian personality is, when as a child you asked your parents 'why'. If they could not think of 'why' they sometimes lost patience and shouted out, 'Do as you're told!' Well, you do as you are told, but you feel baffled, mystified, even perhaps resentful. You have made no progress in your knowledge of your parent or of yourself. We all know the experience of having an unpredictable friend. 'Will you come with me to see such and such a film?' 'No.' 'Why not?' 'I don't know, I just don't want to.' (Later) 'Well, alright I will go.' 'What made you change your mind?' 'I don't know, I just decided.'

Now it is true that God, like all personhood, is mysterious. Not everything in God or about God can be apprehended by reason. But, on the other hand, there is nothing in God or about God which casts reason into confusion. Reason is transcended indeed, but it is never baffled. Reason never retires broken and distracted, although it often bows transcended by wonder. You can and should trust God in the dark, but you cannot and should not trust a dark God. God is light and in him there is no darkness at all. The inquiring faithful spirit, entering into communion with God, is not met by the darkness of an arbitrary will, but is drawn further and further into the dazzling mystery of an eternal light.

The choice is clear. Either God is a dictator or he is not. But what kind of a God are we dealing with in Christian faith? Hopefully, we have to do with a God who gives himself in covenant relationship with men and women whom he calls to walk before him not as slaves but as sons and daughters, advancing in love and trust and responsibility with him, becoming more truly like him, advancing in personhood, as he in heaven is Person. If this is so, it must follow that God, who cannot be inconsistent with himself and with his goals, must not use those means which are compatible with his ends. But his end is person-making. Authoritarianism is hostile towards person-making. If you always respond to your child by saying, 'Stop it or I'll hit you', and never by saying, 'Stop it you're hurting him!', you will never expose your child to consideration of others, to the ethical and rational grounds of behavior, and he will always be dependent upon the external force of your presence which when removed will leave him irresponsible and immature. He will never be anything other than a puppet or an animal controlled by your will or conditioned by the kind of response he expects to receive from you. To advance towards personhood he must advance in responsibility, in rationality, in the exercise of choice, and in the discrimination by the situations which exhibit to a greater or lesser degree criteria which he has come to value for himself. If this is true of earthly fathers, how much more true it is of our heavenly Father. He also, in wishing to advance us in fellowship with himself (and what fellowship can a puppet or a dog have with its master in comparison with the fellowship that a man has with his friend?), commits himself to presenting himself to man not as an authoritarian God but as an authoritative one – one who calls out, 'Come and let us reason together', one who asks of Adam where he is. God has made us for fellowship with himself. But just as the fellowship of heart with heart is love so the fellowship of mind with mind is critical openness, and this because of criteria derived from the notion of mind itself. And our dealings are with a God, and a God man, who is *logos* as well as *agape*.

We can see therefore that just as the Christian who seeks to obey the word of God presented to him in this certain form cannot but be impelled by that very obedience towards criticism of that very word, the Christian who is bound in covenant obedience to a God who presents himself as a God for man, a God who will give himself to man and for man, is committed because of that very obedience to scrutinize, indeed to criticize, that God. For God offers himself in the context of criteria. 'I am the Lord your God who brought you up out of the land of Egypt' – not any old God but this particular God in this particular situation made known in these particular ways by these particular acts which become the criteria for acknowledging and recognizing and obeying him. But if there are criteria, they must be distinguished, understood, arranged and evaluated in order of priority. There was in the history of Israel a movement of prophecy, which very largely consisted of a sustained critique not only of the temple, of the sacrificial system, of the people's patterns of popular piety, but of the popular notion of Yahweh himself, in which earlier and unworthy ideas of God were ousted by more faithful obedience and clear perception springing from richer and more personal fellowship.

We see thus that for the Christian to live the life of critical openness is in no way to exalt human reason above the revelation of God. Rather, it is to exalt God himself who in his wisdom has made man in his image and called him to be his son.

Fifth example: Christian spirituality

It is sometimes thought that the Christian is called to passive obedience. We are a flock, sheep, hence easily lead; we are dependent – branches of the vine; we are to be trustful and accepting like little children; we are to take up our cross not our syllogism. On the other hand, we are called by Christ to be learners, his disciples, 'mathetai', we are to be as wise as serpents; we are to reckon up the cost like the wise king before going out to battle, constantly challenged by the questions and demands of Christ – what think ye?

The spirit of critical openness is not the servile spirit of fear, but it is the humble attitude of the one who knows that he still has much to learn. Far from the spirit of Christian criticism being a proud spirit, it is the very opposite of complacency. It represents the casting off of the old clichés, the old securities and the conventions – which is part of the risk in responding to the challenge of the kingdom.

It is not surprising, in view of these remarks, that religious education as we see it emerging today is found in countries like Newfoundland and England, Australia and West Germany, Scotland, and Holland. I remember being present in the city of Birmingham Council Chamber on the day when the 1975 Birmingham Syllabus was finally accepted. A Moslem member of the committee approached me and a colleague, saying that he and other Moslems were very pleased with the Islamic syllabus in the teacher's Handbook, indeed, he added, they would be perfectly prepared to teach it to their own young people in the mosques. But, he continued, what you must realize is that this syllabus, good in itself, is placed in a context which is Christian through and through. What he meant, I think, is that you do not find in Pakistan Islam taught in the government schools alongside Christianity, Sikhism, Hinduism, Judaism, communism and humanism without commending anyone in particular or attacking anyone in particular. You do not find this kind of religious education in Soviet Russia or in Communist China, in Lutheran Norway (although it is beginning to appear), or in 'Christian' South Africa, but only in the democracies of the West. I believe the reason is that this kind of religious education, along with the two- or three-party system of government and the freedom of the press and the notion of human rights, is one of the basic features of our democracies. This kind of *education* is central to democracy, and religious education as we see it emerging is one of the most characteristic and progressive parts of this form of education. And this also is why in Britain today, where such religious education is perhaps more mature than in any other part of the world, it has been created with the help and leadership of humanists and members of non-Christian faiths, but its principal leaders and defenders have been Christian educators who have seen in this form of religious education an appropriate, indeed the only appropriate, form of the Christian presence in education today. Therefore, it seems inappropriate to compare and contrast religious education with Christian education. I have noticed this contrast made in quite a few discussions here in Newfoundland. I think the expression 'Christian education' may be used in three senses, two of which are misleading. It may refer to that process which intends to create or to deepen Christian faith. I think it is clearer if for this process we use the expression 'Christian nurture'. It may also be used for that religious education which has a study of Christianity as all or part of its content. I think that in this sense it is better to use the expression 'Christian studies'. The third sense is when we speak of a Christian philosophy or theology of education, that education which may or must flow from Christian principles (although we need not be committed to the view that it may flow *only* from Christian principles). In the latter, the only useful sense for the expression 'Christian education', we may see that religious education as an open, critical, descriptive study of world religions, which seeks to advance the humane personal development of children and young people, is a part of Christian education, and indeed as Christian a part as any other part of education could be. It is not the same as Christian nurture; it does not have the same objectives – its content will often differ. That does not make it less Christian. The one who plants, the one who waters, the one who harvests – all have an equal title to the word 'Christian'. Therefore, I think religious educators who are Christians should have no fears about the Christian legitimacy of their work promoting an open, secular, critical view of religious education, which will be fully respectable educationally and will contribute to the developing needs of children and young people. We have good reasons for doing this work, not only as teachers and educators but as *Christian* teachers and educators. This work may be seen as a calling from God. We may indeed fully believe that the decision to promote and defend this kind of religious education rather than the evangelistic or the nurturing kind is a responsibility laid upon us by the Gospel and is part of our obedience to that Gospel.

18. *Christian Nurture and Critical Openness*

Background

The nature of Christian upbringing today needs to be redefined. There can no longer be an easy identification of Christian development with general education. Religious education within the state school systems of modern pluralist democracies cannot be regarded as intending to nurture Christian faith.[1] But how can Christian nurture be distinguished from good education on the one hand and indoctrination on the other?

An outline of the problem was offered in *School Worship, an Obituary* (1975) but in the discussions which lay behind *The Child in the Church* report (British Council of Churches, 1976) it became clearer that Christian nurture must somehow include the idea of critical openness.

> A religion can only encourage the personal freedom of its young people towards their future if the religion is free with regard to its own future. If Christian faith sought merely to reduplicate itself, to form young Christians who were the exact repetition of the previous generation, to pass on Christian faith as if it were like a parcel handed down from generation to generation, then it would be very difficult to distinguish between the passing on of this sort of thing and closed, authoritative instruction or even indoctrination. (para. 59)

The report suggested (para. 60) that the clue lay in the thought that 'Christian faith is constantly critical of itself'. This was seen (para. 62) as the root of the power of the Christian faith to generate an understanding both of general education as open and inquiring, and of Christian nurture as being other than indoctrination.

But *The Child in the Church* does not carry the discussion much further. The section ends with the thought 'that when Christians seek to nurture their young into Christian faith, they ... do not fully know what they are nurturing them into' (para. 63) and with the enigmatic statement, 'What we pass on to our children is not the painting but the paint box.' This was one of the areas in which the working party thought further reflection necessary, 'since the renewal of the Churches' ministry in nurturing both children and adults requires for its support a theology which sees critical openness as springing from Christian commitment' (Recommendation B5). The following remarks are an attempt to carry the discussion a little further.

Section one: The problem defined

We are dealing with a problem in practical theology, or a problem of applicability. We must first place the question of critical openness within the nature of practical theology.

In a changing world an unchanging theology soon becomes irrelevant. A theology which is baldly declared, merely proclaimed or applied without pausing to listen and to examine itself presumes for itself an authority which will no longer be recognized. If practical theology is thought of as theology seeking to be related to the problems and possibilities of human life both inside and outside the community of faith, then critical openness must be a key feature of its method, defining (not exhaustively, of course) the stance it will adopt towards itself and towards the world of human aspiration, achievement and sin, of which it is a part.

Because documents from the past require constant reinterpretation, critical openness is a central feature of hermeneutics, and so becomes relevant to the branches of practical theology concerned with the theological criticism of history and literature. Critical openness is equally relevant in theological appraisal of the physical sciences, where new claims to knowledge are continually challenging the adequacy of existing claims to knowledge. When we come to the social sciences we find that critical openness is significant in the dialogue between theology and all the disciplines which conceive of development as guided by learning. These include aspects of psychotherapy, politics, education (all these are in principle outside the community of faith) and Christian nurture (inside the community of faith).

An instructed person thinks what he is told to think, a socialized person thinks what others think, an indoctrinated person does not really think at all, an educated person thinks for himself. 'Thinking for yourself' certainly does not mean 'thinking whatever you like'. It is neither egocentric nor heteronomous. To think for yourself means that irrational authority (that is, authoritarianism) is rejected, you accept responsibility for your own beliefs and for the actions flowing from them, and you adopt an attitude of appraisal towards your previously and presently held beliefs.[2]

Autonomy of judgment is acquired through a process of growth, so that although it may not make much sense to speak of *training* a person in autonomy it does make sense to speak of his autonomy being fostered, encouraged or *nurtured*. Autonomy may be lost not only to other people but also to your own past self. If my past self directs my thinking to the point of preventing me from responding with suitable creativity to the problems of today, then I have lapsed into heteronomy.[3] We must not only grow to reach autonomy; we must continue growing to retain autonomy.

Other aspects of education exhibit similar features. The very idea of learning implies a willingness to see the limitation of what is known, and to respect the unknown, or be curious about it and so open towards it. Curriculum development requires critical criteria for content selection, and the problem of evaluating curricula also calls for clarification of values. So the educator can be thought of as professionally 'thinking for himself'.

We could build up a picture of education in which critical openness was a distinguishing feature, marking off education from training, which is imitative and thus heteronomous, and from instruction, which is marked by obedience to authority.

'Thinking for yourself' is being used here as a popular slogan including both autonomy and critical openness. Although autonomy (literally 'self-directed law', or 'self-originated principle') requires one to be open to the call of reason, it can suggest a degree of independence and even self-enclosed independence, which the expression 'critical openness' does not evoke. Critical openness suggests listening, respecting, being interdependent, being in relation, and it conveys a meaning which is closer to Christian faith, while retaining the force of the more widely used word 'autonomy'. It would be an oversimplification to suggest that there is only one concept of autonomy in educational philosophy, or one kind of critical openness in religion. Critical openness in Islam may mean the process of drawing contemporary inferences from a received theological structure, or in Hinduism the devotional and intellectual consequences of the relation between the one and the many. But enough has been said to show how the way the idea occurs in modern Western education creates this challenge for Christian thought: can a Christian 'think for himself'? Can he be an educated person? And how can Christian processes of upbringing avoid invidious comparisons with general education, which will seem more noble since it includes the ideal of autonomy?

Christian nurture and critical openness

Christian nurture is offered by Christians to Christians in order to strengthen Christian faith and to develop Christian character. It is easily distinguished from general education, since the latter does not *intend* the building up of Christian faith (although it may in passing have this effect), nor *must* the teachers of general education be Christian (although they may be). It is possible but not necessary to base general education on Christian faith, but it is necessary that Christian nurture should spring from and be defined by Christian faith. It is because Christian nurture is set in a certain community (the Church), the beliefs of which are controversial in society at large, that it may appear to be a form of indoctrination. This is indeed apparently the case with the teaching methods of several religious communities (currently the Korean Moon sect) which attract public attention through their practice of separating young adherents from their schools and families in order to present their teachings with as little distraction as possible, and to avoid the relativizing effect of living side by side with different religious and non-religious communities. It is probably true that the reaction of religious groups to pluralism has usually been to create special residential areas. No doubt the Christian, Jewish and Muslim quarters of cities in the Middle East are not only congenial from the cultural and language points of view, but also simplify the process of passing on religious traditions. But such religious apartheid is ill at ease with the mobility, the mass communications and the common schools of the Western democracies. As *The Child in the Church* report states, 'Any nurturing group which seeks to work in the middle of a plural society in which an open, critical kind of education is functioning will be exposed to the charge that it is indoctrinatory, simply because it selects one possible future (in the case of Christian nurture, a Christian future) and ignores others' (para. 58). In a society where everything is to be examined, how can a process in which some things are not to be examined (if that is what Christian nurture comes to) escape inferior status? At this point, it may look as if Christian nurture has close affinities with anti-autonomous and conformist processes. *The Child in the Church* report argues that 'more open' does not necessarily mean 'better'. This is perfectly correct, but only a closer examination of the relation between Christian nurture and critical openness will dispel remaining doubts.

If Christians were content (as some seem to be) to let education have a monopoly of critical openness and to allow Christian nurture to be assimilated into Christian instruction or even Christian (sic) indoctrination this particular problem would be solved. It would then simply be the case that critical openness had little part to play in Christian upbringing.[4] But other problems would be created. *Either* Christian parents think that critical openness is good for other people's children but not for their own, *or* they think it bad for everyone's children, *or* they think it good in general for other children and for their own but not in areas connected with Christian upbringing. In the first case Christian participation in education becomes more difficult, since a basic feature of education is admitted to be alien to Christian upbringing. We would have Christian children withdrawn from religious education classes or from the public schools altogether.[5] The second position, although more consistent, means the breakdown of the Christian enterprise in modern education and the triumph, in Christian circles, of authoritarian instruction. The last position is the worst of all, since the conflict is internal to the young Christian. He may now think for himself in every area except that which is expected to be his deepest commitment. Such a policy will not attract worthwhile youngsters for five minutes, nor would it deserve to.

If Christian nurture were to be collapsed into Christian instruction the idea of being a Christian person would also have changed. Just as education, instruction, socialization, indoctrination and so on imply different views of man, so Christian nurture, Christian instruction, Christian training and so on imply different views of Christian man. Are Christians to be conformist, passive acceptors of authority, unable to adapt to crises, too set in the received ways to think creatively? Only a Christian nurtured in critical opennness can have characteristics other than these. For those who think (as I do) that this *other* Christian life is essential for the continued vitality and relevance of Christian faith, the problem of how Christian nurture can be like education in possessing critical openness, yet unlike education in intending Christian life and faith, is a central concern.

Section two: Theological notes on critical openness

So far we have been considering critical openness as a problem for practical theology with respect to an area outside the community of faith (general education) and inside (Christian nurture). But difficulties in applying theology usually lead back to problems of conceptual coherence within the belief structure itself. The matter was simpler when upbringing processes within the church were modelled on secular education (theories of psychological development and so on). When an explicitly Christian rationale is sought for Christian nurture today, the main difficulty is whether critical openness can be accommodated within the framework of Christian belief.

Four areas where this tension is apparent are selected for comment. This list is not exhaustive.

1 Finality

If Christian faith is complete and perfect, how can there be room for the exercise of critical openness upon it and within it? One could be critically open towards the outside world, but surely not towards the faith itself?

2 Authority

Does not critical openness seem incompatible with the respectful acceptance which the Christian ought to have towards 'that which has been received from the Lord'? Does it not undermine the teaching office of the church by overemphasizing individual judgment? Is it not far removed from the childlike trust which a creature should have towards the Creator?

3 Revelation

Does not critical openness exalt the reason of man above the Word of God?

4 Spirituality

Is not critical openness hostile to the spirit of discipleship? Surely we are called not to criticize but to follow, to take up our crosses not our syllogisms? Does not the note of detached reserve in critical openness quench the utter abandonment which is demanded of those who would enter the kingdom?

Discussion

1   Finality

Perhaps we could distinguish finality in principle from actual finality. This could give us something like John Henry Newman's understanding of the development of doctrine. What was implicit becomes explicit as the tradition develops. There is a consistent unfolding. In its Protestant form, the approach subjects the ongoing church and its theology to criticism by the Word of God.

> The attitude of the Presbyterian churches towards their Confession of Faith, which they accept and at the same time criticise, may appear to be anomalous, but it is in accordance with the Confession itself. For the central principle of the Reformed faith, which it asserts, is that the Word of God is the only infallible rule of faith and practice, and that no other document ... can be regarded in the same light.[6]

Clearly this approach leaves room for considerable criticism. The actual Church can be assessed by the norms of the real Church. The notion that the faith may be expressed more and more fully means that criteria for its fuller expression have to be considered and so there is scope for creative work in the life and faith of the Church.

But how are the essentials to be criticized? How is the concept of the 'real Church' to be scrutinized? This approach seems to encourage the notion of a permanent essence of Christianity, different from the actual faith which is its temporary linguistic and cultural garb. The distinction between potential and actual finality thus becomes a device for limiting the operation of critical openness.

A second possible approach would be to distinguish the finality of experience from the finality of thought. The idea of the finality of the work of Christ can refer to its experienced religious adequacy. I may find that tomorrow I am even more deeply satisfied. That would not carry the implication that yesterday my satisfaction was less than complete for me as I was then. I may grow in my capacity for experiencing the profound beauty of the cross of Christ, without ever being conscious of dissatisfaction. In this sense, finality and development are compatible. The last coach on the train is always final, regardless of the speed of the train. But if I articulate my experience in propositions, that is, if I theologize about it, then my cognitions of today will be in tension with those of yesterday and I will have to choose. Perhaps this distinction between experienced finality (the lack of any experience of religious dissatisfaction) and reflective infinality (the knowledge that sharper and clearer expression may show me that I was at least partly wrong in speaking about it the way I did yesterday) may help to define the nature of critical openness in relation to the finality and perfection of the Christian faith.

The distinction has its limits however. Can experience and reflection be so neatly distinguished? Does not the distinction lead me to be critically open towards the thoughts of others but self-enclosed as far as *my* experience goes? Does it not fail to open me to the experience of others? And may I not delude myself about my experience, thinking I was satisfied when I was not, or attributing my satisfaction to *this* when later I realize it was *that* which was the true source of my satisfaction? Is there not some danger of absolutizing experience, so that while I may criticize yesterday's theology. I may never theologically criticize yesterday's religious experience, or today's? Is it not easy to see how this approach can be defended any better than the last one from the suspicion that in the end it can become a way for limiting the operation of critical openness.

In discussing the problem of critical openness towards the future of the child, *The Child in the Church* remarks that the Christian nurturer knows what he is nurturing his children out of, but not what he is nurturing them into. 'They know the resources but not the use which will be made of them,' (para. 63). This conception could be compatible with either of the two views discussed above. But whereas the report suggests the metaphor of the paintbox, the metaphor of the hidden time capsule would also fit. Christian faith is regarded as a capsule full of items hidden by Christ and the early Church two thousand years ago. We are learning how to unlock the compartments, and to draw out new items, not knowing what impact they will have upon us or our Christian future. But the truth is more complex. The past of Christian faith is not protected from its environment in a time capsule, to be opened by us, to find each thing as it was when first stored away. The past of Christian faith is available to us only in language and ritual. Both are inescapably imbedded in culture, and demand constant interpretation. No doubt the past is just exactly whatever it was. But we do not know what it was, and as we make it *our* past, our perceptions of it (and apart from these it is only retained in the infallible omniscience of the divine memory) also change. Not only do we not know what we are nurturing the young Christians into; we do not fully know what we are nurturing them out of. Their perceptions of the Christian past may be as different from ours as ours are from the generation of Christians who lived before form criticism. And just as individuals may have false experience, self-deluding experience, only recognized and corrected in the light of a later wholeness, so whole communities and traditions may pass through periods of mistaken experience. What else are prophets for but to awaken people to this?

The only way left seems to be thoroughgoing eschatology. The Christian faith has the promise of finality and completeness within it (and perhaps it is not alone in this respect) because it is pressing on towards finality and completeness. The finality and completeness are perceived in hope and love by faith. We see it through a glass darkly. This eschatological finality is the link with the doctrine of justification by faith, which will be discussed below. It is experienced, in so far as believing in eschatological or teleological finality makes a difference to the way life is lived, but it is not a psychological category, as was our earlier idea of religious experience.

We have discussed three forms of finality – experiential, cognitive and eschatological. The last seems to be the surest ground for a theology of Christian nurture, and the most open to critical openness. But it leads us into the problem of authority.

2 Authority

If religious authority is authoritarianism, it is immune from criticism. If it is authoritative, it demands criticism. For an authoritative view possesses its authority because of reasons – experience, wisdom, character, rationality. There must be criteria. But where there are criteria (unless these are provided in an authoritarian manner) they must be distinguished, weighed, assessed, assented to. Criteria-referenced authority summons the cooperative effort of the one who stands beneath the authority. But the authoritarian decree is right because of its power alone. The authoritarian person is right because he says so, the authoritarian book is true because it claims to be. Here openness becomes disobedience and criticism is impudence. Of what kind is the authority of God – authoritative or authoritarian?

Sometimes an attempt is made to avoid the force of this distinction, and the implications for Christian life which flow from it, by introducing such euphemisms as 'innate authority' or 'self-authenticating authority'.

Innate authority is one which acknowledges no criteria. It remains mysterious, baffling, frustrating. 'Why don't you want to go to London?' 'I just don't want to'. 'But *why?*' There is no *reason* why the friend should not change her mind. 'Oh alright. I will go after all'. 'What made you change your mind?' 'I don't know. I just decided to go after all.' You are pleased with the decision, but as mystified as ever. It is not possible to enter into understanding and sympathetic relations with someone whose decisions are arbitrary. This remains true even if, as in the case of God, the danger of unpredictable ethical changes is removed. Such a God could not be the Thou of man: he could not be the counsellor and guide, for to accept such guidance would be to renounce the status of person and to accept the status of slave.[7] You may trust God in the dark, but you cannot trust a dark God.

The alternatives are clear. Either we have a dictator God, or we are called to the life of critical openness. But God, in declaring himself a God for man, in making himself available to us in personal relation, invites us to accept a reasonable service. Critical openness is the pedagogical technique adopted by a God who is personal and desires us to be persons. Without it, faith in God could not be purged, nor could it be anything other than the confidence of the gambler.[8] What then of revelation?

3 Revelation

The calling of critical openness flows from the nature of the Christian revelation of God as offering himself as a God for man. It is part of the revelation and should not be thought of as being hostile to it. Only when God is thought of as being authoritarian and his self-revealing is thought of as being outside the context of personal life, an imposition external to the person, can critical openness be thought of as exalting the reason of man against the divine revelation. For if God is not authoritarian, then it must be that through his revelation of himself as being not authoritarian he is summoning us to critical openness. God, in willing to bring us to personhood, may adopt only such means as are compatible with personhood and which tend to the creation of persons. But autonomy or critical openness is an essential attribute of personhood. Authoritarianism and autonomy are incompatible. According to the criteria of personhood and what it entails, God is wise – wise in selecting this goal from the lesser goals which might have been selected, and wise in selecting the kinds of relation with his creatures which are best suited to the accomplishment of this goal.[9] It is God's wise decree that his creatures should be critically open. God has called us into fellowship with himself, having made us mind as well as spirit. The fellowship of spirit with spirit is love and the fellowship of mind with mind is critical openness. The criteria for this situation are drawn from the nature of mind itself. Theism without critical openness (a dictatorial God) could empty the Christian view of man of its dignity, the rational soul, the image of God.

But can critical openness be an attribute of God? We must be open because we know that our knowledge is only a fraction of the total sum of knowledge, and we must be critical because we so easily mistake falsehood for knowledge. The divine knowledge is, however, perfect in its quality and in its extent. God knows all there is to be known, and he knows it infallibly and in perfect accuracy of detail.

On the other hand God has ordained a universe in which freely acting agents (persons) other than himself shall be, and this potential for freedom, being in the nature of things as ordained by God, cannot but be actualized in some degree, however slight, at the lowest level of the universe as well as the highest. Details are added to the universe which it previously lacked, and God, although knowing all the details which might conceivably be added, and knowing them infallibly and eternally as soon as they are added, does not know what is not yet there to be known. This is not a limitation on God's knowledge but an assertion about the cognitive expansion which must be the experience of an infallible knower in the presence of an expanding world capable of genuine novelty (freedom) in which there is always more actually to know. Without ceasing to be all-knowing, and possessing no degrees in his omniscience, God is continually receptive and attentive (loving) towards the other centres of value and creativity which have sprung from his own creative work. God is open to the future and to others.

God is critical in the sense that when contemplating the infinite range of possibilities, some but not all of which may be actualized, he exercises discrimination, bringing into being those which are compatible with his general purposes and doing so in a manner compatible with the need to preserve the reality of other centres of consciousness and will. God is also critical in the sense that although no cognition can be lost or be beyond recall to God in the successive stages of his divine life, as the supreme repository of all accumulated value, only cognitions which contribute to that enduring accumulation of value are actively present in the ongoing divine life. 'Your sins and your iniquities will I remember no more.' The divine forgetting is the judgment and the mercy of God towards the world, and the exercise of it requires the divine criticism.[10]

God is thus critical and open in all ways in which we are – towards the future, towards the actions and needs of others, in selecting from present possibilities, in discriminating between values, but without the weaknesses in our criticism imposed upon us by the fact that we are never acquainted with all the facts, and the limitations upon our openness imposed by the fact that we build barriers between ourselves and other creatures. He has the kind of critical openness appropriate to a perfect being. Man therefore in being critically open is, however imperfectly, in the image of God. The thought is perhaps a strange one, because the vocabulary is not the traditional religious vocabulary, but the appeal to be 'perfect as our Father in heaven is perfect' if it means 'be perfect in this respect and in that respect' – whatever these may be which are appropriate perfections for creatures to aspire towards – may be construed as including amongst these many respects this one: to be critically open (within the limits of finitude) as God is critically open (within the limits of infinitude). How are we to live before such a God? This brings us to the next point.

4 Spirituality

People sometimes ask whether we are to be critically open at the expense of our loyalty to Christ.[11] The question arises because critical openness is not one of the traditional Christian virtues but is preconceived as being in potential hostility to Christian commitment. No Christian even asks whether we should be loving at the expense of our loyalty to Christ. To be loving is to be Christian. But, in a less important but still significant way, to be critically open is also to be Christian. Christians have no monopoly of love just as they have no monopoly of critical openness, but the logic of their faith drives them in these directions. But traditional Christian spirituality with its emphasis on such virtues as obedience and submissiveness might seem ill at ease with a spirituality of critical openness. This feeling (for it is no more) arises simply because the implications of critical openness for spirituality are not thought through. So the following comments are offered.

Critical openness is sometimes thought of as if it exhibited a proud spirit instead of a mood of self-repudiating acceptance. This is a mistake. The critically open person cannot but be humble, because in his openness to others he acknowledges his need for help and in his criticism he acknowledges his own fallibility. In as much as critical openness is certainly not thinking what appeals to you or believing what you like or accepting what makes you comfortable, it is a repudiation of self-centredness. The critically open person is the one who knows he has much to learn.

The critically open Christian is far removed from the one who has the 'spirit of fear'. Instead he exercises Christian responsibility, is a son not a slave, and seeks to test everything, in order to hold fast that which is good.

It is true that there is some New Testament imagery which might seem to emphasize the passivity and the dependence of discipleship. We are sheep, a little flock, branches of the vine, we are to leave all and to follow him without question or delay. But other strands emphasize Christian responsibility – we are to count the cost like the king setting out to war, we are to take risks with our talents, we are to be wise as serpents. Moreover, critical openness is part of the abandoning of the old securities which is part of discipleship. How could Jewish men who were not critically open have responded to the question of Jesus about who he was? It should also be pointed out that to belong to the school of Christ cannot be similar to belonging to the school of (say) Aristotle. The follower of Aristotle seeks to elaborate the system of Aristotle. But Jesus founded no system, wrote no book.

Christian autonomy and justification by faith

It may be that critical openness cannot be made compatible with the Presbyterian doctrine of the covenant, as it developed in seventeenth-century Protestant scholasticism, in which the idea that the covenant is bestowed conditionally creates a series of limits, which, if transgressed, place one outside the covenant.[12] But if the older reformed principle of justification by faith is taken seriously and extended into the intellectual realm as well as the moral realm then the Christian, being accepted regardless of conditions, is set free from intellectually inhibiting religious fears. There are no degrees of justification. The justified Christian is thus set free from fear in order to pursue God's path to personhood. In the ethical area, it may be that situation ethics is the life of the conscience flowing from justification by faith. So critical openness is the life of the Christian mind, flowing from the same principle – which itself is open to critical reflection, and so on for ever. We can see therefore that critical openness is not a basic Christian concept (such as the grace of God is) but a derived or consequential attribute of Christian living. It is derived from ideas such as the personhood of God, the nature of the divine image, the Christian hope in the future, the character of discipleship towards Jesus and so on, and we are emboldened to walk this way because of justification by faith. The old Christian symbol of this is not the maze, which presents one with many hazardous choices, but the single-track labyrinth. This is an incredibly convoluted path, with innumerable doublings back, apparent lack of progress, sudden coming near the goal only to be thrust out to the perimeter, and yet a way in which, at the last, there is no being lost.

Is theology made captive to critical openness?

I have tried to show that critical openness is a discipline which the Christian follows not in spite of his faith but because of it. The kind of critical openness which flows from Christian faith has many links with the secular educational ideal of autonomy, and yet, as we have seen from many examples, it has distinctive flavour and colouring which are drawn from the aspects of Christian faith with which critical openness is most closely associated. I do not deny that the secular ideal of autonomy might reveal some important differences if it were examined and compared with greater sharpness, but to do this has not been the purpose of this discussion. Neither do I deny that in other faiths there may be other models of critical openness, which may also be compared with the Christian ideal. But enough has been said, I think, to show that critical openness as described here is sufficient to do the job which was required of it in the opening statement of the problem. Christian theology is not here being reduced to fit the requirements of the dialogue with secular education and the needs of a contemporary Christian nurture. Rather, Christian faith is itself being listened to, in an attempt to hear whether it offers us the resources for this task.

Are there limits to Christian criticism?

To limit criticism would be to resist learning and so to declare that development was complete. But what if criticism were to indicate that all the sacred relics were forgeries, the gospels without historical foundation and the concept of God incoherent? What if criticism explodes the Christian faith? This possibility expresses the ambiguity of faith and it cannot be removed, either by criticism itself or by naive assertion. To restrain criticism because it seemed to be going in the wrong direction would be such an act of intellectual dishonesty that the ethics of Christian intellectual life would be destroyed in any case. One would be left with something more closely approaching the truth than one had before, whereas if criticism is restrained because of fear of unwelcome conclusions, one is left with neither the best truth available nor the Christian faith (since its intellectual calling would have been denied).

Section three: Education and christian nurture – similar yet dissimilar

We have seen that Christian nurture is similar to secular education in that both are committed to inquiry, both are concerned with learning in order to make yet further learning possible. By virtue of this characteristic, Christian faith may provide a rationale for both kinds of processes, since Christian faith is driven towards this position by its own internal logic. We can therefore speak of 'Christian education' in the sense of a Christian rationale for the processes of learning, and of 'Christian nurture' in the sense of a Christian rationale (and in this case there could be no other kind of rationale) for a Christian learning about Christian faith leading to deeper Christian faith. Christian nurture can thus be defended against the charge that it is closed authoritarian instruction, and its humane and ethical status are assured.

But does our discussion prove too much? We began with the problem of how Christian nurture could be like education in possessing critical openness yet remain unlike it in intending the deepening of Christian faith. The likeness is clear; what about the unlikeness? Is the similarity now so close that we might conclude that anything which a child might gain from Christian nurture he could equally gain by education (if it is of good quality in the area of Christian studies) and that there is no particular benefit obtained from Christian nurture as offered by Christian families, churches and other Christian groups and institutions?

I have previously suggested four distinguishing features[13] and I would like to comment on these and add further distinctions.

The first distinction has to do with the differing hopes or intentions of the Christian nurturer and the educator teaching Christian studies. Christian nurture, through its critical openness, can contemplate the possibility of the collapse of Christian faith, but what it expects, hopes for and intends is the strengthening of Christian faith. Critical openness tests, expands and fulfils Christian faith. Christian nurture is based upon the hypothesis that Christianity is true and can be seen to be yet more true. There is nothing odd or illogical about the combination of this commitment with this critical openness. Scientific commitment and inquiry have similar features. Karl Popper has given approval to dogmatism in science, pointing out that only if the adherents of theories defend them vigorously, try by every scientific means to secure them against attack, try to adapt them to meet objections, and set high standards for their overthrow, can science be protected from the situation where theories are lightly advanced and easily given up. The commitment ensures the depth of probing without which the advance of truth would be difficult because the discussion would be superficial.[14] In religion, although the word 'dogmatism' is best avoided because of its pejorative history, the same is true. It is only sensible that there should be a strong commitment to rational religious beliefs provided they are held in the spirit of critical openness and with the contemplation of the possibility (although not the expectation of the likelihood) that they may be false. In the case of the Christian religion, where the commitment and the criticism flow from the same central ideas, the connection is still more evident and coherent.

The educator *qua* educator is not interested in the future of Christian faith. He neither intends to deepen Christian faith nor to overthrow it. There is nothing odd about a Christian being such an educator and nothing odd about Christian theology offering a rationale for such education. The medical doctor as such does not have any particular intentions one way or the other about strengthening Christian faith, but that does not mean that there cannot be a Christian approach to the conduct of medical work.

The second distinction has to do with the relation between Christian theology and education and nurture respectively. It has already been pointed out that there can be no other rationale for Christian nurture than that provided by Christian theology, which is therefore in a necessary and sufficient relationship to the practice of Christian nurture. But Christian theology has but a partial and a possible relation to the practice of education.

Combining these two distinctions, we may say that Christian nurture is a servant of faith, and it is this faithful service which impels it to be critically open towards faith itself, as faith in the Christian sense requires, but education, although also capable of being justified by faith, is an independent activity of secular man. Reversing the servant metaphor, we may say that theology is lord of Christian nurture (Christian nurture is captive to theology) but theology is servant to education. Theology appraises education, tries to illumine, but cannot prescribe, except in circumstances when education becomes itself captive to ideologies hostile to Christian faith, and then education is no longer Christian education, and Christian theology must denounce it. But as long as a Christian rationale for secular education is *possible*, that interpretation remains as a service. There can be necessary attack (where education has become anti-Christian) but there can be no *necessary* support, because non-Christians can be educators. This question has to do with the circumstances when the saying 'He that is not against us is on our side' must be exchanged for the saying 'He that gathereth not with us scattereth, and he that is not for us is against us.' The critical openness of Christian nurture is a Christian critical openness; the critical openness of education is merely compatible with Christian faith.

The third reason for maintaining the education/Christian nurture distinction has to do with the spheres in which the two activities take place, or their social agencies. Christian nurture is a domestic activity of the church; education is a public activity of the state. I am assuming that in certain circumstances the state has the right to educate, although like all the other rights of the state there are limits to its operation.

The fourth distinction has to do with the pedagogical character of the two processes, but is also connected with the nature of the agencies or spheres. In principle (for example, in certain countries of Asia) a satisfactory religious education need make but minor reference to Christianity. And even in Western countries, pupils can become educated concerning several or any religions. But because it is a prolongation of the conditions of infancy (a prolongation which seeks to bring the infant to maturity and not keep him in infancy and yet begins from the conditions of infancy and takes them seriously as the inheritance of the child, whereas education is an initiation into public discourse) a child can only be nurtured in his own religion. You can indoctrinate a child into anything, and in the case of Christianity that would mean alienating him from his Christian family tradition, and you can educate a child into anything worthwhile, and in the case of Christianity that would mean respecting but not promoting his family tradition.

The fifth distinction follows from the fourth. Christian nurture proceeds from an assumption that teacher and learner are inside the Christian faith, whereas education only invites the pupil to *imagine* what it would be like to be inside a faith, or (in the situation where a pupil is being educated in his own faith) education invites the pupil to imagine what it would be like to be outside his faith. The whole environment of the secular school, the plurality present in the classroom, the range of teacher commitments, the nature and style of the public examinations – all contribute to this ethos. Suspension of belief or disbelief is an important part of educational method in the religious area, but has a smaller and different role to play in Christian nurture.

The sixth distinction is that education in religion is appropriate for all, but Christian nurture is appropriate only for Christians. Christian nurture is based upon the belief that there are Christian children.

Finally, Christian nurture takes place in the context of worship (and not merely the study or exploration of worship), in a specialized faith community, where the child, as a Christian, learns from the Word of God. These factors give Christian nurture an ethos, an emotional context, which are quite different from that provided by education.

Of course, it may be the case that these distinctions make little practical difference in some situations, especially with adolescent pupils. It may be that even young people within the churches are so deeply secularized that with them as with the general pupils in the state schools all that the teacher, whether Christian nurturer or educator, can offer is a fundamental pre-catechesis or introduction which will make learning possible in these areas. But even where this were the case, and the starting point thus similar, the ending point would be different. As the processes got under way, the differences would emerge, or, if they did not, the teacher might have succeeded as educator whilst his colleague in the church might have failed as Christian nurturer.

Perhaps this discussion may seem complex, but the problems raised by Christian presence within secular and pluralist culture are themselves complex. There are no easy answers. But if the problems are not to be approached along the general lines discussed in this paper, it is difficult to see how Christian faith can avoid becoming invisible.

Notes

1 For a fuller discussion of this, see chapter 3 above.
2 Dearden, R.F. *et al.*, 'Autonomy as an educational ideal', in Brown, S.C. (ed.), *Philosophers Discuss Education*, Macmillan, 1975, pp. 3–42.
3 Hartshorne, Charles, *The Logic of Perfection*, Open Court, Illinois, 1962, pp. 119–23.
4 Peter Adam, in 'The child in the church', *Churchman*, 91, 4, 1977, pp. 318–28, does not think it possible to establish a middle way between education and instruction. 'Some kind of indoctrination is unavoidable,' (p. 321). Adam seeks an instruction 'which was honest and open about its presuppositions and hopes, and which allowed debate and contrary opinion.' But nothing is said about how Christian theology might thrust instruction in such critical directions.
5 See the discussion on p. 40 above.
6 Hendry, George S., *The Westminster Confession for Today*, SCM Press, 1960, p. 11.
7 In spite of the power and beauty which they often attain, the religious novels of George McDonald yield a few illustrations of this kind of spirituality. See *The Princess and the Goblin* where faith is like following a magic thread in the dark. C.S. Lewis is tempted in this direction, but usually Aslan does not treat his followers in this way, because they have already established a sort of personal relation with him. There are always good reasons for what Aslan does, and they are usually understood.
8 In his *Pedagogy of the Oppressed* (Sheed and Ward, 1972) Paulo Freire discusses the problem of method which faces the teacher who wants to lead oppressed illiterates to freedom without subjecting them to another dehumanizing experience. It would be interesting to consider the problems of God, in his redemptive work with man, in the light of Freire's ideal teacher.
9 Oman, John, *Grace and Personality*, 4th ed., Cambridge University Press, 1942, Chap. VI, 'Autonomy'.
10 Hartshorne, Charles, *Man's Vision of God and the Logic of Theism*. Connecticut, 1964, pp. 98ff.

11 See the letter published in *Learning for Living*, 17, 2, Winter 1977, p. 97.

12 Moller, Jens G., 'The beginnings of puritan covenant theology', *Journal of Ecclesiastical History*, 14, 1963, pp. 46–67.

13 Hull, John M., *School Worship, an Obituary*, SCM Press, 1975, pp. 108–9. The order of the points has been changed in this article.

14 '. . . I have always stressed the need for some dogmatism: the dogmatic scientist has an important role to play. If we give in to criticism too easily, we shall never find out where the real power of our theories lies.' Popper, Karl, 'Normal science and its dangers', in Latakos, I. and Musgrove, A. (eds), *Criticism and the Growth of Knowledge*, Cambridge University Press, 1970, p. 55.

PART V

Christian Theology and Educational Theory

19. *Christian Theology and Educational Theory: Can There Be Connections?*

Introduction

This paper is not concerned with religious education in the curriculum but with the nature of the relation between theology and educational theory. All sophisticated religious belief systems have histories of such relations, the literature of Christianity, Judaism and Islam being particularly rich. Theology of education at the present time is an active field of interdisciplinary study. Recent dissertation abstracts indicate the sort of work taking place[1] in an effort to criticize, clarify and give new directions to education in the light of contemporary religious ideas.

It has now been denied that this activity is a legitimate one.

Exposition

In his book, *Moral Education in a Secular Society* (University of London Press, 1974), Professor Paul Hirst claims that there can be no useful and coherent relations between theology and educational theory. Hirst argues that 'there has now emerged in our society a concept of education which makes the whole idea of Christian education a kind of nonsense' (p. 77). Just as mathematics, engineering and farming are characterized by intrinsic and autonomous norms, so is education. There can no more be a 'characteristically or distinctively Christian form of education' than there can be a 'distinctively Christian form of mathematics' (p. 77). The process of secularization, which has already brought about autonomy in these fields, is now according 'an exactly similar status' to education (p. 68).

Hirst describes two ways in which one might attempt to create a Christian philosophy of education. First, one might start with 'very general moral principles' and seek to draw educational conclusions. But,

Hirst remarks, even although these moral principles might be supported from Christian sources, they are 'usually not in any sense significantly Christian' (p. 78). Second, one might begin with what is said in the Bible about education and try to apply this to teaching today. Problems such as the cultural remoteness of the Bible and the controversies surrounding its interpretation vitiate this enterprise, so that 'a distinctive Biblical or Christian view of education simply is not discoverable' (p. 79).

Hirst then distinguishes two concepts of education. The first is 'primitive' education, which is the view a 'primitive tribe' might have of education as the uncritical passing on of customs and beliefs.[2] There may be distinctively Christian, humanist or Buddhist concepts of this sort of education 'according to which Christians seek that the next generation shall think likewise' (p. 80). The second concept of education is marked by a concern for objective knowledge, for truth and for reasons, and it will set out for pupils the methods and procedures of the various disciplines according to public criteria. But religious and humanist beliefs, continues the argument, must themselves be assessed by such criteria and so the principles of education are 'logically more fundamental' than those of the particular religious communities. Consequently, 'the character of education is not settled by any appeal to Christian, Humanist or Buddhist beliefs' (p. 81).

The autonomy of education is then compared with various other pursuits, such as morality and history; it is concluded that although education may certainly promote an understanding of a faith it may not seek to develop 'a disposition to worship in that faith' (p. 84).

I have no quarrel with this account of the sort of religious education proper to an educational curriculum. It may be worth pointing out that from his 1965 article on religious education[3] through his 1973 article in *Learning for Living*[4] right up to the present book, Hirst has consistently defended the existence of a critical, open study of religion in the schools. Reviewers of *Moral Education in a Secular Society*, confusing a denial that theology of education is proper with a denial that teaching religion is proper, are mistakenly claiming that Hirst is now against any teaching of religion in schools.[5] But Hirst is wrong, in my view, in thinking that in order to protect the independence of secular education against proselytizing groups such as Christians it is necessary to deny the possibility of constructing a useful relation between Christian faith and this concept of critical, open education.

Before we consider his discussion in detail, it may be helpful to distinguish five kinds of possible relations between Christian theology and education.

1   Christian theology might be both necessary and sufficient for an understanding of education.

2   Christian theology might provide a necessary but not a sufficient understanding of education. Theology might, in this case, need assistance from philosophy or psychology.

3   Christian theology might provide a sufficient but not a necessary understanding of education. Other belief systems, including non-religious ones, might also be able to offer sufficient accounts of education.

4   Christian theology might provide a possible and legitimate understanding of education, but one which is neither sufficient nor necessary.

5   Christian theology might be impossible and illegitimate as a way of understanding education. It would have no contribution to offer.

It is the last of these positions which Hirst adopts: '... the search for a Christian approach to, or philosophy of, education [is] a huge mistake';[6] '... judging what is good or bad in education is nothing to do with whether one is a Christian, a Humanist or a Buddhist.'[7] This, for Hirst, is a matter of principle. 'But if I once thought ... the pursuit of a distinctively Christian form of education in principle satisfactory, I have now come to the conclusion that even that is not so.'[8] Moreover, having relentlessly pressed the attack by showing the insufficiency of the Bible for an understanding of education, he will not allow the poor Christian to make a last stand in a tiny corner of the field. 'If one cannot get everything necessary for educational practice from Christian teaching, surely one can get something distinctive' (p. 79). Hirst's reply is that any relation between Christian theology and education will be only with the primitive notion of education. With this area, in which the 'tribe ... seeks to pass on to the next generation its rituals' (p. 80), Christians must be content, and here 'there will be as many concepts of education as there are systems of beliefs and values' (p. 80). This is small comfort indeed, since Hirst goes on to ask whether in this tribal sense the word 'education' should be used at all. 'Indeed I suggest that this pursuit is in fact now increasingly considered immoral.'[9] When it comes to rational, sophisticated education 'dominated by a concern for knowledge, for truth, for reasons' (p. 80) then 'there can be no such thing as Christian education'.[10]

Hirst seems to be reacting against the sort of relations I have set out above as numbers one, two and three. He sometimes uses forensic terminology to describe the improper relations between theology and education. Nothing in education can be 'decided properly by appeal' to Christian sources; 'the issues must be settled independently of any questions of religious belief' (pp. 77f). He not only undertakes to attack the first three positions and to defend the final one but he seeks to commend this fifth relation to the Christian. He agrees that not all Christians will find his approach acceptable, especially those 'who are convinced of the total sufficiency of biblical revelation for the conduct of all human affairs',[11] but there is no 'necessary contradiction between Christian beliefs and education in this [sophisticated] sense, provided Christian beliefs form a rationally coherent system.'[12] Considerable attention is given to the 'secular Christian', to whom Hirst thinks the fifth position should be acceptable.

Hirst does not appear to envisage the modest *modus vivendi* between theology and education suggested in my fourth kind of relation. Hirst and I are in agreement in rejecting the first three models. In what follows the various arguments used to support the 'impossible and illegitimate' relation will be examined. We will then estimate Hirst's success in commending this position to the 'secular Christian'.

Criticism

1 The sociological arguments

The central concept in this opening group of arguments is 'secularization'. This is described in the opening chapter, applied to morals in following chapters and to the relation between theology and education in chapter five. Secularization is regarded as 'a decay in the use of religious concepts and beliefs' (p. 1). This means that 'supernatural interpretations of experience have been progressively replaced by others' (p. 2). The status of science, morals, aesthetics and other modes of thought is now such that 'religious considerations can be ignored'. This does not mean that 'all religious beliefs can be shown to be unintelligible or false. It is rather that [they] come to be seen as of no consequence, having nothing to contribute in our efforts to understand ourselves and our world and to determine how we are to live' (p. 2).

It is difficult to ascertain whether Hirst is merely offering a description of certain historical and social processes, or whether he thinks the processes are significant for the logical relations between religion and other modes of thought. Frequently, the former is the impression given, although conclusions tend to be drawn as if the latter had been established. Thus the decay is in the 'use' of religious concepts. 'There was a time when more people were ... involved' in religion, and religious views are now but 'rarely voiced'. So 'religious understanding has ... come to look more and more redundant' and religious beliefs 'come to be seen as of no consequence'. This is the language of mere description. No doubt such a situation exists, and is quite properly bringing about important changes in the relations between the churches and the schools and the way religion is now taught as a subject in schools.[13] But this has little to do with the logical possibility or the intellectual legitimacy of attempting to formulate conceptual links between theology and theories of education.

Basic distinctions about the secularization processes are ignored. One can usually distinguish between 'secularization' as the historical process whereby social and intellectual life has been freed from dominance by theological concepts, and 'secularism', the stronger claim that this has the (logical or psychological) consequence of rendering religious belief (actually or apparently) meaningless and irrelevant. One can also distinguish between ecclesiastical secularization, which has to do with the relations between institutionalized religion and the rest of society, and theological or conceptual secularization, which has to do with the coherence and vitality of theology in relations with the secular world. These distinctions between the sociology of religion and the logical relations which theology has with other fields are blurred in general descriptions of 'religion' or 'religious belief'. It could be pointed out, for example, that ecclesiastical secularization has been followed by the secularization of theology itself which now exists in a state of secular autonomy similar to that enjoyed by the other intellectual disciplines. Hirst concludes that the autonomy of the secular spheres (he does not reckon theology to be one of them) means that religious considerations 'can be ignored'. Of course they can. Theology is no longer, as it was in the world of the Thomistic *Summa*, both necessary and sufficient for all systematic thought. But must it be ignored? Is the alleged irrelevancy of religious thought a possibility or a necessity? No evidence is offered for believing that the latter is the case, and so Hirst jumps from the first of the five relations between theology and the world of thought to the fourth (or something like it) when considering theology and morals and straight on to the fifth when considering theology and education, without pausing to offer reasons for being required to adopt these later forms of relation.

The second part of Hirst's discussion of secularization has to do with the 'privatization' of religion. In interpreting this discussion, it may be helpful to consider an earlier account of privatization, in which Hirst had suggested that the values upon which the common school must be based should be 'acceptable to all irrespective of any particular religious or non-religious claims'.[14] 'Public values' must be distinguished from these latter 'private values'. The domain of scientific knowledge seems part of the public world but religious beliefs 'which have no generally acceptable public tests of validity'[15] are probably in the private area. Values which 'necessarily rest on particular religious beliefs' are also private, although a citizen may have an education consistent with his private religion. In order not to create the impression that the public school is non-religious or anti-religious, it should be understood that the education it offers can be but partial.

Hirst seems to have held that what the private communities of faith do in their schools is genuinely educational, in that it deals with areas of private values with which the public school cannot deal, and in this way such private education is a necessary or at least a legitimate complement to public education. In the later writings we are considering, the distinction between 'primitive' and 'sophisticated' education seems to take the place of the earlier distinction between 'private' and 'public' value education, and the idea of the religious community offering a legitimate complement to public education, a complement arising directly from its own values yet still being educational, becomes less important, if not immoral.

In the public schools, Hirst continues, methods of teaching must also be in terms of public values. 'Are there Christian methods of teaching Boyle's law which differ from atheistic methods?'[16] Hirst however does not deny that a teacher's private values *may* affect his teaching, only that it can never be claimed that his private values *must* affect his teaching. Hirst seems then at this stage to have had in mind something rather like the fourth of our relations between theology and education, in which religious beliefs could provide a possible but not a necessary or sufficient contribution.

The criteria of knowledge, Hirst continues, are public, and the public school can offer education in at least 'established areas of knowledge'.[17] The idea of the 'autonomy' of a 'domain of knowledge' is now introduced in this 1967 essay. Some agreement, Hirst remarks, is mere consensus but some is 'rationally compelled' on the basis of public criteria.[18] At present, we only have consensus agreement in the moral area. But if moral agreement could be won on the basis of public, rational criteria, then we would have an autonomous basis for the common school. In his 1965 article, 'Liberal education and the nature of knowledge', the idea of the 'autonomy' of the various forms of knowledge does not appear, but in another article from the same year, 'Morals, religion and the maintained school',[19] the idea of 'autonomy' does emerge when discussing the extent to which morals may be regarded as independent of theology. 'Autonomy' and 'privatization' both become key concepts in the 1974 book under discussion. The germs of the 1967 article on 'privatization' are now mature. Morals may at last be justified on independent, rational grounds. Religion however is now severely privatized and the conclusion is drawn that 'when the domain of religious beliefs is so manifestly one in which there are at present no clearly recognizable objective grounds for judging claims, to base education on any such claims would be to forsake the pursuit of objectivity' (p. 81).

So, in a society in which religion has become privatized, 'the widest range of attitudes to religious beliefs is acceptable, provided they are never allowed to determine public issues', and 'it is a mark of the secular society that it is religiously plural, tolerating all forms of religious belief and practice that do not contravene agreed public principles' (p. 3).

One notices the strangely conservative social attitude implied by this approach. Nothing must contravene the public order. We also observe that in discussing society in this way, Hirst is not speaking of the logic or the epistemology of the forms of knowledge, but of convention. The significant 1967 distinction between consensus agreement and rational agreement does not appear. No logical conclusions can be drawn therefore one way or the other about the possibility of relating the conceptual worlds of theology and education on the basis of such an undifferentiated concept of 'privatization'. We observe finally the stringency of Hirst's conditions. Religion must not be allowed to 'determine' public issues. It must not 'contravene' public principles. But may it not even influence them (cf. p. 55)? May it not be allowed to have some legitimate effect? Why, on this argument, *must* it be thought of as having *nothing* to contribute? How can a claim (of whatever strength) that religion must not be allowed to determine public issues such as education lead to the conclusion that there can be no legitimate attempt to construct a Christian philosophy of education in which Christian theology would be but one (influencing but not determining) factor amongst others? What has happened to the private religious values of 1967? A citizen could express these through education provided they did not contravene public values. Must theology now necessarily contravene them? Can Christian faith then never be an ally of the open society?

2   The logical arguments

Hirst claims that the emerging, secular concept of education makes the possibility of a relation between Christianity and education 'a kind of nonsense' (p. 77).

First argument

Education, like mathematics, engineering and farming, is governed by its own intrinsic principles. What is good of its kind in each of these areas is determined by those inner principles and not by reference to theological factors. Bridges stay or fall down for Christians and atheists alike. God, we may add, sends his rain upon the just and the unjust.

But is there really a parallel of this sort between education and mathematics? Does what appertains in the latter, abstract, self-sufficient form of knowledge in which inescapable conclusions are drawn also apply to a value-laden, practical enterprise like education? Education, it must be remembered, is not one of the forms of knowledge. It does not have a unique and distinctive mode of thought nor a characteristic epistemology, but is, like medicine, an applied field in which various other disciplines, some of which are true forms of knowledge, impinge in order to enable the activity to take place. In the cases of medicine and education, these other disciplines are things like anatomy, chemistry, immunology, philosophy and psychology. Medicine and education do not however lack coherence. They derive it not from the structure of their epistemology but from their concentration upon healing or educating people. Their coherence is such as is demanded by a practical enterprise; it is not the coherence of internally self-sufficient principles and it should not therefore be compared to the logical 'autonomy' of mathematics.

In his 1965 article on 'Liberal education' Hirst described political, legal and educational theory as 'fields where moral knowledge of a developed kind is to be found'.[20] Engineering, in the same article, is described as a 'field' and no doubt this would be true of farming as well. We are thus comparing

a   an indisputable form of knowledge in which moral knowledge of a developed kind is not found (mathematics);

b   two fields in which moral knowledge is similarly not well developed (engineering and farming);

c   a field in which moral knowledge is well developed (education); and

d   a disputable form of knowledge in which moral knowledge is well developed (religion).

It is obvious that a, b and c do not exhibit 'exactly similar status' (p. 78) in the kinds and degrees of the autonomy they possess. Their relations both with the moral sphere and the religious sphere will be different in each case. Farming, for example, does not have the self-sufficient logic of mathematics. What is good farming may quite properly be determined by political principles in China, by religious principles in India, and by environmentalist considerations in Western Europe. There will be no clash between the principles of good farming and any of these contexts, because the context has a significant part to play in determining what the principles of good farming actually are. There is, of course, a level of unchangeable circumstances, usually based upon cause and effect sequence in the natural world, at which the techniques of farming and education will be autonomous. Even the devil, if he wants tares, has to sow tares. Wheat produces wheat for angels and devils alike. But whether you pluck the tares up or leave them both to grow together until the harvest is a matter of value judgments and long-term considerations involving questions of religion and philosophy which go far beyond the simple technical level. The objective psychological test will yield the same result for both the Christian and the atheist educational psychologist, and the techniques for the early diagnosis of speech defects are just whatever they are, since speech is just what it is, and defects are defined accordingly. Christians and atheists sharing the same speech conventions will not differ at this level. But to whom the objective test is to be administered, and what use is to be made of the results and why – these problems introduce evaluative questions as well as a wider factual context and at this point the techniques themselves are no longer autonomous. They need the help of sociology, ethics and so on. Secularization has had considerable effect even at this technical level, since the sensible Christian and the sensible atheist agree in using terms like 'emotional disorder' rather than ones like 'demonic possession', and they agree to use the techniques of medical therapy not those of exorcism. There are other Christians who resist this sort of secularization, but neither Hirst nor I is concerned with them. The impact of the secularization process must not be denied, but it must be carefully qualified. Technical autonomy does not bring self-sufficiency to education.

Pedagogy may be described as a conglomerate of technical skills applied in the education of children. Education offers the ideals, the purposes and the values which guide this application. Pedagogy is thus applied education, education is applied philosophical anthropology, and it certainly cannot be claimed that philosophical anthropology is determined by principles which are 'neither for nor against' theological anthropology. Even although philosophical anthropology cannot perhaps be 'settled' by 'appeal' to theological anthropology, or to anything else, theology has a legitimate and perhaps a significant contribution to make to its elucidation. When it comes to the question, what is man?, theologians are also men, and if, like philosophers, they are sensible and rational men, their theological reflections need not be silenced.

Second argument

'On this second view (the sophisticated one), the character of education is not settled by any appeal to Christian, Humanist or Buddhist beliefs. Such an appeal is illegitimate, for the basis is logically more fundamental, being found in the canons of objectivity and reasons, canons against which Christian, Humanist and Buddhist beliefs must, in their turn and in the appropriate way, be assessed' (p. 81). This may be paraphrased as follows. The sophisticated concept of education is governed by rational, objective principles. But these very principles must be used to assess the religious and non-religious belief systems. No such belief system can therefore generate an understanding of such a critical concept of education, because the principles upon which the latter rests are more fundamental than the belief systems themselves.
 But

a   if this is so, education cannot be appraised by anything, since psychology, sociology, and all the rest of the scrutinizing disciplines are also, in their turn and in the appropriate way, to be assessed by rational criteria more fundamental than their particular and distinctive techniques of assessment. Even particular moral criticism is subject to more basic rational moral principles which are used to assess the status of the moral claims being made. This is transcendental autonomy for education with a vengeance.

b   It may be that Hirst is influenced by the thought that theology is in some way a supernatural activity, pretending immunity from rational criticism. If this is in his mind, then it is rather a restricted and perhaps an old-fashioned view of theology. Theology is concerned with the concepts of religion, with their adequacy as expressive of religious experience and with the problems of constructing them into coherent belief systems. It claims validity according to distinctive but not supernatural norms.[21]

c   It may be objected that Hirst does not say 'cannot generate an understanding of' but 'is not settled by any appeal to'. But (i) Hirst does not distinguish between the adjudicating function of a discipline and its illuminating function. This is a major criticism of his approach. The paraphrase, expressing the milder, illuminatory function, does no injustice to his discernible intentions. (ii) If however the stronger interpretation is insisted upon, then point a above not only still holds good but is strengthened. Disciplines which cannot even illuminate certainly cannot adjudicate.

Third argument

'When the domain of religious belief is so manifestly one in which there are at present no clearly recognizable objective grounds for judging claims, to base education on any such claims would be to forsake the pursuit of objectivity' (p. 81).

a   Such a strongly worded, negative conclusion about the possibility of recognizing objective tests of truth in religion appears to be new in Hirst's writings. As recently as 1973, discussing whether religion is a unique form of knowledge in his important article, 'The forms of knowledge revisited', Hirst concluded, 'On the answer to that question few would dare to pronounce categorically. My own view, as in the case of the arts, is that in the present state of affairs we must at least take the claim to knowledge seriously.... Equally, it seems to me unclear that one can coherently claim that there is a logically unique domain of religious *beliefs* [Hirst's emphasis] such that none of them can be known to be true, all being matters of faith.'[22] It would be interesting to know, since we are not told, what further reflections have enabled Hirst to move from the earlier position where the claim to religious knowledge had at least to be taken seriously to the position in the present book where it is 'so manifest' that religion lacks this status. It is difficult to avoid the impression that in order to break the links between theology and education Hirst is slightly exaggerating the clarity and the unanimity of the alleged negative verdict upon the logical status of religious claims.

b   But even if we move with Hirst, although he gives us no reason to do so, to the new, severe position, could it follow that there could be no proper or useful relation between theology and education? Although in the 1973 article just mentioned, religion was still being seriously considered for 'form of knowledge' status, history and the social sciences had already been abandoned. 'I now think it best not to refer to history or the social sciences in any statement of the forms of knowledge as such. These pursuits . . . may well be concerned with truths of several different logical kinds.'[23] (There is, by the way, a parallel here with religion, since 'Christian theology' is regarded by Hirst as a discipline within religion, and religious studies is crossdisciplinary in several senses.[24]) Indeed, the result of Hirst's 1973 revision of the forms of knowledge argument, which is now cast in more strictly propositional shape, is, as Hirst emphasizes, to reduce the forms of the categories of true propositions to only two: 'truths of the physical world' and 'truths of a mental or personal kind'.[25]

It would appear then that *either* not being a domain of knowledge does not vitiate the capacity of an area of enquiry to relate itself meaningfully to the practical field of education *or* if only domains of knowledge may appraise education, then not only can there be no theology of education, but no historical appraisal of education, only a dubious aesthetic scrutiny and no psychology or sociology of education.

c   Hirst remarks that the application of the whole theory of the domains of knowledge to education is strictly limited. It may be then that one contribution of theology (if it were to fail to secure 'domain of knowledge status') might lie in those areas with which the formal epistemological categories do not so easily deal. Hirst mentions several of these.[26]

d   In this argument Hirst again employs the device we find so frequently in the pages we are considering. He sets the most severe conditions, and then allows no place at all in education to a discipline which cannot meet them. So we are required to contemplate the possibility of *basing* education on theology. What does this mean? Does Hirst really anticipate a situation in which Christians would argue that only theists could be educators? This is certainly not what contemporary theology of education seeks to show. Far from insisting that all educators must be theologians, it is only asked that some theologians be allowed to remain educators. Hirst's argument appears then as an unconvincing attempt to establish an excluded middle.

Fourth argument

'. . . an education based on a concern for objectivity and reason, far from allying itself with any specific religious claims, must involve teaching the radically controversial character of all such claims. An understanding of religious claims it can perfectly well aim at, but commitment to any one set, in the interests of objectivity, it cannot either assume or pursue' (p. 81).

This claim about the relationship between the 'basis' of education and the need for a critical curriculum raises two questions. (a) By what characteristic can a theology generate an understanding of the critical, sophisticated concept of education? (b) What is the relation between the aims of theology of education and the aims of teaching religion as a school subject?

On (a), not all theological systems can avoid the difficulty Hirst mentions. There certainly are forms of theology which can lead only to the 'primitive' concept of education in which, for example, the task would be to ensure that subsequent generations of Christians all thought alike. But just as not all theologies avoid the danger, so also not all of them succumb to it. There are forms of Christian theology in which critical enquiry and controversial examination flow directly and necessarily from the values and beliefs to which the theology is committed. It then exhibits these intellectual characteristics not in spite of its commitment but because of it. An alliance (which does not mean an exclusive, unique or necessary derivation of education from this theology) between such theology and such education, far from hindering the critical freedom of education, might do a little to enhance and support it. It is apparent therefore that Hirst does not sufficiently discriminate between the degrees to which different religious belief systems have built into their structures necessary elements of ongoing self-criticism.

On (b), Hirst and I do not disagree about the aims and limits of religious education as a classroom subject. But whereas he thinks the commitment of the theologian in education inhibits him in the carrying out of this critical task, I think it may help him. I agree too that public educational institutions in a pluralist, secular society ought not to be committed to one religion, and consequently that compulsory, unanimous or official school worship is wrong in principle. Again, the question is whether a Christian philosophy or theology of education precludes or advances that view of religious education and of the stance to be adopted by such institutions.

3 The methodological arguments

Hirst claims that even if it were a legitimate enterprise, the methodological difficulties are such that no worthwhile work can be done in this area. (His discussion has been summarized above.)

Naturally, there are difficulties of method in any interdisciplinary study, and the various fields of practical or applied theology are not exempt. Theology receives no special supernatural aid. There is an extensive modern literature dealing with the relations between Christian theology and, for example, culture, the arts, politics, science and medicine. Many of these studies include detailed consideration of problems of method.[27] In theology of education, the two methods discussed by Hirst are by no means the only ones; indeed, they are, as he points out, rather naive and inadequate. This is not the place to enter into a discussion of how it might be undertaken, it being sufficient for our present purposes to remark that it is not appropriate to contrast sophisticated educational thinking with a sample of simple and even crude theological methods.

4 The 'secular Christian'

Hirst suggests that the position he outlines between Christian faith and education is one which ought to commend itself to certain Christians: '. . . it seems to me it is precisely the concept of education an intelligent Christian must accept' (p. 85).

But this Christian presumably accepts this view of education in so far as he is intelligent and not in so far as he is a Christian *per se*. For if the latter were the case, the secular Christian would have been able to understand the critical concept of education from within the resources of his faith and we would then have a Christian theology of secular education which is what Hirst says we cannot have. Nevertheless, Hirst takes some pains to show that the general position in the book is not hostile to Christian faith, and at several points there are quite extended discussions of this matter. It seems to me that in this respect he has failed, and if he had *not* failed, then the position he advocates regarding the impossibility of a Christian understanding of education would have had to undergo revision. In other words, chapters one to four are inconsistent with chapter five, since if Hirst is right in presenting a satisfactory relation between the secular Christian and the secular society with its secularized morals, there remains no reason why he could not also assert a positive relationship between the secularized Christian and secularized education. As it is, he affirms the one and denies the other.

The problems begin in the opening pages. Secular Christians are those 'who seek to go along with the total secularist to the full in all non-religious areas' but continue to maintain that religious beliefs are meaningful. These beliefs 'combine with' or 'complement these other forms of belief in some way' (pp. 2f). But, we observe, before he can go along with the total secularist to the full, the Christian must come to see that his faith has 'nothing to contribute in our efforts to understand ourselves, and our world and to determine how we are to live'. Moreover, if religious beliefs are logically and existentially irrelevant, how can they be intelligibly combined with relevant and intelligible secular concepts? If religious beliefs, on the other hand, are not after all irrelevant, then total secularism is unnecessary. On Hirst's account therefore secular Christians are in an unintelligible position since in seeking to combine intelligible with unintelligible beliefs they are behaving irrationally, or, in insisting that religious belief does have something to contribute, they are refusing to go along with the total secularist.

The discussion of privatization has serious consequences for the Christian, unless, as argued above, it may be thought of as simply a sociological phenomenon. If it is thought to be significant in determining the logical relations between religious beliefs and secular ones, then the privatization of religion separates the Christian, no matter how secular he may be, from rationality, from the secular reality in and around him, from science and (to use the theological word) from creation. No Christian seeking wholeness and truth can accept this account of privatization. But if only the sociological sense is intended, then there is no logical reason why we should not try to construct relations between theology and secular education. Hirst hopes that his argument will be of interest to those who remain convinced 'even perhaps of the truth of certain central tenets of Christianity' (p. 6). How can one be rationally convinced of the truth of private claims? For 'truth is correspondence with reality' (p. 22).

Hirst outlines two traditional Christian approaches towards morals. The first (pp. 18–21) takes the will of God as ultimate in morals. The second (pp. 21–3) sees morality as based on natural law and therefore supposes a degree of natural autonomy for the moral life. This natural, rational morality is based on God's creation of man as free, rational and moral. On this second view the autonomy of science and morals is 'seen as built into Christianity rightly understood' (p. 23). The reader is bound to ask why this argument is not applied to education as well. And then if the autonomy, rationality and secularity of education are similarly built into the structure of Christian faith and can be so elucidated, then the Christian faith does produce a view of education, namely, that it is secular and (in important respects) autonomous. I am not concerned with whether this is a good or bad way to approach the problem; I am merely pointing out a failure in consistency in the argument. Hirst does not seem to see that just as secular Christians like Harvey Cox, whom he quotes, can become advocates of the secular city (an advocacy of which Hirst approves), so they can become advocates of secular education within the secular city,[28] which advocacy Hirst disallows in principle, although it could flow from the very arguments used by him to justify secular morals to the Christian. Whatever secularization may mean to the secular Christian, it cannot mean that the secular and the autonomous fall outside the scope of Christian appraisal.

This inconsistency can be seen clearly when it is understood that what Hirst proposes in his discussion of the Christian and secular morality is in fact a Christian theological rationale for secular morality. '... a coherent Christian view of morality positively requires it' (p. 52). The teaching of the Bible supports this view of natural, rational morals. So the relation between Christian faith and secular morals is that the former leads to the latter, although it is not the only path to it, and the secular morals would still be there even if that particular path to it did not happen to exist. Nevertheless, it remains the case that this is the special kind of morality to which Christian faith actually does lead, and it can be called both the Christian form of ethics and the secular form of ethics. Why then can there not be a Christian form of education which will also be the secular form of education? Hirst thinks that some of 'the most powerful intellectual seeds of secularization' (p. 23) lie within Christian theology, and are so integral to it that the forging of a theology of the secular is necessary to preserve the rational integrity of Christian theology itself. 'Christian teaching can never hope to be coherent if it denies the legitimacy of living in secular terms' (p. 27). Why not admit then that some of the seeds of the secularization of education lie within Christian faith and that the elaboration and further justification of these may constitute a Christian theology of education for today? 'If this emphasizes yet again that certain roots of secularization are to be found in Christianity, let that be recognized' (pp. 26f).

But even in his justification of secular morals to the Christian, Hirst is less ready to grant the full impact of theological ethics than he should be on his own argument. Moral principles have an 'ultimate status' (pp. 46, 50) and morals have to be 'argued back to the most fundamental principles of all' (p. 27). Religion is often described by Hirst as depending upon appeal to authority (for example, pp. 5, 18f, 53). But

Christianity sees morality as having 'its place in some ultimate transcendent scheme of things' (p. 55) and as dealing with 'the ultimate principles of human existence' (p. 55). 'It is in the additional emphasis that religion brings to the development of appropriate moral aspects of the personal life, by seeing them within beliefs, dispositions, and emotions of a wider and metaphysically more ultimate nature, that the religious impact upon morality is centred' (p. 75). Religion thus appears to offer a wider and more coherent pattern of justification for morals. Surely one is morally obliged to accept the most coherent frame of reference provided that frame is not irrational? Although he writes as if privatization has the effect of isolating religion and depriving theology of applicability, Hirst also speaks of theology as coherent, rational, a systematic whole from which conclusions can be drawn and impetus discovered for other forms of life. Religious morality is concerned with life's 'ultimate metaphysical understanding, its ultimate source and character' (p. 73). Enquiry into theological ethics would appear then to be morally obligatory since it must be a principle of rational morals to seek the widest possible framework and the most ultimate basis. The insistence that what theology contributes to morals is its metaphysical belief system (that is, its religious doctrines) and the repeated denial that religion has anything other than the purely rational (that is, not religious doctrines) to offer cannot be easily reconciled in Hirst's discussion. His thought about the relation between theology and secular ethics is ambivalent rather than ambiguous.

Conclusions

I have tried to show that the arguments which Hirst uses to disallow the possibility of connections between Christian theology and educational theory are unconvincing in themselves and inconsistent with his arguments elsewhere in the book about the relation between Christian theology and other spheres such as ethics. I have also tried to show that he does not succeed in commending this approach to the secular Christian, let alone the more traditional Christian, because the notion of a secular Christian is, in his account, not intelligible, and because the consequences from that part of his argument which is intelligible would be unacceptable to any Christian in pursuit of rational wholeness. It remains to ask why Hirst should make such genuine efforts to commend his view of ethics to the Christian but remain so adamant about the impossibility of a relation between Christianity and education. I can only assume that an educational philosopher in Britain today, being well aware of the rather unhappy history of some attempts by some churches and of some aspects of theology to control education and to retain it at a 'primitive' level, is particularly sensitive in this area. This is an understandable attitude, but not a philosophical one.

Notes

1 Daines, J.W., 'A review of unpublished theses in religious education 1968–72', *Learning for Living*, 12, 4, 1973, pp. 16–21; Webster, Derek, 'American research in religious education: A review of selected doctoral theses', *Learning for Living*, 14, 5, 1975, pp. 187–93; Steward, David S., 'Abstracts of doctoral dissertations in religious education 1971–72', *Religious Education*, 69, 4, 1974, pp. 475ff.

2 Cf. '. . . the older and undifferentiated concept which refers just to any process of bringing up or rearing', Hirst, Paul, H., and Peters, R.S., *The Logic of Education*, Routledge and Kegan Paul, 1970, p. 25.

3 Hirst speaks of 'thoroughly open instruction about religious beliefs' and adds a note to the 1974 reprint which reads, 'My view then is that maintained schools should teach "about" religion, provided that it is interpreted to include a direct study of religions, which means entering as fully as possible into an understanding of what they claim to be true', Hirst, Paul H., 'Morals religion and the maintained school', *British Journal of Educational Studies*, 19, 1; now in Hirst, Paul H., *Knowledge and the Curriculum*, Routledge and Kegan Paul, 1974, pp. 186f.

4 '. . . there is a proper place in the maintained school for religious studies', 'Religion, a form of knowledge? A reply', *Learning for Living*, 12, 4, 1973, p. 10.

5 See the review in *Education for Teaching*, 97, Summer 1975, pp. 88–90.

6 Hirst, Paul H., 'Christian education: A contradiction in terms', *Learning for Living*, 11, 4, 1972, p. 6.

7 *Ibid.*

8 *Ibid.*, p. 7.

9 *Ibid.*, p. 10.

10 *Ibid.*, p. 11.

11 *Ibid.*, p. 7.

12 *Ibid.*, p. 11.

13 I have discussed such matters in 'Worship and the secularization of religious education', Chapter four of my *School Worship, an Obituary, SCM Press, 1975,* and in 'Religious education in a pluralistic society', in *Progress and Problems in Moral Education* Taylor, Monica (ed.), NFER Publishing Co., 1975, pp. 195–205.

14 Hirst, Paul H., 'Public and private values and religious educational content', in *Religion and Public Education*, Sizer, T.R. (ed.), Boston, 1967, p. 330.

15 *Ibid.*, p. 331.

16 *Ibid.*, p. 332.

17 *Ibid.*, p. 333.

18 *Ibid.*, p. 335.

19 Both articles are now available in *Knowledge and the Curriculum*, cf. note 3.

20 Hirst, Paul H., 'Liberal education and the nature of knowledge', in *Philosophical Analysis and Education*, Archambault R.D. (ed.) Routledge and Kegan Paul, 1965, p. 131.

21 See, for example, Lonergan, Bernard, *Method in Theology*, Darton, Longman and Todd, 1972; Hart, Ray L., *Unfinished Man and the Imagination*, Herder and Herder, 1968; and Tillich, Paul, *Systematic Theology*, Nisbet, 1968, for characteristically modern approaches to theology, and Schleiermacher, F., *The Christian Faith*, T. and

T. Clark, 1928 for a now classical example of theological method from the early nineteenth century in Germany.

22 *Knowledge and the Curriculum*, p. 88.
23 *Ibid.*, p. 87.
24 *Ibid.*, p. 97.
25 *Ibid.*, p. 86.
26 *Ibid.*, p. 96.
27 Illustrations, from theology of culture, of method in modern applied theology are Tillich, Paul, *Theology of Culture*, OUP, 1964; Ong, Walter J., *The Presence of the Word*, Yale University Press, 1967; and Spiegler, G., *The Eternal Covenant*, Harper and Row, 1967.
28 See the symposium, 'Religious education in the secular city', by Cox, Harvey, *et al.* in *Religious Education*, 61, 2, 1966, pp. 83, 113.

20. *What Is Theology of Education?*

Preliminary remarks

An understanding of the nature of theology of education, as of any other field of applied or practical theology, will spring from some previous understanding of the nature and functions of theology itself. But here the theorist in the interdisciplinary field is in something of a dilemma. If he fails to make it clear that theology of education rests upon an interpretation of the nature of theology, his treatment will tend to be superficial. He will be exploring the theological implications of education, but he will not have shown himself aware of the implications for theology of the methods he uses in his exploration. Since his aim is to elucidate implications for theology, he must turn his scrutiny inwards towards himself as theologian, as well as outwards towards education. On the other hand, in setting forth the understanding of theology which informs his work in applied theology, he makes his work more controversial, since there will be other understandings of theology, and other understandings of applied theology will flow from these to relativize his own methodology. Or it may be thought that the interdisciplinary field necessarily rests upon this and only this understanding of theology, and then those whose understanding of theology differs will conclude that the whole interdisciplinary enterprise is misconceived. A relatively underdeveloped interdisciplinary field such as theology of education is particularly susceptible to this misunderstanding.

So, does he elaborate the view of theology which he finds most useful, or does he not? The dilemma is inescapable, but the former alternative is slightly less uncomfortable than the latter. Failure to particularize theological premises hinders further discussion, and theology of education should be guided by this educational consideration, as well as by theological ones. But it should be made perfectly clear that there are almost as many theologies of education as there are theologies, the only restriction (and it is an important one) being that some theologies are incapable of generating an understanding of education, but tend, in their reflection about education, to turn education into something else. We must therefore distinguish between theologies of education and theologies of Christian nurture, theologies of preaching, or theologies of indoctrination. In so far as the processes of education, nurture, preaching and indoctrination differ, theologies will differ in the extent to which they can appraise them successfully. Nevertheless, it remains the case that a variety of theologies could certainly yield a variety of valid approaches to education. The approach offered here claims to be no more than one possible approach, and is offered as illustrative rather than stipulative.

Would it not be possible to overcome the particularities of given theologies by abstracting from a number of such illustrations the methodological features common to them all, thus arriving at something like a general method of applied theology? That may perhaps be possible in the future. But since the structure of theology of education has as yet received rather slight attention, it seems necessary at this stage to begin with the examination of concrete specimens.

How should we decide what theology is?

Is it legitimate to allow reflection about the nature of theology to be influenced by the use to be made of the resulting concept? For surely norms intrinsic to the nature of theology must be logically prior to any use made in applying those norms to other fields? And yet it is by no means a simple matter to distinguish between what is intrinsic to the nature of theology and what is merely an influence from some applied field. Success and failure in applying theology reveal problems in the conception of the nature of theology, and so theology is always made up of many layers of previous insights and revisions resulting from attempted applications. In other words, there is an intimate connection between historical theology, systematic theology and applied theology. It is a relationship of mutual interdependence. But are not the decisive factors for the nature of theology derived from considerations of a theological kind rather than from education, politics or science? Even if Christology in the first Christian century developed as a result of a failure of the inherited christological conceptions to be successfully applied to Jesus, at least the impetus for the development came from Jesus, already conceived as a theological category, and not from some secular sphere. But this is too simple a view. The criteria for what is to count as being theologically significant are not so self-evident. Why, after all, did Israel take the Exodus events to be theologically significant rather than significant as natural history, politics or climate? It could not have been because of the application of the criterion 'miracle', for (a) non-miraculous events were also accepted as being theologically significant and (b) classification as 'miracle' often follows the judgment of theological significance rather than preceding it.

The criteria for judging theological significance can be thought of as derived exclusively from previous theological formulations only if theology is conceived of as being a logically self-sufficient field of successive deduction, perhaps a little like mathematics, although even mathematics forms new mathematical concepts to interpret new non-mathematical data. But if, as seems more probable, theology operates both at an inductive, experiential or empirical level and at a level of very great generality and abstraction, then what is reckoned to be theologically significant will not be confined to what was thought of in that way by previous theologians. There is therefore a place for allowing insights and experiences drawn from both the natural and the social sciences to affect our judgments about what is theologically significant, in so far as these new, initially non-theological materials show themselves to relate meaningfully to previous theological formulations, so contributing to the ongoing theological task.

The nature of the theology which will serve us best in theology of education is therefore partly influenced but not wholly determined by the requirements of the task in hand. The history of theology of education shows many examples of applied work being integrated into a reformulated systematic and philosophic theology. Augustine's use of reflections about the learning process in *On the Trinity* is a case of such mutuality between materials which at first sight might seem readily distinguishable into 'intrinsic' and 'applied' or into theological and non-theological data.

What is theology?

The view of theology of education which will be outlined below rests upon the idea that theology is a form of thinking, a kind of rationality. Its distinctiveness lies in its subject matter. There may be certain forms of thought which will be especially appropriate to articulate the peculiarities of religion, and so, for example, theology may make considerable use of analogical and symbolic forms. But the analogical thinking will adhere to whatever norms there might be for such thinking. There are peculiarities about religious language, and probably distinctive criteria for meaning, but when the theologian or the philosopher of religion elucidates these, he will seek to show that the peculiarities are comprehensible, that they perform certain tasks and follow certain rules. If this were not the case, theology could not communicate with other fields; it could only consume or be consumed.

But what *kind* of religious thinking is involved in theology? For when a person prays, he is also engaged in thinking. If he prays for God to have mercy on him, he not only believes that there is a God who may have mercy on him, but is actually thinking it as he prays. In such thinking, the thinking serves the purposes of the praying. But in theology, thinking occupies a more primary position. In prayer, thinking may be systematic, as when it moves from praise to petition and to intercession. But such systematic thought is an elaboration of the concept of prayer; it is not a critique of the concept of prayer. One does not, one logically and psychologically cannot, both intercede and critically consider the concept of intercession simultaneously. The adoration of God requires, as long as it specifically continues in prayer and worship, that the adorer should bow in humility and commitment. Only at another time may he critically and systematically think about God as an object of adoration. In theological thinking, thought is controlled by the characteristics of thought as such – criticism, coherence, judgment, selection, formation of hypotheses and so on.

What is the subject matter of theology? The subject matter of theology is the contents of the religious consciousness, that is, the characteristics of the self-awareness in so far as these are knowingly influenced or formed by participation within a religious tradition. We may assume that few people in the Western world escape some influences from Christianity and Judaism, and that these continue to mould Western views of time, death and nature. We may, however, distinguish between those who know this and those who do not. Within the former group, who know that their self-consciousness is moulded by religion, we may further distinguish between those who confirm these influences, identifying with the religion, and seeking to be further moulded by their participation in it, and those who reject these influences and seek to refashion their personhood along different lines (for example, the thoughtful humanist). The tasks of theology of education can best be understood if we confine the area in which theologizing takes place to those who know they are influenced by the religious tradition and wish that influence to continue. Theologizing (which must be distinguished from the *study* of theology) thus takes place within the community of faith, and its subject matter is the experience of the faithful, or of those

252

who, knowing they are unfaithful, see even in this self-recognition a summons to faith.

The subject matter of theology is thus not the New Testament but the Christian religious experience in understanding and interpreting the New Testament, the religious consciousness in so far as it is determined by the New Testament. The critical study of the Bible through such disciplines as philology, archaeology and textual criticism is important to theology (and there are theological reasons for this) but theology itself is concerned with hermeneutics, with the way in which the Bible does or should or might impinge upon the religious consciousness. Similarly, the subject matter of theology is not initially God but the religious apprehension of God, and this is one of the features which differentiates theology from philosophy. Leonard Hodgson has shown the way the doctrine of the trinity was the result of a conflict between a monotheistic theology and a trinitarian religion.[1] Theology thus deals with the revelation of God in so far as that revelation is subjectively (individually and corporately) realized within consciousness. Its task is to articulate, to clarify and to conceptualize that consciousness.[2]

Doing theology and studying theology

If theology is the critical, systematic conceptualization of the religious consciousness it can take place only where there is access to religious consciousness. One can really *do* theology only upon the subject matter of one's own religious consciousness, whether individually in a search for one's own wholeness, or as a member of a religious community on behalf of the wholeness and integrity of the community. Otherwise, one is *studying* theology. If the theological reflection of a simple believer is deepened by the questioning of a sympathetic enquirer who does not share the experience of the believer, the enquirer would be helping the believer to do theology but would himself be studying the believer's theology. There will be other borderline situations. The student may begin by studying the theology of a community and find himself engaged in an enquiry after his own religious coherence. The move between objectivity and subjectivity is familiar to every theological student. It is appropriate in university and in school to study theology without insisting that theology be actually *done*, since the latter insistence would require religious tests for admittance. But like any teachers who believe in the beauty and value of their subject, those who teach students to study theology hope quite properly that the study will be of some personal significance to the student, whether this can ever be described as doing theology or whether it results in a more meaningful coherence of the student's secular consciousness. In other words, doing theology is characterized by participation in the intentionality of theologizing but studying theology is examination of the phenomenology of that intentionality and is thus characterized by empathy rather than by sympathy.

The reason for this discrimination between doing and studying theology is that it is necessary to emphasize the nature of theology as an existential activity which demands commitment, and to see that this commitment springs from its home in the religious self-awareness. Theology becomes uncommitted and disengaged only when it becomes isolated from the religious consciousness of the enquirer. Doing theology and studying theology are, however, complementary. Both have their advantages. It is both possible and necessary, by imaginative suspension of belief, to study one's own theology. But without some such distinction, it becomes difficult to provide a rationale for the place of theology in public educational institutions, whether schools or universities.

Problems in theology

Since theology of education sets out to deal with certain problems which arise in and for theology, we must next ask how problems *can* arise in theology. What is it about the nature of theology which allows problems to emerge, or what is meant by a theological problem? Our understanding of theology enables us now to describe various kinds of theological problems so as to define the sort with which theology of education is concerned.

We may distinguish between two kinds of problem. The first (problems of coherence) arises out of the quality of the thinking as thinking. The second (problems of applicability) arises out of a dissonance between the thinking and the subject matter, that is, a failure to correspond with the religious consciousness which is being conceptualized.

A problem of coherence arises when the clarity and the distinctness of a theological concept are in doubt. The concept of God might be such a case. Or the distinctions and relations between two similar concepts might be unclear, such as the relation between the human spirit and the divine spirit in prayer, or the distinction between procession and generation in the Trinity. In more severe cases, the coherence of the theological system as a whole might be under threat, either internally (the problem of evil and the goodness of God) or externally, as when two apparently rival theological universes converge (Christianity and Islam).

The second kind of problem concerns the applicability of theological concepts. The possibility of applying theological concepts at all arises from their origin in the religious experience. From thence they come, and there they must return. The need for applying them is built into their function as the clarification of aspects of that experience. Their applicability verifies their meaning and establishes their relevance. Theology of education deals with certain problems of applicability.

Two areas of applicability may be distinguished. The first arises when theological concepts are applied *within* the community of faith. There may be dissonance between the objects of credal confession and the popular objects of devotion, or the theological concepts may appear to be devoid of ethical significance, or they may be significantly different from the previous conceptualizations arrived at by the same community. If theology is to retain its role as the critical servant of the religious consciousness, it must strive to retain unity with what it purports to be articulating. The drive towards wholeness is a feature of mature religious consciousness, as well as a necessary feature of rationality. Ethical responsibility is another aspect of the religious consciousness, and a theological concept unable to relate itself to ethics would fail in its claim to be a valid theological articulation. The subject matter and the results of reflection must always be in a relationship of mutual support and intermingling, and if this cannot take place, we have a problem in theology. Cognitions as well as affections are part of the experience of being religious, and it is the task of theologizing to purify and integrate them conceptually. Other activities, such as worship, purify and integrate them in different ways.

The problems with which theology of education is concerned lie in the second area of applicability, when theological concepts are applied *beyond* the community of faith. If this cannot be done, we have this variety of theological problem. Religious faith seeks to comprehend and unite all experience, and the universal applicability of its critical conceptualized form (theology) is an aspect of this desire to unify. There may be aspects of human experience, whether within the community of faith or outside it, which resist this. From outside the community there may come a new style of art, a new kind of novel, which has not been understood theologically because it is too new. There may be other aspects of experience which pose a mild problem just because they seem to be lacking in religious or theological significance, such as the areas of pastimes, play and sport.[3] Strong forms of this kind of problem arise when the secular areas of experience and interpretation actively resist theology. This may be the case with certain scientific or political theories. The secular world may appear to offer rival worlds of meaning, such as humanism and communism. When such influences originating beyond the community take the initiative, the problem may be transformed from one of applicability beyond the community into a problem of theological coherence. So the Darwinian controversies began as a problem of applicability beyond the community (relations between Christian faith and biology) but became a problem of theological coherence (hermeneutics and the Christian concept of man). Relations between Christianity and the other world faiths at one time took the form of a problem of applicability, since the question was the place of the non-Christian religions in the Christian view of the plan of God for the world. If one now speaks of the possibility of a world religious history and a universal theology, the definition of the 'community of faith' is enlarged, and the problem is then one of coherence within the community of religious mankind. Indeed, since problems usually begin with the observation of unusual phenomena and the discovery that these cannot be fitted into existing frames of reference, we may say that most theological problems begin as problems of applicability and become problems of coherence if they cannot be resolved through application. This illustrates the earlier claim that successful applicability is a major form of theological truth testing. A persistent difficulty in applying a concept will almost always be found to spring from some deeper incoherence, or it will lead to the emergence of a dissonance between theology and other experience not perceived before. Here then we have a further reply to the question whether it is legitimate to allow the needs of theology of education to influence our definitions of what theology itself might be. If education could not have such an influence, it would demonstrate that something was wrong with the understanding of theology. The two types of problems, coherence and applicability, must constantly be in communication with each other.

The work of theology in applying its concepts to areas beyond the community of faith has given rise to a number of special branches of theology. So we have theology of culture, theology of history, theology of the arts, theology of play, theology of world religions and so on. These expressions describe forms of theological enquiry which seek to resist an attack mounted from a hostile sphere, or meaningfully to relate and interpret the concepts within an alien but not hostile sphere, or to bring out the theological significance of an apparently passive, inert and theologically irrelevant sphere. These objectives are indicated in the use of the word 'of'. The implication is that the concluding word in the phrase, whether it be culture, art or history, despite its hostile, alien or passive appearance, does contain within it material significant to theology, or an implicit theological structure, or even resources for theological construction, and that there can be a theology of culture just as truly as there can be a theology of revelation or a theology of the sacraments. Theology of culture or of art will normally be more peripheral than theology of revelation or of the sacraments, in that the former are in the applied area and the latter within the area of specific theological concepts themselves, but in view of the inner relation between the two areas there may be occasions when theology of culture (church-state relations in Nazi Germany) or theology of world development (the revolutionary ecclesiastical movements in South America) may take on an urgency which will bring them within the central concern of religious faith, and make them into a powerful force for reshaping basic theological concepts.

The word 'of' also indicates that these are convergent disciplines, in which the practices and theories of the final term (culture or art) are interpreted and appraised by the norms and concepts of theology. This does not imply that the theology of culture is critical of culture but not critical of theology. Indeed the dominant mood of all these interpretative theological disciplines is that of a dialogue in which theology is also seeking to appraise itself and to reformulate itself. Theology of culture is thus also cultural theology, that is, the theology implicit within culture made explicit.

Theology of education is one such branch of theology. Its work and the problems it encounters fall within the attempt of theology to apply itself to areas which lie mainly beyond the community of faith. Some of its concerns will, however, be related to the attempt of theology to apply itself within the community of faith, and here we would find catechetics and religious nurture.

Theology of education as an educational discipline

The nature of theology of education must be considered not only in relation to theology but also to education. Education, like medicine, is a field upon which a number of disciplines converge. These disciplines are ruled by their own norms and procedures, but come together in order to facilitate or improve the practical enterprise of educating people. Although this convergence creates a number of areas of enquiry peculiar to education (for example, curriculum theory), education does not constitute a distinct and unique form or domain of knowledge like mathematics, physical science or aesthetics.[4] The main contributory disciplines are psychology, sociology, history and philosophy. There are other disciplines also involved, such as social administration and statistics, but these are less fundamental in the appraisal they offer. Theology of education has similarities with the former group; it is certainly not at all like the latter group (statistics). It claims to offer a fundamental appraisal of education. The closest parallel is with philosophy of education, which, in its major British form, seeks to clarify the concepts of education. Naturally, philosophy of education cannot avoid working from within a particular philosophical tradition, and in so far as it is critical of itself as well as critical of its subject matter, philosophy of education will be aware of this particularity. The present dominant British school is using the techniques of philosophical analysis, and is thus primarily interested in linguistic philosophy.[5] There are also existentialist philosophies of education, pragmatic ones, idealist ones and so forth. Because of its nature as related to a particular religious consciousness, theology of education cannot avoid working within the belief structure of a particular theology or ranging from one particular theology to another. So there are well-developed Islamic and Jewish theologies of education, and within Christianity there are confessional (denominational) theologies of education such as those of Lutheranism or Catholicism. The relations between philosophy of education and theology of education will be like the relations between philosophy and theology, mediated and complicated by the third term, education.

The main difference of principle between philosophy of education and theology of education is that the latter, because of its distinctive position as an articulation of an aspect of the religious consciousness, permits a distinction between *doing* and *studying* which philosophy of education does not. Theology is concerned with a more specific aspect of human consciousness, that is, the consciousness as religious and as religiously involved in education. Philosophy is secular in that it is concerned with nothing but good thinking of a philosophic kind. Theology is concerned with good thinking about the religious kind of experience. This does not make theology any less critical of its subject matter or of itself but it always starts with that subject matter. The thinking of theology thus occupies a middle position between the thinking of prayer and philosophical thinking. The difference between theology and philosophy of religion is that theology is working deliberately within the religious tradition which has moulded the consciousness in question, whereas philosophy of religion stands further back, and assesses the success of theology in articulating the contents of that religious consciousness not in terms of faithfulness to the tradition and the present consciousness, but in terms of wider philosophical criteria. The difference between philosophy of art, philosophy of science and so on and theology of art or theology of science is that the former are as central to philosophy as anything else in philosophy. Philosophy of science is as much philosophy as is philosophy of mind. There is no division of philosophical problems into those that deal with matters within the community and those that deal with matters beyond the community, because there is no community, or because it is simply the community of all rational people. Similarly, there is no difference in philosophy between problems of coherence and those of applicability. Philosophy of education is not applying philosophical concepts to education and scrutinizing education in the light of them. It is not applying coherence from another realm ('philosophy') but it is seeking coherence within education by philosophical means.

Although we can say that there is some truth in the suggestion that in philosophy of education the tools are those of philosophy (for example, philosophical analysis) but the concepts are those of education (for example, 'learning') whereas in theology of education one is concerned with the relation between theological concepts (for example, 'grace') and educational concepts (for example, 'learning'), even this must be qualified.

The perennial problems of philosophy, such as perception, mind, knowledge, the status and function of language and so on, are already of an educational kind. But there is a difference between theology of the sacraments and theology of education, in that the former deals with concepts which are themselves already part of the theological sphere, whereas the latter is seeking to comprehend, from within that sphere, concepts which lie beyond it. Theology of education is a frontier discipline in that it seeks to extend the theological system. Although integrated with the rest of theology, it is logically more peripheral to theology than philosophy of education is to philosophy. You can thus do philosophy only if you are rational but you can do theology only if you are religious. Being rational is a defining attribute of the human, but being religious (in the sense in which I am using it, as possessing a consciousness knowingly and willingly moulded by participation within a religious tradition) is not. But if anyone claims that being religious *is* a defining attribute of the human, then it would seem difficult to distinguish philosophy from theology, and philosophy of education from theology of education. We might, of course, say that there could be a difference between doing philosophy and studying philosophy in that the former supposes a greater degree of commitment on the part of the student. But the commitment is to nothing but his rationality, and since everyone engaged in philosophy should be committed to rationality, we would be justified in saying that all students of philosophy *ought* to be *doing* it, and that if they are not prepared to be rationally *engaged* in it, that is, thinking about it for themselves, they ought not to be doing it at all, or perhaps they could be described as, in fact, not doing it *at all*. All philosophizing should be a doing since all are rational. But not all are religious, and it would not be proper in a public educational institution to urge upon a student that he ought not to be taking an interest in theology unless he was personally religious. It is, we normally believe, intellectually legitimate for him to be rationally engaged in the study of theology even if he is not religiously engaged. He may study it even if he does not do it. The distinction between studying theology and doing theology is thus pointing to the nature of religious discourse as characteristic of a particular 'form of life' in Wittgenstein's sense, with its particular contexts and rules. Because it is thus particular, it can be examined either from the outside or from the inside. But nobody could *examine* philosophy from the outside of rationality.

This distinction, if it is clear and valid, poses the major problem for the viability of theology of education as an educational discipline. For how can a discipline which is characteristic of a particular form of life legitimately scrutinize one (education) which, in so far as it is a rational activity, is universal? Two kinds of reply to this are usually given. In the first reply, the independent rationality of education is denied. Education, in some way or other, is dependent upon religion, or is a means to achieving a religious end; thus education cannot be thought of as a secular activity. All education, rightly conceived, is religious education (because all education ought to make people religious). This kind of reply causes education to set goals related to particular religious forms of life, and, in the end, causes education to be conceived not in the open, critical sense, but as nurture into one of the particular religious traditions. Thus, most theological writing from previous centuries about 'Christian education', as it is normally called, is more correctly described as being about Christian nurture. So what this first reply tries to do is to remove the problems of theology of education from the area of applicability *beyond* the community of faith and to place them as problems *within* the community of faith, within actual or intentional Christendom. Such an approach cannot hope to succeed because it fails to take the secularization process seriously, and fails thus to take modern education seriously. It refuses to scrutinize education, but merely tells education it should be something else. Since it cannot succeed, it will inevitably lead to a breakdown in relations between theology and education.[6] We may observe in passing that because of the emergence of secular education in our century, education has become an urgent theological problem.

The second customary reply to the objection that theology cannot scrutinize education is to deny the distinction between studying theology and doing theology, making some claim for the necessity of religion as being as constitutive of humanity as reason, and thus pinning one's hopes on some kind of *homo religiosus* argument. Whereas the first reply domesticates education, the latter universalizes religion. All education, rightly understood, is religious education (because all people are already religious). It all depends on how you 'rightly' understand education. This approach is certainly preferable to the former, and there are possibilities of a satisfactory theology of education through the work of Max Scheler, Martin Heidegger, Mircea Eliade, Martin Buber and others. Certainly, philosophical anthropology is a very significant level of thinking both in education, philosophy and theology, and some of the most important work has to be done here.

But if we stick to the distinction between studying and doing theology, approach the problem through linguistic analysis, agree with Wittgenstein about the particularities of forms of life and games of language, and take the secularization of education seriously, what then?

The legitimacy of a theological scrutiny of education can be maintained only if the purpose and limits of that scrutiny are clearly stated. Theology cannot seek to absorb education; it cannot seek to establish a view of education such that the principles of education flow necessarily and exclusively from theology. This would mean that only theists, or believers in whatever kind of theology was being set forth, could take part in education. On the other hand, theology cannot admit that it has no right to an influence upon education; for then no theologian could be engaged in education and still preserve his integrity. Theology would fail to articulate the whole of his religious experience, or his experience would be wider than his religious experience. The aim of theology of education must therefore be to show that theology can provide a legitimate and a possible source of understanding for education but not a necessary one. In this way the dignity of education as a secular sphere of human expertise is secured, but it is made clear that such secularity does not carry with it immunity from criticism from other forms of life such as religion and art. This is not the place to ask what kind of theology might generate this kind of understanding of this kind of education, since we are here concerned with the nature of theology of education in principle not in substance.

What this means is that anyone engaged in education must, in preserving his integrity, seek to make sense of his work in terms of the rest of his outlook on life. If he is a humanist, he must develop a humanist understanding of education. If he is a communist, he will develop a communist understanding of education. We should not speak of *theology* of education in the case of such teachers since it would not articulate a *religious* consciousness, but it will be a related activity of some kind. But because communist values are not those of our democracy as a whole, and therefore a communist would be limited in the extent to which it would be proper for him to exercise communist theories of education in the state schools, that does not mean that the attempt to relate communism and education is wrong in principle, or that taking place within a democracy ought to protect education from scrutiny and critique by Marxists. This example is relevant, because it is precisely on the ground that it is a minority pursuit or a set of 'private' values that the legitimacy of theology of education is assailed.[7] In a pluralist society, we are all minorities. But to insist that comment on public affairs shall be couched only in terms which win the consent of all is to refuse to live with genuine and actual plurality. We are fond of saying that religious education as a subject of the curriculum cannot be justified theologically but only educationally if it is to be a valid educational activity. If this means that there was a time when theological justification was such that the nature of the activity as *educational* was obscured, then this protest is quite proper, because such theological justification would be improper. But that does not carry with it the implication that when the proper educational justification is provided, it must then be immune from theological scrutiny. The educational justification cannot be *based* on the results of such theological scrutiny, and in that sense, theology of education will not be intellectually imperialistic. It has no right to dominate, or to insist that it be satisfied. But it has a right to enquire, a right to be heard and a right to seek to influence. If that is not granted, there can be no place for the thoughtful Christian in education today.

We conclude from this that theology of education is justified as a branch of educational study in two main ways. (1) In so far as it is the *study* of the relations between various theologies and education, it is a perfectly normal and proper intellectual activity open to all rational people involving examination of what theologians have said about education, what might be inferred about education from various religious belief systems and so on. It is a perfectly respectable activity for a university department or faculty of education to engage in. (2) In so far as it involves the *doing* of theology of education, it is a minority activity, relevant in the first place to those who are religious and wish to articulate their participation in education in terms of their religious consciousness. This is not a proper activity for a university, since it would require tests of religious faith from students, but ought to be conducted in theological colleges and the church colleges of education, and on the part of the various churches and other religious communities. But it has a wider importance in so far as many persons engaged in education are Christian (or of other religious persuasions) and it is in the interests of a more reflective and sophisticated teaching profession that such individuals should be helped to reflect about their professional work in the light of their faith. As far as Christianity is concerned, there is no reason to believe that such reflection would hinder them in their critical educational tasks. On the contrary, it should help them. But it remains a carefully limited enterprise, which must not, in criticizing education, lose respect for the secularity of education. Secularization is a theological category, but that does not mean that the items within that category are not genuinely secular.

Theology of education in practice

The study of theology of education has received but little attention in Britain, although there have been a few important contributions.[8] More work has been done in North America[9] and in continental Europe. In 1972 the University of Birmingham began the first course in theology and education to be offered as part of a British Master of Education degree by course work and dissertation. It is anticipated that in 1977 it will be possible, in the new Birmingham University Faculty of Education, to take an MEd degree entirely in theology and education. The main difficulties are to do with methods and resources. Some of the conceptual difficulties in method have already been touched upon. How does one work on this subject? By what criteria are areas of education selected for theological study? How does one elucidate the insights for education offered by a certain theological doctrine? Can a theological problem in education be solved? Is it any different when it is solved? The difficulties in resources are mainly to do with the paucity of literature or its inaccessibility. A large amount of material is in the form of unpublished dissertations and theses.[10] Significant areas of study exist in other languages. The educational writings of Schleiermacher have never been translated into English and the critical literature relating to his theology of education is almost entirely in German. Often the researcher is faced with a theological work on one hand and an educational work on the other, and must simply begin to do his own bridge building. Not many students, even at quite a mature stage, are capable of this sort of work.

There will not be a single method to be applied to all problems. Some methods will suit some problems. Beneath the difficulties of method and resources lies the task of creating a list of problems. Only then can one distinguish the problems which differ from each other in principle. Similarly with resources one must isolate the problems before one can begin to marshal the resources in an orderly fashion. The right order for theology of education is therefore first, to draw up a list and if possible a taxonomy of problems, then to distinguish the methods appropriate to the resolution of the various problems, and finally to marshal the resources for the task. Only then can the substance of the work begin.

The list which follows is a first attempt to make some of these distinctions. It is certainly incomplete in several respects even as a list of problems, the most important of these being that it is deliberately limited to problems in the Christian theology of education. It might well be that taxonomies presented in terms of other faiths would present different areas or different emphases. One hopes for the day when specialists in Islam and education will produce a list of problems in the Islamic theology of education thus making it possible for us to begin systematic work in the field, including both comparative religion and comparative education. In the meantime, we must begin to study what lies closest to hand, Christian faith and Western education.

Use of the list of problems

Apart from its theoretical use as a conceptual map of the area, which has already been mentioned, the list may serve as an indication to research workers of the range of subjects requiring investigation and enable a student to plot some of the connections between his problem and related ones. It may also serve as an outline syllabus for those involved in teaching theology of education. The list is a guide to the study of theology of education for everyone, and to the *doing* of theology of education for Christians.

The comments are intended simply to indicate the sort of problems which are in mind. These are necessarily fragmentary and the reader will notice many aspects to which no reference has been made. To improve it as a working tool, the list should be followed by bibliographies which would indicate the extent to which the area has already been recognized as a problem and the progress already made in dealing with it. In spite of its limits, the list does claim to offer a grid which in principle includes all the possible problems which might arise between Christian theology and education.

Taxonomy of problems in the theology of education

Part I: Problems of formal principles

This is the first of the three main sections of the taxonomy. It deals with formal, theoretical or conceptual problems arising out of the relations between education and theology, and is thus the largest and most important of the three sections. The distinction between formal and material principles is that the latter, in the second main section, have to do with content in the teaching situation, whereas the former, although often having a bearing upon content and method in teaching, are not immediately concerned with this application of their theoretical constructs.

The first part begins with problems arising from education and continues with those arising from theology.

Part 1A: Problems arising from the formal principles of education
This is divided into problems arising from the main disciplines through which education is studied, namely philosophy, psychology, sociology and history. Educational administration and comparative education are listed under sociology.

Part IA1: Problems arising from the philosophy of education
The list which follows is suggestive not exhaustive. It may well be possible to arrange them in a more satisfactory way. Fields like these tend to 'fan out' into various interlocking theological problems when examined by someone very familiar with the area.

IA1a: The concept of education
Problems of the nature of education, its aims and objectives, its autonomy or otherwise, distinctions between education and other related processes such as training and indoctrination, and the various theological rationales for each of these different processes. The nature of education and the nature of religious education as a part of it.

IA1b: Values in education
This obviously springs out of the previous category. Education and the nature of man, education and the person. What is a person? Authority, discipline, punishment. Theological ethics and educational values. Rationality. Relations between religious education and moral education, in principle.

IA1c: Epistemology
Education and the nature of knowledge. Religion as a form of know-

ledge. Relations between forms of knowledge. Theological epistemologies and educational ones.

IA1d: Particular philosophies of education
Analytic philosophy; platonism, pragmatism, existentialism. The theological significance of the work of Rousseau, Dewey, Heidegger. Marxist and Maoist philosophies of education and theology. Paulo Freire.

Part IA2: Problems arising from the psychology of education
Here we have listed some of the aspects of psychology which either implicitly (social learning and behaviourist theories of learning) or explicitly (Freud) impinge upon the concerns of theology. Theological concepts of learning will be contrasted. Theories of child development, the theological interpretations of childhood, and the psychology of moral development with special reference to conscience, freedom and autonomy arise. This also seems the right section to place study of the psychology of religion, theological and psychological estimates of religious experience and conversion. So we have:

IA2a: Learning theories
IA2b: Communication theories
IA2c: Child development
IA2d: Psycho-analysis. Freud
IA2e: Analytic psychology. Jung
IA2f: Counselling psychology. Rogers. Maslow.
IA2g: Logotherapy. Frankl.
IA2h: Moral development
IA2i: Psychology of religion and religious experience

Theological consideration of the implications of the work of Ronald Goldman, for example, would appear under Piaget in IA2c. Formation of a Christian existentialist philosophy of education would combine IA2g with IA1d on existentialism.

Part IA3: Problems arising from the sociology of education
The questions relating to secularization should be placed here. What theological problems are raised by the independence of educational institutions and activities? What is the nature of Christian presence within a secular educational system? In what senses may religious education be secularized? Questions concerning the nature of church-state relations in education also arise at this point. The second main area might be that connected with deschooling, with social revolution and the school, and with progressive education and political theology. Theology of culture and the social context of learning, the implication for theology

and education of the sociology of knowledge and so on. Finally, we ask to what extent is theology interested in the principles and values of educational organization? Questions of Christian social ethics also arise in consideration of such issues as private schools and streaming. So would we have:

IA3a: Secularization
IA3b: Social revolution and the school
IA3c: Theology of culture and the social context of learning
IA3d: Comparative education and educational organization and administration

Part IA4: Problems arising from the history of education
A good deal of research work has dealt with the relations between theology and education in the past. Here then we have such questions as the degree to which Pestalozzi was influenced by the theological thought of Rousseau and Schleiermacher, the theological factors at work in the educational activities of the English evangelicals in the eighteenth and nineteenth centuries, and so on.

Part IA5: Problems arising out of curriculum theory
Here we must examine the objectives of the curriculum and its various parts, theories of curriculum development, the basis of integration in the curriculum and so on. There may be some overlap here with IA1c: Epistemology. Curriculum theory presents theology with the truth that it is one kind of knowledge amongst many. Since the collapse of the great romantic and idealist syntheses of the early nineteenth century, theology has been wrestling with the problems of the diversity of knowledge. The curriculum presents not only a complex form of this problem but one of practical urgency.

We now turn to the second half of this first section of our taxonomy.

Part IB: Problems arising from the formal principles of theology
It would be a mistake to think that in passing from the principles of education to those of theology we are moving from problems to resources. It has already been shown that in theology of education theology is affected as well as education, and in its encounter with education, theology asks itself new questions about its viability and relevance. Of course, there is a sense in which theology must ultimately find within itself the resources to interrogate education, but this will present problems too. If a theology were hostile to education, or should prove itself uncongenial to educational thinking,[11] this must raise a host

of questions for educators who hold such a theology. But then if the whole nature of theology were conceived of differently, theology of education might be a different sort of undertaking. This taxonomy, it should be remembered, is based on a certain view of theology which is not uncontroversial. Not only might different taxonomies flow from non-Christian belief systems, but different premises within Christian theology would change the nature of the interdisciplinary dialogue.

As with education, the formal principles of theology are regarded as the ideas, constructs, insights, concepts derived from systematic theology, biblical and historical theology, confessional and practical theology. 'Contemporary theology' is used to gather together conveniently several current concerns which are generating an educational literature.

Part IB1: Problems arising from systematic theology
Ib1a: God
If education is founded upon ideas about man and if theology holds man to be made in the image of God, then theology must be concerned with the foundations of education. What might flow from the concept of God in the thought of Teilhard de Chardin or Charles Hartshorne for education? What are the implications of the doctrine of the trinity for education?

IB1b: Revelation
To what extent is the concept of the 'closure of revelation' hostile to education? To what extent is the divine revelation thought of as the education of man? What theories of revelation underlie religious education? Gabriel Moran.

IB1c: Man
The question of man and his destiny is perhaps the most crucial of all theological areas for education. Problems of sin and punishment also arise. Must an educational theory necessarily be Pelagian?

IB1d: Creation
The relation between theology and education enters an interesting stage when we move to creativity. What is the significance for syllabus construction of the idea that all creation is revelatory? This begins to overlap with Part II of the taxonomy.

IB1e: Christology
What does the lordship of Christ mean for the Christian in education? To what extent should the image of man underlying education be moulded by the image of Christ, for example, his love? Questions regarding the incarnation and the atonement enter here.

IB1f: The Holy Spirit
Does Christian education need the Holy Spirit? To what extent is

religious nurture a special means of grace? Note that this last question takes us into the area of applied problems arising within the community of faith.

IB1g: Ecclesiology
What is the mission of the church in education, and through her own institutions of education? What is the educational value of the liturgy and the sacraments? Penance in particular is an educational sacrament. What is Christian community?

IB1h: Eschatology
Where does education stand in an ethic such as that of Bonhoeffer who distinguished between the ultimate and the penultimate things? What are the consequences of the theology of hope for education? Note the impact of Teilhard de Chardin's eschatology upon education.

IB1i: Hermeneutics
In religious education, experiential methods are a form of applied biblical hermeneutics in existentialist terms. What problems does this present? This leads us to Part III of the taxonomy. But theology has a wider interest in the principles of hermeneutics expressed in literary criticism and historical studies, so this opens up important areas of discussion which impinge upon Part II of the taxonomy.

Part IB2: Problems arising from biblical theology and from historical theology
Here we come to the individuals or the writings which deal explicitly with education, or from which implications for education may be drawn. Only illustrations are offered, as elsewhere in the taxonomy.

IB2a: Education in biblical thought, Old Testament and New
IB2b: Education in patristic thought. Catechesis in the early church. Irenaeus, Clement of Alexandria and Augustine
IB2c: The scholastic theology, especially Aquinas
IB2d: The protestant reformers, especially Luther and Calvin, and the Catholic reaction, especially the Jesuits
IB2e: Modern theology. Schleiermacher, Kierkegaard, Horace Bushnell, Karl Barth, Martin Buber, Paul Tillich *et al*.

Part IB3: Problems arising from confessional theology
Here we find denominational theories of education. The most distinctive seem to be from Catholicism (for example, Maritain, Moran, the Vatican Documents), Orthodoxy, and, within Protestantism, the Lutherans, the Quakers, and the conservative evangelicals. But there is ample scope for study of the educational theologies of almost all the denominations, for

example, there is quite an extensive literature from the Brethren movement.

Part IB4: Problems arising from trends in contemporary theology

Here we list, for convenience of treatment, such movements as process theology, radical, secular theology, and political theology, which seem significant for education. How one categorizes particular studies depends on their emphasis since there are obviously areas of overlap here with other sections. This is true of the distinction between parts A and B of this first section as a whole. There are frequent overlaps between problems arising in the history of education and in the history of theology. The usefulness of the distinction holds good in spite of this.

Part IB5: Problems arising from practical theology

Other areas of practical theology (apart, that is, from theology of education) offer possibilities for cross-fertilization.

IB5a: Catechetics and religious nurture

Here we have the problems associated with the church's own treatment of its own young. The bulk of the Protestant writing from North America and the theological debates within Catholicism about catechetics fall here. Indeed, theology of education is sometimes spoken of as if this was all it contained. In this list, however, it is not part of theology of education proper, but only a related field. The question then is what theology of education can learn from the theologies of Christian nurture.

IB5b: Pastoral care, health, medicine

The problems of theology in relation to the world of healing are often similar to those in this present field of theology and education. More work needs to be done in relating them. What relations are there between concepts of education, salvation, wholeness and healing?

Part II: Problems of material principles

Since we now come to questions of the content of education we can abandon the formal distinction between the concepts of education and those of theology, moving directly to consideration of the subjects of the school. (An alternative arrangement would be to move IA5 down, to begin this part.) It is enough to remark that the teaching of history, geography, English literature, art and science all present matter with which theology has a concern. Questions about the content of religious education, the theological rationales for the teaching of world religion, the relations between theology and the content of moral education classes, and a host of other questions come to mind. For the sake of brevity, I have compressed this second main part of the taxonomy, but probably as much has been written in Britain under this Part II as under the whole of Part I.

We now come to the third and final part of the list.

Part III: Problems of pedagogical method

Our three sections thus cover the concepts, the content and the methods of education. It is important to distinguish the theological consequences or implications of method from those of content, although in practice they often overlap. The methods of education are just as full of values and assumptions as anything else in education and perhaps more so. It is in the methods of the teacher that his educational theories come most immediately to the pupil. Most of the work has been concentrated on method in the teaching of *religion* but in principle there is no theological reason why this should be so. We can distinguish the direct method, the 'discussion 'method, the experiential method, life-themes, the theological implications of the use of audio-visual media (for example, Desmond Brennan, Pierre Babin, Marshall McCluhan and Walter Ong) and finally the theological significance of the use of dance, drama, play and story.

Notes

1 Hodgson, Leonard, *The Doctrine of the Trinity*, 1943, p. 103.
2 Note the centrality of phenomenology in much contemporary work on theological method. Human intentionality, imagination and judgment are central in, for example, Hart, Ray L., *Unfinished Man and the Imagination*, 1968, and Lonergan, Bernard, *Method in Theology*, 1972.
3 Rahner, Hugo, *Man at Play*, 1963, is a good example of a theological work which falls within this area.
4 Hirst, Paul H., *Knowledge and the Curriculum*, 1974, p. 46.
5 For example, Hirst, Paul H., and Peters, R.S., *The Logic of Education*, 1970.
6 As an example of this, see Chapter 5 of Hirst, Paul H., *Moral Education in a Secular Society*, 1974. I have discussed Hirst's arguments in 'Christian theology and educational theory: Can there be connections?' in *The British Journal of Educational Studies*, 24, 2, June 1976. See also the Editorial in *Learning for Living*, 15, 2, Winter 1975 and Professor Hirst's reply in 15, 4, Summer 1976.
7 Hirst, Paul H., *Moral Education in a Secular Society*, pp. 3, 54, 74 and 80f.
8 Most recently, Smith, J.W.D., *Religion and Secular Education*, St. Andrew Press, 1975; Davies, Rupert E. *A Christian Theology of Education*, Denholm House Press, 1974; and Ramsey, I.T. 'Towards a theology of education', *Learning for Living*, 15, 4, Summer 1976.

9 Webster, Derek 'American research in religious education: A review of selected doctoral theses', *Learning for Living*, 14, 5, May 1975, pp. 187–93.

10 The principal British resource for the recovery of these is Daines, J.W., *Religious Education, a Series of Abstracts of Unpublished Theses in Religious Education*, University of Nottingham School of Education, in four parts, 1963-.

11 See the comments by Derek Webster, 'Theory in religious education: Criticism and prospect', *Learning for Living*, 15, 3, Spring 1976, p. 85b.

21. *The Value of the Individual Child and the Christian Faith*

It is surprisingly difficult to provide satisfying reasons for some of the most deeply held moral beliefs. Why is it sometimes wrong to kill people? Why it is wrong to eat people but right to eat animals? What makes this particular mentally deficient child so valuable? There is nothing he can do which a normal child cannot do better, and even if his potential is fully realized he will never be able to offer society anything which will compensate for the resources devoted to caring for and teaching him.

This paper will discuss the problem of the value of the individual child, first with reference to non-religious arguments, and then in relation to various observations drawn from Christianity.

Part 1: The value of the individual child in non-religious discussion

The problem of particularity

We sometimes defend our concern for a particular handicapped child by saying, 'Well, he's human like the rest of us'; or 'People matter, children are people, this is a child'; 'All personality is precious' and so on.

This kind of observation appeals from the general to the particular. There is a general quality (humanity, personality, rationality,[1] etc.) which is to be valued. But (the implication could be developed) this valuable quality or attribute is only to be found in the individuals of the class. Universal properties only actually exist when exemplified in particular entities. Hence individuality is to be valued.

We must distinguish however between giving a reason for valuing individuality, and giving one for valuing a particular individual.[2] No doubt the individual soldiers of the army are valuable because 'army' is nothing without its soldiers. Nevertheless, when one soldier falls another takes his place. Certainly, the army is depleted by the loss of any individual, but this does not confer any value upon a particular soldier *as an individual*, but only in so far as he instantiates the 'army', a quality he shares, no more and no less, with every other individual soldier. One individual is replaceable by another, the only loss being the diminution of the aggregate.

If we turn from individuality to think of the attributes which individuals have together with the other members of their class, then the aggregate could be considered to have increased even if an individual were lost. Suppose the place of a *less* courageous soldier were taken by one who was more than twice as courageous, and who had not previously joined up. The total courage of the army is increased.

In order to clarify the idea of the value of this particular individual, as opposed to the value of individuality in general, we need to introduce the idea of irreplaceability and to distinguish between substitution and representation.[3] Your substitute, on the committee, in the team, at your place of work, takes your place. He takes the place which was once yours. He replaces you, making your potential redundancy apparent. But your representative speaks for you, acts on your behalf. His importance depends on your continued importance. There are many aspects of our lives for which a substitute can be found, but surely it is in those for which no substitute is adequate that our value as individuals is to be found. Can you be substituted for, as father to your children, as lover and friend?

We see then that the difficulty about justifying the value of a particular individual by reference to a quality he possesses in common with his class lies in the move from the abstract to the concrete.[4] If we value snow, any loss of a snowflake is to be regretted since snowiness as a whole is depleted. But there is no loss if two flakes form where one disappears. Each flake is replaceable. The problem is precisely how to value the particular, and not merely the abstraction, 'snowiness', as expressed through individuality which is merely another abstraction.

The problem of uniqueness

Sometimes when we are challenged as to the value of this particular child, we say, 'No one sings just like Tracy!', 'He has a lovely smile', or simply 'Each child has something special and different to contribute.'

Here, instead of emphasizing what the individual has in common with the species, we draw attention to his uniqueness, that which he alone has. But the value of uniqueness is not obvious. Each snowflake is unique, not only in its pattern, but in the time and place of its descent and its relation to other snowflakes. Just as we saw that the *idea* of 'concreteness' is a very abstract idea, so we now see that there is hardly anything as common as uniqueness. Moreover, qualities can be uniquely bad and ugly as well as uniquely beautiful and attractive, so uniqueness itself can hardly be a reason for valuing this particular individual.

If I value Penny's smile, surely this is not because it is unique, but because it is Penny's. I am not a collector of smiles but an admirer of Penny. This does not mean that Penny's uniqueness is of no importance. It would at first be rather confusing if I met someone else with all of Penny's attributes including her smile (her twin sister, Jane). But I would soon realize that the story of Penny was not the same as the story of Jane, and that it was Penny I admired. Her uniqueness lies in her story, perhaps. But without uniqueness I could not distinguish one from the other, unless they were together, and then I could distinguish but not identify them. It would not matter however because in that case (as in science fiction stories of cloning) each could substitute for the other. Uniqueness is thus a necessary condition for valuing Penny as an individual, in the sense of creating irreplaceability, but it is not a sufficient reason, for Jane is as unique as Penny. Uniqueness alone will thus not offer a reason for valuing this particular individual.

The problem of élitism

Sometimes we add to our claim about the uniqueness of this child other details which show why this particular uniqueness is to be valued. 'If only you knew what this child has had to put up with!' 'He said something the other day which showed quite a lot of insight.' But as soon as we begin to spell out such details, to fill out the unique story of this child, questions of comparison inevitably enter for now we are again dealing with attributes, the distinctive attributes of this unique child, certainly; yet unless we give such random defences as 'I just love the sound of her name!' the question of the degree to which the valued attribute is present relative to other individuals must arise. For we do not want to value this individual more than that one, if we are teachers, but we want to value each one for himself and equally. Otherwise, the sub-normal child always loses out. If he shows courage, someone else shows more courage. If he has potential, some more able child has more potential. Perhaps, since we do not know the potential of any individual, and some apparently retarded children have made remarkable artistic and literary creations later in life, we should treat all alike, like the Calvinist who does not know which of his congregation may be elect. But the differences will steadily appear as time goes by and with them differences of value. And should not less care be taken with the less valuable?

Rights and values

Can the élitist tendencies created by the necessarily preferential concept of value be alleviated by using the idea of rights?

Let us distinguish (a) the degree to which a quality or attribute can be realized by an individual; (b) the degree to which a quality or attribute can be valued by an individual, and (c) the manner in which the right to pursue or have that valued quality or attribute may be possessed by an individual.

Under (a), some qualities, such as beauty, happiness and goodness, permit of degrees; indeed it is hard to conceive of their absolute presence or total absence. Others, such as the attribute 'being a twin' or 'having £100 in the bank', permit of no degrees. They are either present or absent. Under (b), whether the attribute itself permits of degree or not, its value will not only permit but demand degree. To value is to discriminate, to exercise preference, and to arrange in hierarchies. 'Being a twin' is valued *more* or *less*, and so is happiness. Under (c), the right to pursue or have the valued attribute does not seem to permit degree. To have the right is to have the key to the door. How far the right itself is valued, how far the attribute to which the right grants access is valued and desired and how far the attribute is actually acquired (unless it is an attribute like 'being a twin' which cannot vary) will vary. But either one has or has not the key.

This is not to deny that the precision with which the right is defined may not vary, and as critical cases arise, the conditions in which the right may be forfeit will appear. It is not to deny that the criteria for possessing the right may vary from time to time, and that there will be ambiguous cases when it is not clear if the criteria are met or not. But none of this alters the fact that once the right is granted, and as long as it continues to be possessed, it is held without degree. If Mr A and Mr B both possess the *same* right, then that right is possessed equally. It does not increase Mr A's right to life because he is Prime Minister while Mr B is only a man in the street. That is not to say that the life of the Prime Minister may not be valued more highly by the community, but that is to introduce other considerations. As far as the right itself is concerned, they possess it equally, if both meet the criteria. If there is a right to education, and if mentally deficient pupil Frank meets the criteria for possessing the right just as does gifted pupil Paul, Frank's right to be educated is exactly the same as Paul's, regardless of any difference in the degree to which they may value the right or the degree to which they are in a position to pursue that to which the right grants access. Their *claim* upon the community for education is, in principle, an equal claim. If this is so, the right of the handicapped child (if he has the right at all) is the same as the right of the child who has more potential, more talents, more beauty (if he has the right at all) and so élitism is excluded. If this is *not* so, then the concept of rights does no more than the concept of values to help us avoid the perils of élitism and we are back where we were.

There are however certain drawbacks about the use of rights as a way of explaining our concern for this particular child.

First, the attitude evoked by rights is one of respect. Not only are the rights of the individual to be respected, they are to be defended, protected, and everything possible is to be done to ensure his unhindered exercise of them. One can even speak of loving rights – one loves freedom, and so one loves the right to freedom. But it does seem odd to speak of loving the individual because he possesses the right. Because the idea of a right is an idea of an obligation which an individual can levy upon his fellows, the response of love seems inappropriate.[5] Does the concept of rights lead us to the idea of the irreplaceability of a particular individual, which we previously isolated as being the heart of what it is to treat someone as an individual? The very equality of rights, their virtue which enabled us to escape from élitism, seems to deprive us of that very treasuring of this individual, the sense that there is no one quite like him, which is the attraction of value language.

We can see this by considering the relation between rights, values and death. Doubtless there is a right to a decent burial, and we acknowledge other obligations towards the dead. But on the whole, it is absurd to think that the individual continues to possess his rights after his death. This is perhaps because the basis for the possession of rights is the capacity to form life purposes which ought not to be unwarrantedly frustrated.[6] This right clearly ceases at death. A widow would feel an obligation to continue to promote her late husband's purposes by publishing his book, but his own right to create, to freedom of speech and so on ended with his death. But the value which we place upon a person may increase after his death. He is treasured, recollected, his sayings lovingly stored up in memory, his music played and esteemed more and more. The notion of value leads us towards this view of the irreplaceable individual as the notion of rights does not.

The second disadvantage of speaking of rights rather than values is that rights are possessed conditionally. This is so in two senses. (a) Having once possessed the criteria for the right, I may subsequently lose some or all of the criteria; and (b) it is at least arguable that certain rights, perhaps even the right to life itself, may be forfeited if I deprive or threaten to deprive others of their rights.

Under (a) if the right to life is based on awareness of, or the potential for having life purposes (the point about potential protects the unborn child), what is the status of those who once had such awareness, but, because of accident or extreme old age, have it now no longer?[7] Under (b) if I attack someone else's life, my right to life may be forfeit to his right to self-defence. If I deprive others of their freedom, my own is lost.

But does the loss of rights (themselves values) carry with it the loss of all values? Surely not. The condemned man on his way to the death cell is still loved by his mother. We intuitively believe that there is something superior about unconditional acceptance, about being the recipient of a love which cannot be forfeited. But this brings us back to the problem of giving a reason for such unconditional value. Is this a weakness of rights language, or may we speak of an unalienable right to be loved? St Paul thought so: 'Owe no one anything, except to love one another, for he who loves his neighbour has fulfilled the law' (Rom. 13:8) The right to be loved, thought of as a 'debt of love' which is owed to the neighbour, is the other side of the duty to love. But here we have passed from rights talk to theological ethics.

Values and the evaluator

We have seen that when values are located in the valued one, the self as moral object, it is difficult to avoid either loss of particularity through abstraction, or the making of distinctions of value, which nearly always disadvantage the mentally handicapped child. But the dominant tendency in moral philosophy since Kant has been to stress the self as moral agent, and to locate values in the will, the moral decision of the evaluator.

So, this mentally handicapped child, whether more or less talented and lovely than other children, and whether instantiating the higher values of his species or not, is precious because I love him. I love this particular child, who is thus irreplaceable, and I love him regardless of his failure or success in meeting any criteria of love which depend upon his own achievements. There is an immediate strength about this move from the qualities of the valued to the will of the evaluator.

Here are the problems presented by this view.

First, if this child is valuable because I love him, then he is only valuable *to me*. Others may respect him for my sake, just as someone may esteem a painting although unable to 'see anything in it' himself, knowing how much it has meant to a loved friend. For those other people, respect for the child becomes respect for me, but it is hard to see how any one can love the child *for himself* because of his love *for me*. Each adult has to decide whether to love. I have. Don't ask me why; I just love him. But will others decide to love him?

Second, am I capable of such a love? Will not my steadfastness falter? Might I not be fickle? Might not someone more beautiful come along, and (on platonic grounds) should I not decide to love the new one more? Does not the value of this handicapped child thus fluctuate with the variations of my love?

Third, when someone who loves us dies, we suffer a felt loss of value. We are diminished. We are bereaved. Now Mozart is not very vulnerable to such loss of value (and if value is in the evaluator such loss would be real, not only felt) because his music is enjoyed by thousands, and it is unlikely they will all die and not be replaced. But his orphan child has only me. If I dropped dead, she would be bereaved indeed, since she would be deprived of most of, if not all, her value.

Part II: The value of the individual child in Christian faith

In dividing this paper into non-religious and religious parts, it is not my intention to suggest that secular ethics having failed we must look to religion. My belief is that the secular and the religious gain mutual benefit by association. I have not claimed that the non-religious reasons for valuing this particular child have failed, only that they present difficulties. Perhaps the various secular arguments combined might each compensate for some weakness in the others. But it is also possible that they will be strengthened (not abolished) by association with theology. Theological observations have their own kinds of difficulties, so, to underline the point, we are not now moving from problems to answers, but trying to see the value of the individual child in a wider and richer historical, imaginative and conceptual universe of symbols[8] than that which is offered by the secular arguments alone. What we need is not two halves, but a network or pattern in which the value of the child will be secured from as many sides as possible. All that the first part of the paper need show, for my argument, is that secular discussion is amenable to supplementation, not that it is wholly or even largely inadequate.[9]

Reflections on theism

The God of the particular

Modern metaphysical systems, such as those of A. N. Whitehead[10] and Charles Hartshorne[11] have emphasized the centrality of individuality in nature, God himself being seen as the sole universal individual.[12] Such philosophy is the modern heir of the individualistic theology and philosophy of the late Middle Ages, especially that of Nicholas of Cusa[13] who taught that the universal is manifest only in particularity, each particular sharing the characteristics of the whole, and each being as near and as far from God as any other particular. This view overthrew the older conception of a graduated universe in hierarchies, in which lower entities were further from God, and defined by reference to their class or grade of being rather than as individuals, which had come from neo-Platonism and pseudo-Dionysius. The medieval concern to establish a place for the concrete particular against such classification theories of reality sprang from the Hebrew-Christian tradition,[14] in which God was conceived of as the one who had created each thing, called all the stars by name (Isa. 20: 46) and noticed the fall of the sparrow (Matt. 10:29). In Christian faith, this emphasis upon the concrete becomes an imperative,[15] because of the concern for this particular man, who 'suffered under Pontius Pilate' and who had been this particular child, the babe of Bethlehem.

The God who knows

God is thought of as the one 'unto whom all hearts are open and all desires known'. Whereas in my care and appreciation of this child I am hindered by my ignorance, God not only knows every detail of this child's rich experience of life but knows it infallibly, completely and eternally. This knowledge can never be lost, and so nothing of value will ever be lost. In this sense, as Jewish ritual expresses it, 'He will endow our fleeting days with abiding worth'.

The God who loves

What would it do to the value of this child if there were, after all, one who, knowing this child with perfect knowledge, loves him with perfect love, a love which never fluctuates, which is extended equally to all, which is offered unconditionally and which can never cease, it being the love of one who is invulnerable to death?

The God who calls

Conceptions of the divine election, whereby God is thought of as calling individuals, nations or humanity and nature to fulfilment, vary widely in Christian thought. But whether, as in Calvin's teaching, God calls some individuals and not others, or in Karl Barth's, where all humanity is both called and judged in the person of Jesus Christ, one thing is clear. God's call is without respect of persons, God's call does not reckon with human achievements but is the overflow of his grace and love. Indeed, the values are inverted. God called Israel not because it was the greatest nation 'for you were the fewest of all people' (Deut. 7: 7); he called not the wise, the powerful and the noble, but the foolish, the weak, the low and the despised (I Cor. 1: 26–9). In the teaching of Jesus, the first become last, the leaders become servants and the Kingdom of God belongs to children (Mark 9: 35f; 10: 14).[16]

It is important to realize the nature of these kinds of theistic ethics. It would not only be rather offensive to say to someone, 'Although you are quite uninteresting to me in yourself, I value you because God values you'; it would also be to misunderstand the theistic inference. I may, as we discussed previously, respect someone for the sake of someone else who respects or loves the person, but to say, 'God loves this child' is logically different from saying, 'The headmaster loves this child'. The latter offers a reason of some sort for adopting a certain attitude to the child which is extrinsic to the child, and it would be quite in order to object that one ought to love the child, or at least respect him, for his own sake, as an individual, and not as a means of expressing our respect for someone else, such as the headmaster. But when it is said that the child is a creature of God, is known by God, loved and called by him, this is offered as an understanding of self-hood. This is a statement about the nature of the child. He is a moral object, but in a way (because of the nature of God who forms the child in this way) which frees the child as object of value from the problems which seem to remain in purely non-religious discourse. Other problems are of course created, but this particular one is not amongst them. When self-hood is defined, and regarded as being constituted by environment, heredity, social relations, moral attributes or whatever, these theories of self are intrinsic to the self because they offer themselves as attributes to the self. To say that the child is a child of God is similarly to offer an attribute of all children and is no more and no less external to the child than any other understanding of self-hood. So when the child is regarded as a child of God, he is being regarded precisely as an individual, and the one who loves the child *for these reasons* is loving the child *as he is* and for his own sake, and as an individual.

There are secondary senses in which one should respect and love beings respected and loved by God *for God's sake*, and one ought to seek to deepen one's own appreciation of God by acting more and more *as if* God's attitudes were normative. But these considerations are less significant for value theory than the view that what theism offers is a theory of self as such.

Theism not only offers a view of self[17] which enriches our evaluation of the self as moral object but also, accepting the view that values also lie in the evaluator, gives us an evaluator whose judgments and will are immune from the weaknesses of non-divine evaluators.

Reflections of Jesus Christ

The all-important factor in determining Christian evaluations of childhood has been the belief that God was manifest in childhood, in this particular child, the baby of Bethlehem and the boy in Nazareth.[18] This has been interpreted in widely differing ways. In the Christmas sermons of the Church Fathers, the child Jesus is mainly regarded as a guarantor of Nicene orthodoxy – before his adult life, from the beginning, he was already true God. In the Christ Child cult of the Middle Ages, a more practical, as well as more mystical, note was struck, which reached its climax in seventeenth-century France[19] where, in the teaching of the 'French School' of spirituality, the insignificance and helplessness of the child was the inspiration for Christian self-renunciation, and later in the century the Infant-King was adored as the representation of supreme glory combined with littleness and weakness. The impact of such ideas upon the treatment of children was considerable, as is indicated by the many schools, orphanages and hospitals founded for poor children in the name of the Holy Child Jesus.[20]

As is witnessed by the many legends and folk-tales on the subject, the connection between the Christ Child of Palestine and the poor contemporary child was made by means of the idea of the Christ Child incognito. This was based upon such sayings as 'Whoever receives one such child in my name receives me, and whoever receives me receives not me but him that sent me' (Mark 9: 37) and 'See that you do not despise one of these little ones; for I tell you that in heaven their angels do always behold the face of my Father' (Matt. 18: 10) and 'As you did it to one of the least of these my brethren, you did it to me' (Matt. 25: 40). The lonely and desolate child carried by St Christopher over the swollen torrent is not only the Maker of all; he is every poor child.

Behind this vivid imagery lies the thought that God is not absent from the world he has made, but is present within it all, as the logos and 'light of everyman' (John 1: 4) but especially present in those who as children share in his own childhood and receive his special blessing and as poor children share in the lowliness of his own infancy. He continues to live in them and takes their form. If the poor of the world are his body, then the poor children of the world are his child-body, both generally and individually, for he was, and remains, this very particular child.

It would be easy enough to give many more illustrations from Christianity of the special status and significance of children. Some could be drawn from ecclesiology, where we could consider the implications of the classical Protestant doctrine of the child in the church, in which children of Christians were regarded as being 'children of promise' and as being included in the covenant with God, so claiming their baptism as a right which the church could not deny them. We could also consider the implications for the status of the child of his treatment in the sacraments, especially in the Orthodox churches, where baptism, confirmation and first communion all take place in earliest infancy. We could consider the implications of even such a doctrine as the Trinity for the value of childhood. Clement of Alexandria regards the eternally begotten son of the Father as the principle of constant renewal such that God, Father and Son, is forever old and forever young.

Part III: The significance of theological ethics for childhood

Christian faith, like the other great religions, can be expressed as a more or less coherent belief system; indeed, each religion has generated many such systems. But the actual life of any religion is vastly more complex, less ordered, more exuberant. Instead of trying to present a systematic account of a theology of child-value, I have deliberately selected a range of materials, some metaphysical,[21] others historical, or symbolic, or perhaps no more than whimsical, in the folk-story tradition. My intention has been to show what feelings for, duties towards, vision of this particular child a teacher might have if he were somewhere within range of the power of these ideas. Clearly, the capacity of such ideas to illuminate contemporary action depends initially upon the general plausibility[22] of Christian faith. It must be remembered that the success of a religion in showing its ethical relevance is part of its general plausibility. It is not a matter of first coming to conclusions about the coherence of the concept of God and then relating it to the education of children. The coherence of the idea of God is part of a pattern which includes children and education.

Is there a problem of 'is' and 'ought' in all this? Are we not drawing ethical conclusions from assertions about states of affairs?[23] It seems to be recognized that the relationship between 'is' and 'ought' is more subtle than had been thought a few years ago,[24] and in any case, since theological discourse, however factual it might appear, is already evaluative, this is not a matter of simply drawing evaluative conclusions from non-evaluative data, but rather a matter of establishing links between two kinds of evaluative statements. The building up of networks of relations between religion and ethics has been strangely neglected in moral philosophy where most of the interest has been concentrated on whether the divine command equals ought.[25] I have made no reference in this study to the idea of divine command, because religious value systems cannot be expressed in such narrow terms.

There seems little doubt that the status of this particular child is both more secure and richer in the Christian value system (and perhaps in other religious value systems) than it is in merely secular ethics. In a time when there is a tendency to look upon children as a national resource, this is a gain which is at least worth exploring.

Notes

1 For a discussion of this problem in Kant, see Pollock, L., 'On treating others as ends' *Ethics*, 84, 1974, p. 260f.
2 The failure to make this distinction is a serious flaw in John Dewey's much quoted *Individualism Old and New*, Allen and Unwin, London, 1931.
3 Sölle, Dorothee, *Christ the Representative*, SCM Press, London, 1967, Part 1.
4 'We can only grade them with respect to their qualities, hence only by abstracting them from their individuality', Vlastos, Gregory:, 'Human worth, merit and equality' in Feinberg, Joel (ed.), *Moral Concepts*, OUP, 1969, p. 143.
5 In Downie, R.S., and Telfer, Elizabeth, *Respect for Persons*, Allen and Unwin, London, 1969, respect is equated with the love (*agape*) of the New Testament p. 29 but if the context of love in the teaching of Jesus and Paul were given its proper emphasis, this identification might seem questionable.
6 See Young, Robert, 'What is so wrong with killing people?', *Philosophy*, 54, October 1979, pp. 515–28.
7 For an argument which denies the right to life of the foetus and the infant, see Tooley, Michael, 'A defence of abortion and infanticide' in Feinberg Joel (ed.), *The Problem of Abortion*, Wadsworth Publishing Co., Belmont, California, 1973, pp. 51–91 and also McClosky, H.J., 'Moral rights and animals', *Inquiry*, 22, 1979, especially p. 51.
8 Apart from the length of this paper, there is no reason to confine religious symbols to Christianity. See Rotenberg, N., 'Alienating individualism and reciprocal individualism: A cross-cultural conceptualization', *Journal of Humanistic Psychology*, 17, 1977, pp. 3–17 for a Jewish critique of Christian individualism.
9 Reviews of theologies and philosophies which have influenced the place of individuality in education are provided by Hill, Brian V., *Education and the Endangered Individual*, Teachers College Press, Columbia University, 1973.
10 Parsons, H., 'God and man's achievement of identity; religion in the thought of

Alfred North Whitehead', *Education Theory* 11, 1962, pp. 228–54.

11 Hartshorne, Charles, *A Natural Theology for our Time*, Open Court, Illinois, 1967.

12 Sontag, F., 'Universal categories and one particular being', *Religious Studies*, 9, 1973, pp. 437–48.

13 Cassirer, Ernst, *The Individual and the Cosmos in Renaissance Philosophy*, Blackwood, Oxford, 1963.

14 Coplestone, F., *A History of Philosophy*, Vol. III, Burns, Oates and Washbourne, London, 1953, p. 49.

15 As one example of the extensive scholarly literature on biblical individuality, see Moule, C. F.D., 'The individualism of the Fourth Gospel', *Novum Testamentum*, 5, 1962, pp. 171–90.

16 For the child in the teaching of Jesus see *The Child in the Church* (Working Party Report), British Council of Churches, 1976, paras 31–3, and Weber, Hans-Ruedi, *Jesus and the Children*, World Council of Churches, 1979.

17 For a bold and rather idiosyncratic study of theism, life after death and individuality, see Witcutt, W.P., *The Rise and Fall of the Individual* SPCK, London 1958. A more profound and less polemical study of the two types of theistic individuality is Babcock, W.S., 'Patterns of Roman self-hood: Marcus Aurelius and Augustine of Hippo', *Perkins School of Theology Journal*, 29, 1976, pp. 1–19.

18 *The Child in the Church, op. cit.*, paras. 34–8.

19 Noye, Irénée, 'Enfance de Jésus', *Dictionnaire de Spiritualité Ascetique et Mystique*, Beauchesne, Paris, 1969, cols. 652–82.

20 Bremond, Henri, *A Literary History of Religious Thought in France*, Vol. 3.

21 For a recent discussion of the value of human life in which the need and legitimacy of metaphysics is emphasized, see Brody, Baruch, *Abortion and the Sanctity of Human Life, a Philosophical View*, Massachusetts Institute of Technology Press, 1975, especially p. 95.

22 'There certainly does not seem to be any unanswerable objection to non-naturalism, and the phenomenology of moral experience ... seems to make its presupposition at least plausible', Downie and Telfer, *op. cit.*, p. 151.

23 For an example of how theology is coping with this, see Bresnahan, James F., 'Rahner's Ethics: Critical natural law in relation to contemporary ethical methodology', *Journal of Religion*, 56, 1976, pp. 36–60.

24 Hudson, W.D. (ed.), *The Is-Ought Question*, Macmillan, 1969.

25 See the comments by Sutherland, Stewart, in 'Ethics and transcendence in Bonhoeffer', *Scottish Journal of Theology*, 30, 6, 1977, p. 554.

Author Index

Approach → as if you & I are
finding out 1) ps that rel
is + why people are rel
+ that being rel involves
    doing.

Identify el in & community
 -buildings.
Survey people on their rel
beliefs + what they feel
being religious is (Perhaps
use one of & CU members, or one
of & ps in & dao).

Subject Index

Agreed Syllabuses, 1, 8–9, 17, 24, 29, 30–42, 46, 49–50, 61, 62, 65, 73–92, 103–12, 113–16, 117, 118, 119, 123–5, 137, 140, 144, 178–9
  see also Birmingham Agreed Syllabus
Australia, 27, 28, 29, 45–6, 54
authority
  and God, 202–4
  religious, 212, 215–16
  and religious education, 57–71

Bible, 50, 64, 75, 76, 123, 124, 129–32, 136–42, 149–61, 175–6, 190–4, 199–202, 253, 269, 280–2
Birmingham Agreed Syllabus, 1, 29, 30–42, 82–91, 103–12, 113–16, 117, 118, 119, 178–9
  see also Agreed Syllabuses
Britain
  religious education in, *passim*
British Council of Churches, 1

Canada, 27, 28–9
children
  and Christian faith, 273–85
  and the church, 207–25
Christian commitment
  and religious education, 173–225
Christian Education Movement, 2, 90, 119, 185
convergent teaching, 175–85, 189–95
  see also divergent teaching
Cowper-Temple clause, 60, 65, 74, 88
curriculum
  and religious education, *passim*
  see also Agreed Syllabuses

divergent teaching, 175–85, 187–95
  see also convergent teaching

Education Act (1944), 5–9, 28, 49, 55, 65, 73, 80, 82, 85, 97, 103, 105, 110–12, 113, 116
experiential religious education, 19–20, 135–46, 150–61

humanism, 28, 35, 38, 39, 43, 82, 87, 88–9, 103–12, 115, 118–19, 198, 205–6, 230–1, 238, 261

individual
  and Christian faith, 273–85
International Seminar on Religious Education and Values, 1
life themes
  see themes

New Zealand, 27, 54
non-Christian religions, 6, 14–15, 27–8, 31–3, 37–8, 40–1, 45–55, 61, 80, 82–8, 114–16, 117, 175–85, 187–95, 199–201, 205–6, 210, 229, 230–1, 238, 256, 258, 264, 268
  see also pluralist society
Norway, 45–6

pluralist society
  religious education in, 37, 39–40, 42, 45–55, 187–95, 207, 262
  see also non-Christian religions
religious education
  aim of, 19–21
  and Christian commitment, 173–225
  content of, 18–19, 24, 50–1, 60–2
    see also Agreed Syllabuses
  and indoctrination, 103–12
  integration of, 57–71, 159–61
  nature of, 25–119